Transforming Sudan

Following the conclusion of the Second World War, the nature of inequality in Africa was dramatically altered. In this book, Alden Young traces the emergence of economic developmentalism as the ideology of the Sudanese state in the decolonization era. Young demonstrates how the state was transformed, as a result of the international circulation of tools of economic management and the practice of economic diplomacy, from the management of a collection of distinct populations, to the management of a national economy based on individual equality. By studying the hope and eventual disillusionment this ideology gave to late colonial officials and then Sudanese politicians and policymakers, Young demonstrates its rise, and also its shortfalls as a political project in Sudan – particularly its inability to deal with questions of regional and racial equity, showing how it fostered not only state formation, but also civil war.

Alden Young is an assistant professor of African History and the Director of the Program in Africana Studies at Drexel University, Philadelphia. He was previously a post-doctoral fellow in the Africana Studies Department at the University of Pennsylvania, and holds a Ph.D. in History from Princeton University, New Jersey.

African Studies

The African Studies series, founded in 1968, is a prestigious series of monographs, general surveys, and textbooks on Africa covering history, political science, anthropology, economics, and ecological and environmental issues. The series seeks to publish work by senior scholars as well as the best new research.

Other titles in the series are listed at the back of the book.

Transforming Sudan

Decolonization, Economic Development, and State Formation

ALDEN YOUNG
Drexel University, Philadelphia

CAMBRIDGE
UNIVERSITY PRESS

CAMBRIDGE
UNIVERSITY PRESS

University Printing House, Cambridge CB2 8BS, United Kingdom

One Liberty Plaza, 20th Floor, New York, NY 10006, USA

477 Williamstown Road, Port Melbourne, VIC 3207, Australia

314-321, 3rd Floor, Plot 3, Splendor Forum, Jasola District Centre, New Delhi - 110025, India

79 Anson Road, #06-04/06, Singapore 079906

Cambridge University Press is part of the University of Cambridge.

It furthers the University's mission by disseminating knowledge in the pursuit of education, learning and research at the highest international levels of excellence.

www.cambridge.org
Information on this title: www.cambridge.org/9781107172494
DOI: 10.1017/9781316779071

First published 2018

A catalogue record for this publication is available from the British Library

ISBN 978-1-107-17249-4 Hardback
ISBN 978-1-316-62384-8 Paperback

Contents

Acknowledgments

I first became interested in the questions that motivate this book as I watched my parents take part in Black urban politics from the 1970s until the early 2000s. Living in New Orleans and then Detroit, I was fascinated not only by the voting rights movement but also by what followed its achievement: the successes and failures of local governance, in particular economic governance. Similarly, this book is concerned primarily not with the heroes of the independence movement in Sudan, but with the officials who strove to govern Sudan after January 1, 1956.

Princeton University gave this project its initial home. There, I was fortunate to receive the support of the Princeton History Department, the Davis Center for Historical Research, the Princeton Institute for International and Regional Studies, the Department of Near Eastern Studies, and a Fulbright-Hays Critical Language Grant. For Bob Tignor's ability to constantly point me in new and fruitful intellectual directions, I will always be grateful. I am indebted to the care he demonstrated for my work and for my personal development as a young scholar. Similarly, Emmanuel Kreike is a model teacher and scholar. He constantly held me to the highest standards of scholarship. At Princeton, an amazing community of mentors such as Jeremy Adelman, and Michael Laffan, continue to influence me until today. I would also like to thank David Candidine, Molly Greene, William Chester Jordan, Stephen Kotkin and Brad Simpson for their mentorship. Adrienne Brown, Will Evans, Caley Horan, Victor Marsh, Jack Tannous, and NurFadzilah Yahaya were unflinching friends during my time at Princeton. Mary Morgan of the London School of Economics supported my project at a critical moment, and she continues to be a mentor and an intellectual role model. I would also like to thank Carolyn Brown of Rutgers University. All along this journey my two comrades in arms have been Mike Woldemariam and Onur Ozgode. I wouldn't have been able to do it without them.

Next, I want to thank Eve Troutt Powell and the Department of Africana Studies at the University of Pennsylvania for providing me with a two-year Mellon Humanities postdoc, during which I had the opportunity to reformulate my project for publication and to become immersed in Black Studies. I would also like to thank Herman Beavers, Camille Charles, Dorothy Roberts, Barbara Savage, Deborah Thomas, Robert Vitalis, Heather Williams, and Tukufu Zuberi. I was fortunate to be among the greatest group of postdoctoral fellows that one could imagine, including Garry Bertholf, Darius Bost, Clem Harris, Grace Sanders Johnson, Oliver Rollins, and Keren Weitzberg. While at Penn, I also had the pleasure to work with exceptional graduate students, including Celina De Sa, Jacob Feygin, Rasul Miller, and Zachary Mondesire.

Finally, I would not have been able to complete this project without the warm support of the History Department at Drexel University. I want to thank my senior colleagues Scott Knowles and Amy Slaton for their enthusiasm and kind support, which included generous leave and financial support as I completed the book. I have also been fortunate to have the support of a generous faculty cohort, particularly, Debjani Bhattacharrya, Gabriel Rocha, and Tiago Savaria. As Director of Africana Studies, Jackie Rios has supported my efforts, as well as Kate Hughes and Jessica Kratzner. I would also like to thank Rogelio Miñana, Julie Mustov and Dean Donna Murasko.

Many others have helped me formulate my thoughts either during invaluable conversations or by diligently reading drafts. Thank you to Aasem Ali, Sara Ansari, Hannah Appel, Beth Baron, Una Barrett, Edna Bonhomme, Michelle Bourbonniere, Jeffrey Byrne, Raph Cormack, Rohit De, Laura Dean, Maria Margarita Fajardo Hernandez, Romain Ferrali, Jeremy Friedman, Nils Gilman, George Hatke, Kevan Harris, Peter Hudson James, Saarah Jappie, Sheila Jasanoff, Morten Jerven, Cherry Leonardi, Joanna Lewis, Zack Kagan-Guthrie, Khoolod Khair, Jamie Kreiner, Laura Mann, Wendell Hassan Marsh, Jamie Martin, Tom Meaney, Houda Mechtaly, Moritz Mihatsch, Sam Moyn, Nicholas Mulder, Karam Nachar, Tinashe Nyamunda, Vanessa Ogle, Pandora O'Mahony-Adams, Donna Patterson, Jemima Pierre, Noah Salomon, Tehila Sasson, Logan Schmid, Kirsten Schulze, Manuel Schwab, Melissa Teixeira, Adam Tooze, Alton Torregano, Christina Tobajas Schmid, Gerardo Serra, Heather Sharkey, Justin Willis, Peter Woodward, and Harry Verhoveon.

My journey to Sudan would not have been possible without the Durham trio of W. J. Berridge, Zoe Cormack, and Christopher Vaughan. In Sudan many people opened their doors to me, introducing me to their families, friends, and colleagues: Osman Saleh Eldawie, Khalel Adam Idriss, Nagla Hussain, Sulafa Kamel, Ahmed Sayed Ahmed, and Musa Ahmed Osman. I would also like to thank ElSadig Muhammad, Muhammad ElSanousi, and Muhammad Badri.

I would like to express my gratitude to the staff of the Sudan Archives Durham, particularly the chief Sudan archivist Jane Hogan, who pointed me to the then-uncataloged files of John Carmichael. I would also like to thank Dr. Awatif, Abd al Moneim, and Muhammad Azraq in the National Record Office of Sudan. At the University of Khartoum's Development Studies and Research Institute, I would like to thank Ismail Elkhalifa Suleiman, who sponsored my initial visit to Khartoum. Additional thanks go to the indomitable politician and activist Mansour Elagab.

This project has also benefited greatly from the kind support and generous feedback of numerous colleagues around the world. Parts of this project were presented at the "Ninth Annual International Seminar on Decolonization," National History Center, Library of Congress, July 6–August 2, 2014; "Institutions, Credit, and the State: A History Project Conference," Yale University, October 17–18, 2014; "The Nation-State and the World Economy between Two Eras of Globalization, 1913–1975," (YSI) Institute for New Economic Thinking, Scoula Superiore Sant'Anna, July 14–16, 2015; Science and Technology Studies Circle, Harvard Kennedy School, April 4, 2016; Scales of the Economy, Laureate Research Program in International History, University of Sydney, July 27–29, 2016; and Emancipation and Empire: Africa and the Project of Black Studies, Department of African American Studies, UCLA, December 5, 2016. The work that follows has benefited greatly from the suggestions, comments and reviews of the editors, anonymous reviewers, and readers of the following publications in which portions of the work that follows have previously appeared. I would like to thank the editors of the following publications for allowing substantially modified versions of work previously published to appear in these pages: "African Bureaucrats and the Exhaustion of the Developmental State: Lessons from the Pages of the *Sudanese Economist*," *Humanity: An International Journal of Human Rights, Humanitarianism and Development* 8:1 (Spring 2017): 49–75 and "Measuring the Sudanese Economy: A Focus on National Growth Rates and a Blindness to Regional Inequality, 1958 to 1964," *Canadian Journal of Development Studies* (April 1, 2014): 44–60. The cover photo of the Al Jazirah Scheme is used courtesy of Al Jazirah, Sudan; NASA/METI/AIST/Japan Space Systems; and U.S./Japan ASTER Science Team. I would also like to thank Jake Riley for producing the maps that appear in this book.

Khalil al-Salem, his family, and his many friends in Jordan first introduced me to the Arab world, and the perspective they granted me continues to shape my understanding of politics and the universal nature of day-to-day life. Of course, I want to thank my cousin Courtney Bryan. The integrity with which she approaches her work and her family sets a standard to which I am always pushing myself.

This book is dedicated to my mother and father. My mom was a great example of scholarship and civic and familial dedication. Though she did not live to see me enter Princeton, her passion and spirit inspire me today. My father is my intellectual hero; this book builds on questions that he introduced me to years ago. I would not do what I do without him.

Finally, I am happy to share this book and the long journey that it took to complete it with my wife Nafeesa Syeed, who has been in my life since I first saw the Nile in 2003. Her dedication and unflinching sense of integrity have made this journey worthwhile.

Introduction: The Economizing Logic of the State

From the beginning, policy makers' visualizations of the Sudanese economy were marked by curious absences. Certain activities did not count and certain transactions were not calculated. Estimating conservatively, there were at least two and a half times as many heads of livestock in Sudan as citizens, yet economic planners focused on cotton, rather than cattle, sheep, or camels.[1] Explaining this discrepancy requires that we examine the history of planning in Sudan. In 1961, after years of effort and funding expended first by the colonial and then the postcolonial state in Sudan, Director-General Abdel Rahim Mirghani and his team at the Economic Planning Secretariat announced that they had created a scientific plan that would ensure that the country achieved "the first phase of [its] long-term objectives for development extending over a generation or so."[2] Abdel Rahim Mirghani and his colleagues believed that economic planning would allow the Sudanese economy to grow at an "accelerated rate" and "reach the stage of self-sustaining growth."[3] Much of the book that follows details the story of the construction of the economy as a calculative machine through the government's surveillance, classification, data

[1] Republic of Sudan, *The Ten Year Plan of Economic and Social Development 1961/62–1970/71* (Khartoum: Government Printing Press, 1962), p. 31.

[2] Abdel Rahim Mirghani, "Introduction," in Republic of Sudan, *Ten Year Plan of Economic and Social Development 1961/62–1970/71*, p. 2.

[3] Ibid. "In addition to my regular duties as Deputy Under Secretary, Ministry of Finance and Economics, I was Director-General of the Economic Planning Secretariat, which was set up towards the middle of 1961 to formulate the Seven Year Development Plan which was later extended to become the Ten Year Plan of Economic and Social Development 1961/62–1970/71. Soon afterwards, I became the Under Secretary of the Department of Economic Planning in the Ministry of Finance and Economics and held that post for the whole of the first five years of the Ten Year Plan." Abdel Rahim Mirghani, *Development Planning in the Sudan in the Sixties* (Khartoum: Graduate College Publications, University of Khartoum, 1983), p. 1.

gathering, budgeting, and finally economic projections.[4] This work allowed Sudanese and international experts to speak with authority about the Sudanese economy.[5]

The contrast between the ways that cotton and cattle were dealt with exemplifies the dilemmas confronted by officials striving to plan Sudan's economic future. While the production of cotton, primarily grown for export on state-managed or private commercial farms, was meticulously tabulated, cattle production – even when those cows were commercially exported – was only haphazardly counted by state officials. This dichotomy led to strange patterns of staff activity within the Ministry of Finance and Economics. For instance, finance officials and economic planners spent hours and hours writing documents debating how to increase their surveillance of cotton production, while they remained largely silent about livestock, noting cattle production only in passing in the *Ten Year Plan for Economic and Social Development 1961/62–1971/72*:

> Livestock constitutes one of Sudan's main potential sources of income. Although no reliable livestock population figures are available, it has been roughly estimated to be over 25 millions...The development of livestock has been hampered by the social habits of livestock rearing population, mostly nomadic and semi-nomadic, to whom possession of livestock is more a sign of social prestige than of economic value and by the paucity of water and grazing facilities.[6]

Why was livestock relatively ignored in the planning efforts of Sudanese officials and their international advisors? The first reason was the limited capacity

[4] For a discussion of the work that goes into making an economy calculable, see Mary S. Morgan, "Seeking Parts, Looking for Wholes," in Lorraine Daston and Elizabeth Lunbeck, eds., *Histories of Scientific Observation* (Chicago: University of Chicago Press, 2011); Mary S. Morgan, "'On a Mission' with Mutable Mobiles." Working Paper on the Nature of Evidence: How Well Do "Facts" Travel? No. 34/8 (London: London School of Economics, 2008); Morten Jerven, *Poor Numbers: How We Are Misled by African Development Statistics and What to Do about It* (Ithaca, NY: Cornell University Press, 2013); Gerardo Serra. "The First Modern Census of Contemporary Africa: Population Counting and Postcolonial State Building in 1960s Ghana" (PhD diss., London School of Economics, 2015); and Wolfgang F. Stopler, *Planning without Facts: Lessons in Resource Allocation from Nigeria's Development* (Cambridge, MA: Harvard University Press, 1966).

[5] Timothy Mitchell, "Fixing the Economy," *Cultural Studies* 12:1 (1998): 82–101. For a discussion of the different ways in which one can study the economy as an object of historical inquiry, see Quinn Slobodian, "Which 'the Economy'? Complicating the Timothy Mitchell Thesis," Comment at "Historicizing "the Economy" Workshop" (Harvard University, September 2016). www.academia.edu/28948215/Which_the_Economy_Complicating_the_Timothy_Mitchell_Thesis [accessed July 17, 2017].

For a very provocative reading of different conceptions of the economy, see Adam Tooze, "The Crisis: The Unmaking of the Economy?" Working Paper (London: London Foucault Working Group, April 2016): www.adamtooze.com/wp-content/uploads/2016/03/Tooze-Unmaking-the-Economy-2016.pdf [accessed January 20, 2017].

[6] Republic of Sudan, *Ten Year Plan of Economic and Social Development 1961/62–1970/71*, p. 31.

of the state. At independence in 1956, Sudanese officials inherited from Britain and Egypt a vast country, the largest in Africa, but with an attenuated infrastructure, built primarily in the central region of the country and along the banks of the Nile – the very areas from which cotton was exported. Meanwhile, the great herds of livestock resided primarily in the western and southern regions of the country where the state's infrastructure was lacking and its ability to survey economic activity was weakest.[7]

Yet, the reasons for the lack of attention to livestock production were not merely technical; they were also epistemological.[8] Cotton, unlike food or livestock, was grown for markets controlled by the state. Therefore, finance officials found it easy to calculate the amount of cotton produced in Sudan and to tabulate the numbers of transactions related to its export. In contrast, with food, cattle, camels, or sheep, planners found it very difficult to distinguish economic transactions – those transactions that formed the modern, public, monetary economy – from those that were non-economic or were part of the traditional, familial, subsistence economy. Yet neglecting the livestock sector and ignoring the question of how to distinguish economic cattle from non-economic cattle – those animals not intended for sale in the market – would have an impact on the political future of Sudan for decades to come.

This book demonstrates how the economic imagination of Sudan's planners expanded or constrained the visions of Sudan's politicians. Sayyid Saadiq al-Mahdi, the scion of the powerful Mahdi family, encapsulated the contradictory ways that northern politicians imagined the economic potential of the southern provinces when he wrote in 1964 that the southerners are mostly poor, hungry, sick and dependent on cattle, fish, and wild fruits. Yet, referring to British reports from the late colonial period, Saadiq al-Mahdi argued that the southern provinces were the key to Sudanese economic independence, potentially supplying the country with coffee, tea, and sugar, as well as fruits and rice.[9] The oscillating visions of southern Sudan as alternatively the key to the country's future prosperity or a barren and lawless land influenced political debates in Sudan about whether to attempt to unify and develop the whole territory,

7 Peter Woodward, *Sudan, 1898–1989: The Unstable State* (Boulder, CO: Lynne Rienner, 1990); "Economic policy over the period from 1956–1969 was geared mainly towards expansion within the framework established prior to 1956," in Tim Niblock, *Class and Power in Sudan: The Dynamics of Sudanese Politics, 1898–1985* (Albany: SUNY Press, 1987), p. 231; Martin Daly, *Darfur's Sorrow: A History of Destruction and Genocide* (Cambridge: Cambridge University Press, 2007).

8 S. Herbert Frankel was a South African economist who held a professorship at Oxford University. His writings were influential within the Sudanese colonial administration, and in this essay he offers a provocative description of the problems associated with using the tools of economic measurement to assess value. S. Herbert Frankel, "'Psychic' and 'Accounting' Concepts of Income and Welfare," *Oxford Economic Papers* 14:1 (1952): 1–17.

9 US National Archives and Records Administration (NARA), RG 59/Pol 17–2/2667, Letter From Embassy, Khartoum to Department of State, "Book on the Southern Sudan by Sadeq al Mahdi" (April 30, 1964).

two-thirds the size of India, or to retreat, defining the nation-state as only the prosperous regions around Khartoum.

During the 1960s, Sudanese politicians also disagreed ferociously about the ideological character of the nation. For instance, Sayyid Abdullahi al-Fadl al-Mahdi, one of the senior leaders of Ansar, the political, religious and social organization built around the Mahdi's family, argued that the country was lost as long as it ignored its Islamic character and that Black African states lacked civilization. In contrast, southern politicians such as Luigi Adwok Bong and Clement Mboro saw the only hope for Sudan as forming a federation of its Black African peoples.[10] In July 1965, the Sudanese Armed Forces killed more than a thousand southerners in clashes in Juba, and by 1966 upward of 125,000 southerners had fled the country, with possibly a million moving into northern Sudan.[11] The clash over the identity of the Sudanese state had become a hot war.

Yet, while differences in how politicians imagined the political identity of the state fostered Sudan's civil wars, it would be a mistake to believe that the only obstacles confronting the Sudanese were political. The willingness of successive Sudanese regimes to engage in extreme violence has made it very tempting to search for structural explanations for Sudan's wars and to look for continuity in the underlying rationale of the various regimes that have ruled the Sudanese state.[12] However, while violence itself is endemic in the historical record, its justifications have changed over time, and understanding and explaining acts of violence and exploitation necessitate an approach to historical interpretation that is sensitive to the intellectual ideas that allowed officials and other actors to behave as they did.[13]

[10] NARA RG 59/Pol 17–2/2667, Letter From Karl F. Mautner, First Sec. American Embassy Khartoum to State Department, "Ansar Leader Criticize Abboud Regime" (February 23, 1964) and NARA RG 59/Pol 17–2/2667, Memo, Ethiopian Embassy, "Luigi Adwok Bong's Views on the Southern Problem" (July 10, 1965).

[11] "Luigi Adwok Bong's Views on the Southern Problem" and NARA RG 59/Pol 1–2, "Incoming Telegram Department of State" (October 1966) from the Ethiopian Embassy.

[12] Alex De Waal, "Sudan: The Turbulent State," in A. De Waal, *War in Darfur and the Search for Peace* (Cambridge, MA: Global Equity Initiative, Harvard University, 2007), p. 32.

[13] There are many competing explanations for what has been referred to as the instability or turmoil of the postcolonial state, although the debate has often been characterized by a search for unitary explanations. In part, this debate has rested on more general questions about the colonial legacy and whether or not the colonial period was decisive in creating new political, social, or economic institutions. Frequently the literature on Sudan has sought "root causes" in the colonial period or in the Ottoman-Egyptian conquest of Sudan, which began in the 1820s. In recent years, this issue has been explicitly recast in debates about the land tenure system in Darfur and whether colonialism created new political identities there, or if identities dating to before the colonial period were retained and continue to explain current political cleavages. Mahmood Mamdani, *Saviors and Survivors: Darfur, Politics, and the War on Terror* (New York: Pantheon, 2009); for an opposite position on the survival throughout the British colonial period of older forms of land tenure and political identification, see R. S. O'Fahey, *The Darfur Sultanate: A History* (New York: Columbia University Press, 2008).

To explain the violence of the Sudanese state, writers such as Douglas Johnson and Jok Madut Jok have focused on the persistence of patterns of exploitation by northern riverain communities of the rest of Sudan. The northern elites derived from the tribes first conquered by the armies of Mehmet Ali, such as the Ja'alin, Shaigiya, and the Danagla. While acknowledging that the mechanisms of exploitation changed over time – the most flagrant example being the institution of slavery[14] – these writers argue that the elites' self-image of cultural supremacy allowed them to justify their exploitation of the rest of Sudan.[15] The most compelling explanations of Sudan's turmoil point back to the nineteenth century and argue that colonialism left Sudan marred by a series of incomplete nation-building projects during the last quarter of that century. Examples include the rise of the Mahdiyyia movement, transformations within the Mirghani Sufi order, and the growing mobilization of southern communities.[16]

Yet, by emphasizing long historical continuities over the last one to two hundred years of Sudanese history, most historians of Sudan have neglected

[14] Jok Madut Jok, *War and Slavery in Sudan* (Philadelphia: University of Pennsylvania Press, 2001). An explicit statement of the thesis that the Arab elite has sought to hinder Africans' economic development can be found in Benaiah Yongo-Bure, *Economic Development of Southern Sudan* (Lanham, MD: University Press of America, 2007); see also Abdullahi El Tom, *Darfur, JEM and the Khalil Ibrahim Story* (Trenton, NJ: Red Sea Press, 2011). Fatima Babiker Mahmoud has emphasized the privileged connection of traders and officials from the Ja'alin, Shaigiya, and Danagla tribes to the outside world and wider trading networks. These connections made it both possible and profitable for members of these northern groups to create commercial networks that spanned the whole scope of the country and, in the process, to build a state that could protect their privileged position. Fatima Babiker Mahmoud, *The Sudanese Bourgeoisie: Vanguard of Development?* (London: Zed Books, 1984).

[15] Johnson notes that the Sudanic states began systematically raiding their peripheries in the fourteenth century. Johnson continues by asserting, "The southern Sudan had been largely unaffected by the succession of early states in the North. By the early eighteenth century, southward expansion was effectively halted by the Shilluk kingdom…and by the Dinka living along the Kiir…White Nile, or the Sobat…The Turco-Egyptian conquest of the Sudan upset this regional balance…It was during this period of the nineteenth century that we can identify the beginning of a North-South divide." Douglas Johnson, *The Root Causes of Sudan's Civil Wars* (Bloomington: Indiana University Press, 2003), pp. 2–4.

[16] "The Khatmiyya refused to join the Mahdist forces, unlike some smaller orders, on two grounds: the leader of the Order did not believe in the religious mission of the Mahdi as the 'Expected One' and the Khatmiyya saw in the political domination of the Mahdist a threat to its position and privileges. This opposition has continued into the present-day politics of the Sudan." Later both the Mahdist and the Khatmiyya would serve as intermediaries for members of the Native Administration and the educated urban elite, allowing both to represent themselves to the colonial state or, after independence, to the popular masses, particularly in the countryside.

Ahmed Al-Shahi, "A Noah's Ark: The Continuity of the Khatmiyya Order in Northern Sudan," *British Society for Middle Eastern Studies Bulletin* 8:1 (1981): 17–18; see also Muhammad Abu Salim, *Buhuth fi Tarikh al-Sudan: al-Aradi, al-'Ulama', al-Khilafah, Barbar, 'Ali al-Mirghani.* (Beirut: Dar al-Jil, 1992), 172–173; Muhammad Abu al-Qasim Hajj Hamad, *Al-Sudan: al-Ma' ziq al-Tarikhi wa Afaq al-Mustaqbal* (Beirut: Dar al-Kalimat lil Nashr, 1980), pp. 254–256. The classic work on the Mahdi era remains P. M. Holt, *The Mahdist State in Sudan, 1881–1898* (Oxford: Clarendon Press, 1958).

the particularity of the decolonizing moment, a period that extended in Sudan from the 1930s until the mid-1960s.[17] Consequentially, Sudanese scholars have deemphasized the distinctiveness of the late colonial and early postcolonial state.[18] This study aims to correct this error by demonstrating that the nature of the postcolonial Sudanese state was determined by policies enacted during the twenty years following World War II. In addition these policies cannot be explained simply as the inheritance of the nineteenth century or of the colonial period: they must be understood as the outcome of contingent decisions made by mid-twentieth-century policy makers in Sudan.

Imagining the Sudanese State

To develop the Sudanese state, colonial officials, postcolonial politicians, policy makers, and their international advisors were forced to align their sociopolitical imaginations with two different infrastructures.[19] The first was the physical infrastructure left behind by the colonial state at independence. For example, Sudan's elite inherited a massive territory with a railway network that extended to hardly any of its borders (Map 1). The second was the cognitive infrastructure provided by the development economists of the 1950s and 1960s, who theorized, for example, that capital investment was the engine of economic growth. The globally circulating doctrines of development, which became hegemonic within the Sudanese Ministry of Finance between 1956 and 1966, frequently equated development with production and asserted that the pace of development was controlled by the rate of capital investment.

Encouraged by cultural prejudices, the legacies of these two infrastructures led Sudan's leaders to focus their efforts on the most developed region of the country. Sudan's economic planners promised that investment would flow

17 Those scholars who focus on the particularities of war, famine, and political Islam begin their narratives in the 1980s, Alex De Waal and A. H. Abdel Salam, "Islamism, State Power and Jihad in Sudan," in A. De Waal, ed., *Islamism and Its Enemies in the Horn of Africa* (London: Hurst, 2004), pp. 71–114; Alex De Waal, *Famine that Kills* (Oxford: Oxford University Press, 2005); David Keen, *The Benefits of Famine: A Political Economy of Famine and Relief in Southwestern Sudan, 1983–1989* (Princeton, NJ: Princeton University Press, 1994).

18 D. A. Low and J. M. Lonsdale, "Introduction: Towards the New Order, 1945–1963," in D. A. Low and Alison Smith, eds., *History of East Africa Vol. III* (Oxford: Clarendon Press, 1976), pp. 1–63. For a discussion of how the symbols, institutions, and metaphors of the colonial state lived on into the postcolonial state, see Crawford Young and Thomas Turner, *The Rise and Decline of the Zairian State* (Madison: University of Wisconsin Press, 1985).

19 Emmanuel Kreike, *Environmental Infrastructure in African History: Examining the Myth of Natural Resource Management in Namibia* (New York: Cambridge University Press, 2013), pp. 21–22. "Infrastructure is both relational and ecological – it means different things to different groups and it is part of the balance of action, tools, and the built environment, inseparable from them. It is also frequently mundane to the point of boredom, involving things such as plugs, standards, and bureaucratic forms." Susan Leigh Star, "The Ethnography of Infrastructure," *American Behavioral Scientist* 43:3 (1999): 377–391. I would like to thank Oliver Rollins for this citation.

MAP 1 Map of railways in Sudan

toward the less developed parts of the country in stages after development of the core regions of the country. Once politicians and finance officials began to challenge the Sudanese development narrative in the wake of the October Revolution of 1964, the notion that the provinces of Sudan needed to wait for investment gave way to the image of those regions as irredeemable badlands.[20]

To understand policy making during the decades before and after Sudan's independence, it is necessary to place the policy makers back in their intellectual environment and to remember the optimism of the decolonization era, an optimism that engulfed the Sudanese. Today, the Sudanese government is often seen as petty, corrupt, and neopatrimonial. The international media frequently associate poverty, famine, and civil war with the band of Sahelian states stretching from Senegal on the Atlantic Ocean to Sudan along the Red Sea. In the post 9/11 era, simplistic explanations for the wars that have ravaged Mali, Chad, the Central African Republic, and Sudan have frequently been offered, reflecting the late Samuel Huntington's *Clash of Civilizations*, which posited a new cold war between a westernized sub-Saharan Africa and the Islamic world.[21]

A constant barrage of media reports and also scholarship thus has obscured the success the Sudanese state did achieve in the 1950s and 1960s.[22] Morten Jerven argues that this is part of a broader trend in which scholars of African economic development project backward the economic failures experienced by many African states during the 1980s as an accurate description of postcolonial Africa's economic trajectory, ignoring the economic growth that was achieved in countries such as Sudan from the 1950s to the 1970s.[23] After all, when Sudan became independent in 1956, observers believed that the country's economic prospects were bright. In 1958, as World Bank officials wrote up

20 Alden Young, "African Bureaucrats and the Exhaustion of the Development State," *Humanity* 8:1 (2017): 49–75.

21 Samuel P. Huntington, *The Clash of Civilizations and the Remaking of the World Order* (New York: Simon & Schuster, 1996); Robert D. Kaplan, *Surrender or Starve: Travels in Ethiopia, Sudan, Somalia, and Eritrea* (New York: Vintage, 1998).

22 The largest body of scholarship on Sudan focuses on the civil wars. James Copnall, *A Poisonous Thorn in Our Hearts: Sudan and South Sudan's Bitter and Incomplete Divorce* (New York: Hurst Press, 2014); Matthew LeRiche and Matthew Arnold, *South Sudan: From Revolution to Independence* (London: Hurst, 2013); Ann Lesch, *The Sudan: Contested National Identities* (Bloomington: Indiana University Press, 1998); Christopher Clapham, ed., *African Guerillas* (Oxford: James Currey, 1998); Peter Adwok Nyaba, *The Politics of Liberation in South Sudan* (Chicago: Fountain Press, 1996); Scopas S. Poggo, *The First Sudanese Civil War: Africans, Arabs and Israelis in the Southern Sudan, 1955–1972* (New York: Palgrave Macmillan, 2009); and Oystein H. Rolandsen, "A False Start between War and Peace in the Southern Sudan, 1956–1962," *Journal of African History* 52:1 (2011): 105–123.

23 Morten Jerven, *Africa: Why Economists Get it Wrong?* (New York: Zed Books, 2015); Jerven, *Poor Numbers*.

their initial impressions after their first mission to an independent Sudan, they happily reported that the Government of Sudan gave "evidence of a rather sound grasp of development." And they attested to the fact that the Government of Sudan "followed a conservative financial policy."[24]

Generations of primarily political scientists have defined neopatrimonalism as the replacement of the public interest with private interests. Returning to the archives of the early independent Sudanese state and carefully examining its policy documents, the historian is not met with the impression that its bureaucrats were in the thrall of private interests.[25] In fact, in the 1950s traces of neopatrimonialism were found more frequently in the records of the departing British colonial officials, who were often more concerned with their pensions, rather than of the earnest Sudanese who replaced them.[26] Still, narratives of African officials' corruption, which were spread initially by the retreating colonial state, have since become received wisdom.[27]

In the 1950s Sudanese officials were not seen as corrupt or incompetent. As mentioned, World Bank officials believed that Sudan was led by very competent senior Sudanese officials, though they were concerned about the lack of technical expertise and mid-level administrative talent following the departure of the British from most administrative posts in 1954. Thus, at least according to informed outside observers such as those stationed at the World Bank, Sudan was expected to make an easy transition to independence.[28] Moreover, World Bank officials also agreed with the direction of Sudan's economic policy: to increase the amount of land cultivated by farmers to raise cash crops, particularly cotton, for export. The government used the majority of the income earned from cotton exports to purchase additional land to bring under cultivation and to develop complementary import-substitution industries, such as food processing or textile manufacturing.[29]

The Economizing Logic

Reflecting on the economic policies that Sudan and a number of African countries pursued in the decades after independence, Robert Bates in 1981

24 Sudan Archive at Durham University, UK [SAD] 593/8/1–61/, International Bank for Reconstruction and Development, "The Economy of the Sudan" (February 25, 1958), p. 1.

25 SAD G//S 1166, J. Carmichael; Box 3/2; General Review of Financial and Economic Problems.

26 Thandika Mkandawire, "Thinking about Developmental States in Africa," *Cambridge Journal of Economics* 25:3 (2002): 289–313, and "Neopatrimonalism and the Political Economy of Economic Performance in Africa: Critical Reflections," *World Politics* 67:3 (July 2015): 563–612.

27 Robert L. Tignor, "Political Corruption in Nigeria before Independence," *Journal of Modern African Studies* 31:2 (1993): 175–202.

28 SAD 593/8/1–61/, International Bank for Reconstruction and Development, "The Economy of the Sudan" (February 25, 1958), p. 1.

29 Ibid.

provocatively asked, "Why should reasonable men adopt public policies that have harmful consequences for the societies they govern?"[30] Unlike Bates, I do not feel that the economic planners replaced public interests with private interests; my contention is that decisions about how to allocate resources in the twenty years after 1945 were vested in an economizing logic. The ideology of development entrenched a future-oriented vision of cost and benefit as the paramount logic of the state.[31] In part, this book records the actual distribution of resources to the different regions of Sudan, but I focus not on the enumeration of budget figures, but instead on the new ways of thinking that began to emerge during the two decades on either side of independence. Certainly, the politics of distribution has fueled conflict among the regions of Sudan.[32] However, it is not merely that provincial elites vied for resources; there was a deeper conflict over how the state would decide which claims on its resources were valid.[33]

But how did the economizing logic become the policy-making lens in Sudan? There are three ways that a sociologist of knowledge might understand economics and economists' influence on policy: as the result of professional authority, institutional position, or cognitive infrastructure.[34] In the chapters that follow, I discuss the growing professional authority of specific economic policy makers and their shifting institutional positions as a way to demonstrate the growing power of finance and economic officials in the Sudanese government from the 1940s until the 1960s. However, my argument hinges not on the influence of specific officials, but on the spread of new types of cognitive infrastructures among economists and non-economist policy makers throughout the Sudanese government. I trace the emergence of new styles of reasoning and "economic policy devices that produce knowledge and help make decisions."[35] This economizing logic became the framework in which British and then Sudanese officials wrestled with what it meant for Sudan to possess

30 Retrospectively, two of the classic criticisms formulated by later generations of scholars were first, that redirecting the profits from the agricultural sector toward state-sanctioned developments would destroy the incentives for farmers to farm, and second, that extensive exploitation of resources simply made Sudan, as well as many of its fellow African states, vulnerable to the vagaries of world markets. Robert Bates, *Markets and States in Tropical Africa* (1981; repr. Berkeley: University of California Press, 2005) p. 3; Giovanni Arrighi, "The African Crisis: World Systemic and Regional Aspects," *New Left Review* 15 (May–June 2002), https://newleftreview.org/II/15/giovanni-arrighi-the-african-crisis [accessed June 17, 2017].

31 Timothy Mitchell, "Economentality: How the Future Entered Government," *Critical Inquiry* 40:4 (2014): 479–507.

32 Catherine Boone, *Property and Political Order in Africa: Land Rights and the Structure of Politics* (Cambridge: Cambridge University Press, 2014), p. 60.

33 James Ferguson, *Give a Man a Fish: Reflections on the New Politics of Distribution* (Durham, NC: Duke University Press, 2015), p. 10.

34 Daniel Hirschman and Elizabeth Popp Berman, "Do Economists Make Policies? On the Political Effects of Economics," *Socio-Economic Review* 12 (2014): 781.

35 Ibid.

a sovereign economy. Policy making in Sudan meant constantly "improvising within tight corners."

Understandably, anticolonial leaders across the world rejected the idea that their societies' poverty was natural. Therefore, they latched onto the new science of economics, which, during the two decades following World War II, became the paramount political science. Both racial/ethnic and structural explanations for Sudan's turmoil ignore the shifting intellectual environment in which mid-twentieth-century Sudanese leaders and intellectuals lived. Beginning in the 1930s, intellectuals – born colonial subjects such as W. Arthur Lewis, Eric Williams, and Samir Amin – began to fashion theories of economic development that charged the colonizing powers such as Great Britain with gross negligence when it came to the poverty of their colonial possessions. This poverty was newly visualized using the global accounting techniques of statisticians such as Colin Clark. Even more challenging for colonial ideas of racial and civilizational superiority, intellectuals such as Lewis argued that there were readily applicable theories of economic development that could be implemented to address the poverty and lack of industrialization that plagued large parts of the colonized world.[36] These views challenged long-held tenets of colonial economics developed by imperial economists such as Sally Herbert Frankel and P. T. Bauer, who largely believed that economic development efforts directed toward the territories of British Africa would be in vain.[37] In their view, economic development could not be stimulated by government action. Thus, the task before the colonial state was principally to maintain order among backward peoples until such a time as natural processes brought them to a higher stage of knowledge.[38]

Those who spoke the language of economics not only rearranged the world in the imperial and industrial cores of the interwar period but also altered the

[36] Frederick Cooper, "Commentary on the Essay of Joseph Hodge," *Humanity* (May 3, 2106): http://humanityjournal.org/blog/commentary-on-the-essay-of-joseph-hodge [accessed July 16, 2017]. Robert L. Tignor, *W. Arthur Lewis and the Birth of Development Economics* (Princeton, NJ: Princeton University Press, 2006). The extent to which independence leaders in the Caribbean and Africa sought to imagine an international order that would uphold the values of universalism and antiracism can be seen in the recent work of Steven L. B. Jensen, *The Making of International Human Rights: The 1960s, Decolonization, and the Reconstruction of Global Values* (New York: Cambridge University Press, 2016).

[37] S. Herbert Frankel, *Capital Investment in Africa: Its Course and Effects* (New York: Oxford University Press, 1938), pp. 30–60; P. T. Bauer, *West African Trade: A Study of Competition, Oligopoly and Monopoly in a Changing Economy* (New York: Cambridge University Press, 1954). For context see Helen Tilley, *Africa as a Living Laboratory: Empire, Development and the Problem of Scientific Knowledge, 1870–1950* (Chicago: University of Chicago Press, 2011); John Toye, "Herbert Frankel: From Colonial Economics to Development Economics," *Oxford Development Studies* 37:2 (June 2009): 171–182.

[38] For a critique of development thinking during this period, see William R. Easterly, *The Elusive Quest for Growth: Economists' Adventures and Misadventures in the Tropics* (Cambridge, MA: MIT Press, 2002).

visions of state-makers across the decolonizing world after World War II. When economics entered into the sinews of government, it provided a lens through which to frame the plethora of information flooding across the desk of postwar policy makers. Promoting the health of the economy – a proxy representing the collective well-being of a particular society – became the hallmark of an economized politics.[39] The propagation of a system of national income accounts made it possible to replace the hierarchy of civilizations, which had a now discredited racial component, with an index of states ranked according to their wealth.[40] However, the more things changed, the more they stayed the same, as Daniel Speich noted: "The national income view of global inequality did not force Western politicians to reconsider the colonial logic of domination fundamentally. Notions of supremacy, which used to be grounded in cultural considerations, found easy expression in the statistically based language of economic strength."[41] Nevertheless, development as a new formulation gained worldwide acceptance because, unlike the old scales of civilizations, which appeared immutable, the new rankings of states, according to each one's national income, offered a path for improvement, for development. While from the very beginning, there were doubts about the quality of the measures of income across societies and disagreements about how development should proceed, the very image of mobility that economic development promised ensured its popularity among colonial officials, nationalist leaders, the technical experts of the two superpowers, and ultimately the burgeoning international bureaucracy that sprang up to manage the Bretton Woods world economy.[42]

Sudanese policy makers were well aware of the vast inequalities that plagued their country, yet the tools of mid-twentieth-century macroeconomics helped them justify ignoring them in favor of the goal of catching up economically with the states that they aspired to have as peers. The central triangle from

[39] Timothy Mitchell, *The Rule of Experts: Egypt, Techno-Politics, Modernity* (Berkeley: University of California Press, 2002), p. 272.

[40] First developed in 1953, the UN System of National Income Accounts allowed economic activity to be compared internationally. Daniel Speich, "The Use of Global Abstractions: National Income Accounting in the Period of Imperial Decline," *Journal of Global History* 6:1 (March 2011): 7–28; and Morten Jerven, "Users and Producers of African Income: Measuring African Progress," *African Affairs* 110: 439 (2011): 169–190.

[41] Speich, "The Use of Global Abstractions," p. 21. I am thankful for my correspondence with Hannah Appel, who suggested this quotation, December 6, 2016.

[42] Frederick Cooper, "Modernizing Bureaucrats, Backward Africans, and the Development Concept," in Frederick Cooper and Randall Packard, eds., *International Development and the Social Sciences: Essays on the History and Politics of Knowledge* (Berkeley: University of California Press, 1998), pp. 64–84; Joseph Hodge, "British Colonial Expertise, Postcolonial Careering and the Early History of International Development," *Journal of Modern European History*, Special Issue on "Modernizing Missions: Approaches to 'Developing' the Non-Western World after 1945," 8:1 (2010): 24–46. For a discussion of the continuing significance of race in the postcolonial world, see Jemima Pierre, *The Predicament of Blackness: Postcolonial Ghana and the Politics of Race* (Chicago: University of Chicago Press, 2012).

Omdurman to Kosti and Sennar not only dominated the nation's politics but also was significantly richer than the rest of the country, with a per capita income more than three times that of parts of southern and western Sudan.[43] Nevertheless, it was the central region of the country that received most of the development funding allocated by the Sudanese government in Khartoum. This inevitably led to unrest in 1955 at Torit in the Equatoria province of southern Sudan, where a rebellion broke out over the failure of the central government to include southerners in the civil service list. Later in the early 1960s rebellions broke out throughout the southern provinces protesting neglect, exclusion from development decision making, and a general unwillingness on the part of the central government to interact with southerners political ambitions except through a militarized counterinsurgency.[44]

During the two decades after World War II, the quest for societal mobility underlay the Sudanese story. For the political class and the technocratic elite ensconced in Khartoum and the major provincial towns, transforming Sudan from a poor country to one that rivaled its middle-income Arab neighbors was a clear goal. In favor of this goal, Sudanese officials were willing to delay investment in the majority of the country.

Economic Imaginaries

One of my major goals in this work is to demonstrate how globalized conceptions of development interacted with local utopias in the minds of policy makers. Sudan was created through the interaction of imaginaries both globalized and nonglobalized.[45] The practical tools of development are built on cognitive infrastructures, and when policy makers used those tools in their decision-making processes, the cognitive infrastructures encoded in them defined what was thinkable and reasonable.[46]

[43] Daly, *Darfur's Sorrow*, pp. 185–189.

[44] Oystein Rolandsen and Cherry Leonardi, "Discourses of Violence in the Transition from Colonialism to Independence in Southern Sudan, 1955–1960," *Journal of Eastern African Studies* 8:4 (2014): 609–625. For a discussion of the extent to which the Government of Sudan in Khartoum was part of a wider mid-century tradition of combining counterinsurgency and the discourse of development, which continues until today, see Mortiz Feichtinger and Stephan Malinowski, "Transformative Invasions: Western Post-9/11 Counterinsurgency and the Lessons of Colonialism," *Humanity*, 3:1 (2014): 35–63, http://humanityjournal.org/issue3-1/transformative-invasions-western-post-911-counterinsurgency-and-the-lessons-of-colonialism [accessed July 16, 2017].

[45] Samuel Moyn, "On the Nonglobalization of Ideas"; see also Emma Rothschild, "Isolation and Economic Development in Eighteenth Century France," *American Historical Review* 119:4 (2014): 1055–1082.

[46] Bruno Latour, *Science in Action: How to Follow Scientists and Engineers through Society* (Cambridge, MA: Harvard University Press, 1988), pp. 68–69, and "Visualisation and Cognition: Drawing Things Together," *Knowledge and Society Studies in the Sociology of Culture Past and Present* 6 (1986): 1–40; Peter A Hall, "Policy Paradigms, Social Learning, and the State: The Case of Economic Policymaking in Britain," *Comparative Politics* 25:3 (April 1993): 275–296.

I distinguish two types of imaginaries in the documents of policy makers.[47] The first are the cognitive infrastructures baked into the very tools that these officials were adopting, such as national development programming and their assumption of the nation-state as the unit of financial analysis. The second type of imaginary is the social world of the planners who are manipulating these tools in order to make decisions. Which assets does an official see as economic capital, for instance? Which investments appear risky and which safe? These questions are intimately entwined with the sociological imagination of the person making these decisions. At the same time, there is a reality to the economy that cannot be ignored. Sudanese officials inherited a particular physical infrastructure; the railroads, for instance, only connected certain parts of the country. Likewise, Sudanese officials understood that the margins of maneuverability within which to experiment with the state's current account surplus or its development budgets were necessarily narrow.[48] These officials also operated within an international network of peers that socialized their views of the economic world.

In many ways, the representation of an independent Sudanese economy was the unintended byproduct of policy makers' attempts to define their own authority by melding their visions of the future with the cognitive and physical infrastructures at their disposal. Once economic independence had been asserted, policy makers discovered that factors beyond their control severely constrained their power to govern and shape the direction of Sudan's economy. Frederick Cooper and Gary Wilder recently highlighted several ways that West African intellectuals imagined alternatives to the nation-state as independence approached: actually, independence for Sudan as a nation-state was not the original demand of the anticolonial leaders as they began to fight Britain in the 1920s. By the 1940s in the parlors of Omdurman, proposals for Sudan to be a part of a supraterritorial unit found vibrant support. Many anticolonial leaders championed the concept of the "Unity of the Nile Valley," while British officials were enthralled with visions of a Central African Federation or an East African High Commission. Yet the feasibility of these alternatives was undermined, because tools such as national budgets limited what it was politically possible to execute.[49] For instance, once two distinct budgets are created, each representing different territories, the divergences in wealth between the two become visible to alert publics; this makes it almost impossible to

47 Sheila Jasanoff, "Future Imperfect: Science, Technology, and the Imaginations of Modernity," in Sheila Jasanoff and Sung-Hyun Kim, eds., *Dreamscapes of Modernity: Sociotechnical Imaginaries and the Fabrication of Power* (Chicago: University of Chicago Press, 2015), pp. 1–34.

48 Adam Tooze, "Trouble with Numbers: Statistics, Politics, and History in the Construction of Weimar's Trade Balance, 1918–1924," *American Historical Review* 113:8 (2008): 678–700.

49 Cooper, *Citizenship between Empire and Nation*, and *Africa in the World: Capitalism, Empire, Nation-State* (Cambridge, MA: Harvard University Press, 2014), and Gary Wilder, *Freedom Time: Negritude, Decolonization, and the Future of the World* (Durham, NC: Duke University Press, 2015).

recombine these entities without raising difficult questions of redistribution. Despite all of the political and intellectual activity that aimed to find alternatives to the nation-state, it still emerged as the chosen, almost ready-made, or modular solution at independence, as one country after another emerged from European colonialism.[50]

Why Sudan?

Sudanese nationalism was at once liberatory and exclusionary. From its origins in the 1920s until the nationalists came to power in the mid-1950s, Sudanese nationalism situated itself within two transnational movements. The anticolonial movement was popularly framed as the quest for development.[51] The second social movement that Sudanese nationalists were swept up in was the battle against racism.[52] In the case of Sudan, the bilingual riverain elite, which inherited control of the state, felt that they were the target of racism on the part of both the British and the Egyptians. Yet, each of the three parties attempted to emphasize the prejudices of the others for its own advantage during the run-up to independence.[53] To this day, many Sudanese point to the deposal of Muhammad Neguib as the first president of the Republic of Egypt following the Free Officer Coup as an example of racial prejudice on the part of Gamal Abdul Nasser and his fellow Egyptians. They often say that was the moment when they knew they could never be part of a federation with Egypt.[54]

The movement for economic development, when combined with combating racism, created a strong emphasis on national sovereignty, which played out in a very specific manner that continues to haunt the country until today. First, despite the fact that a narrow segment of Sudanese society took power at independence in 1956, that small group, the elite, came to see themselves as the

50 Benedict Anderson, *Imagined Communities: Reflections on the Origins and Spread of Nationalism* (New York: Verso, 2006), p. 137. For a discussion of some of the earlier visions of Sudanese nationalism, see Elena Vezzadini, *Lost Nationalism: Revolution, Memory and Anti-Colonial Resistance in Sudan* (Rochester, NY: James Currey, 2015), and Mohamed Omar Beshir, *Revolution and Nationalism in the Sudan* (London: R. Collings, 1974).

51 Mahmood Mamdani, "Beyond Settler and Native as Political Identities: Overcoming the Political Legacy of Colonialism," *Comparative Studies in Society and History* 43:4 (October 2001): 651; Frederick Cooper, "Modernizing Bureaucrats, Backward Africans, and the Development Concept," in Frederick Cooper and Randall Packard, eds., *International Development and the Social Sciences: Essays on the History and Politics of Knowledge* (Berkeley: University of California Press, 1998), pp. 64–84.

52 Tukufu Zuberi, *African Independence: How Africa Shapes the World?* (New York: Rowman & Littlefield, 2015), pp. 13–14, and Robert Vitalis, *White World Order, Black Power Politics: The Birth of American International Relations* (Ithaca, NY: Cornell University Press, 2015).

53 Justin Willis and Atta Batthani, "'We Changed the Laws': Electoral Practice and Malpractice in Sudan since 1953," *African Affairs* 109:435 (2010): 191–212.

54 Mohamed Ahmed Mahgoub, *Democracy on Trial: Reflections on Arab and African Politics* (London: Andre Deutsch, 1974), pp. 11–63; A. R. al-Mukhtar, *al-Harif al-Farah: Asrar al-Sudan, 1950–1970* (Khartoum: Dar al-Sahafah, 1978).

emblems of *Sudani-ness*, a creole identity to which it was possible for them to assimilate the other peoples over whom they ruled.[55] This then created a situation in which Sudanese nationalists, unlike their peers in countries such as Nigeria or Kenya, refused to countenance ideas of regional autonomy or ethnic federalism.[56] Using the language of economics, officials even argued that since all Sudanese citizens were formally equal, there was no reason to make policy accommodations for historical grievances and group identities. Paradoxically, the principle of equality enshrined in the national imagination and economic policy making allowed the officials of the newly independent Sudanese state to reinscribe regional and individual inequality, while simultaneously defining as illegitimate claims for redress by marginalized communities. Thus, as Sudanese nationalists gradually assumed power between 1945 and 1966, the project of governing Sudan was transformed from the management of a collection of distinct populations, each with its own attributes, to the management of a national economy made up of equal individuals, whose preferences policy makers assumed could be aggregated and even maximized.

Even as the 'Abboud regime, a military dictatorship that came to power in November 1958, spoke of establishing a relationship with its citizens that would not rely on the intermediation of the traditional parties, it fetishized the "economy," represented as a combination of the aggregate figures collected by the state's statistical agency.[57] The GDP calculated as a result of national income accounts became a novel means of representing the economy and economic progress. Increases in the rate of economic growth became the measure of a successful government. Statistical and planning offices worked to manufacture new economic tools.[58] Yet despite the great effort expended by Sudanese officials to see their country through an economic lens, the economic was always refracted through their own social imaginations. Therefore, they read agriculture carried out by peasants without government assistance as helplessly disorganized, they saw the great cattle herds of the southern and western provinces as non-economic assets, and they always believed that significant capital investments in regions distant from Khartoum would underperform, contributing next to nothing to the state.

55 Heather Sharkey, *Living with Colonialism: Nationalism and Culture in the Anglo-Egyptian Sudan* (Berkeley: University of California Press, 2003), pp. 16–40.

56 This became a distinct problem in regard to southern Sudan, because as Amir Idris explains, "Southerners do not regard the mainstream culture that is Arab-Islamic as superior to their own. Moreover, the assertion of Southern Sudanese distinctiveness is not the result of an inability to merge into what is perceived to be mainstream Sudanese culture." Amir H. Idris, *Sudan's Civil War: Slavery, Race and Formational Identities* (Lewiston, NY: Edwin Mellen Press, 2001), p. 7.

57 Mitchell, "Fixing the Economy," pp. 82–101.

58 "[An instrument] can be a piece of hardware like a telescope, but it can also be made of softer material. A statistical institution that employs hundreds of pollsters, sociologists and computer scientists gathering all sorts of data on the economy *is* an instrument if it yields inscriptions for papers written in economic journals with, for instance, a graph of the inflation rate by month and by branch of industry." Latour, *Science in Action*, pp. 68–69.

The economic imaginary of their country that Sudanese officials possessed guaranteed that the peripheries would continue to be neglected.[59] In the eyes of Sudanese officials, even violent unrest did not fundamentally alter the need to concentrate investment in a few massive, but potentially highly profitable, projects located in the Sudanese core. However, in October 1964, the equation of economic growth with the legitimacy of the regime did not survive riots and unrest in the capital.[60] Even so, the failure of the 'Abboud regime did not destroy the legitimacy of economic expertise; rather it further entrenched planning and the discipline of economics in Sudanese affairs as tools capable of explaining the failure of the military regime's economic policies and offering a way forward.[61] In particular, former officials such as Hamza Mirghani Hamza returned home from working for international financial institutions (IFIs) to argue that the Sudanese state could not be expected to control its economic destiny in isolation. With the support of the International Monetary Fund, he used the instability of the global commodity market and the limits that the markets placed on Sudan's ability to plan as an argument for greater transparency within the government of Sudan. The implicit promise was that transparency would allow Sudan to receive the support it needed from the IFIs to develop. Even though the drive toward greater transparency placed a disproportionate share of the burden of economic reform on countries such as Sudan, it reflected the realization that only the further integration and transformation of the international system could propel development.[62]

When one moves from an approach based solely on interests and identity politics and toward one that foregrounds changing approaches to development, it becomes clear that the shifting ideas held by senior policy makers on how to manage the economy propelled the political conflicts that have dominated Sudanese history since independence. Many of these policies, in turn, were the direct result of the adoption of particular economic tools. For instance, state officials conceived of development planning and budgeting in 1946 in ways that were dramatically different from the practices associated with development planning in the 1960s. Changes in the state's style of planning played a large role

59 Jasanoff, "Future Imperfect," pp. 1–34.

60 For a description of the events leading up to the October 1964 uprising, see Yusuf Fadl Hasan, "The Sudanese Revolution of October 1964," *Journal of Modern African Studies* 5:4 (December 1967): 491–509 and Peter K. Bechtold, *Politics in the Sudan: Parliamentary and Military Rule in an Emerging African Nation* (New York: Praeger, 1976).

61 The chief of the Economic Planning Secretariat charged with writing the ten-year plan wrote one of the most important retrospectives of this period. It continues to be an important economic text used today to train the country's economic planners. See Mirghani, *Development Planning in the Sudan in the Sixties*. See, also, Rolf Gusten, *Problems of Economic Growth and Planning; The Sudan Example: Some Aspects and Implications of the Current Ten-Year Plan* (New York: Springer-Verlag, 1966) and journals such as the *Sudan Journal of Administration and Development*, which was first published in 1965.

62 Nils Gilman, "The New International Economic Order: A Reintroduction," *Humanity* 6:1 (2015): 1–15.

in determining the types of investment considered economically rational, and the resulting patterns of investment directly affected Sudan's political stability.

Finally, Sudanese economic and financial policy makers, like their peers in many other African countries, have succeeded according to some of the metrics that they set for themselves. The devices that policy makers used to help them formulate policy allowed Sudanese officials to navigate the state's position within the world economy, even as their use pushed the voices of a multitude of communities into the shadows, allowing inequality to fester and grow.

Methods and Sources

By writing a narrative that combines political history with a cultural history of political economy, I explain how a small group of colonial and postcolonial officials in Sudan were able to justify ever-increasing economic inequality in the name of state- and nation-building.[63] As a political history, my story explains both the scramble to create the Sudanese state and the confusion about where to locate it as the British and Egyptian Empires came undone. It then describes the struggle to create a centralized state in a territory made up of numerous overlapping and centrifugal political communities, culminating in revolt and civil war. Using insights from science and technology studies, I analyze plans, budgets, and forecasts as artifacts of thinking and illuminate the implicit biases embedded in each of these objects. Development planning, budgeting, and forecasting are useful sites of investigation, because these instruments track and shape elite aspirations about the structure of the state.[64] The rules and tools of economic planning structured which decisions the officials were able to imagine as reasonable.[65] Planning, due to its future orientation, public nature, and repetition, captured the aspirations of senior bureaucrats to legitimate the state.[66]

The administrative, political, and economic history of the Sudanese state during the two decades after 1945 has largely been ignored. This is part of a larger neglect of the administrative history of African states during the early years of independence. Historians' neglect of this period until recently has allowed political scientists such as Robert Bates, Jeffrey Herbst, and Crawford Young to

63 Caitlin Rosenthal, "From Memory to Mastery: Accounting for Control in America, 1750–1880," *Enterprise and Society* 14:4 (2013): 732–748

64 Mitchell, "Economentality," 479–507; Jenny Andersson, "The Great Future Debate and the Struggle for the World," *American Historical Review* 117:5 (2012): 1411–1430; Debjani Bhattacharyya, "Interwar Housing Speculation and Rent Profiteering in Colonial Calcutta," *Comparative Studies of South Asia, Africa and the Middle East* 36:3 (2016): 465–482.

65 For a discussion of how national statistical offices functioned and of how the technical aspects of planning often interacted with its political aspects, see Jerven, "Users and Producers of African Income." Also see Vincent Bonnecase, *La Pauvreté au Sahel: Du Savoir Colonial à la Mesure Internationale* (Paris: Karthala, 2011).

66 For a discussion of the legitimating function of internationally comparable measures of development, see Speich, "The Use of Global Abstractions."

provide the most useful explanations of why independence-era African politicians enacted the economic policies that they did. Yet, while my work builds on their contrasting theories about the African state and the role of its policy makers, it adds an archivally grounded specificity that previous accounts have lacked. By doing so it seeks to counteract the tendency of scholars to imagine the African state as rapacious and predatory, with official institutions serving little purpose other than legitimization and patronage. The point here is not to argue that postcolonial states are not rapacious, but to question whether the study of their institutions can be dismissed so easily.[67]

One of the problems with studying bureaucracies, rule making, and the immediate post-independence generation is that each of these often takes on an ephemeral quality. Oral interviews or narrative accounts written today tend to gloss over the activities of the post-independence generation with an affectation of boredom.[68] Therefore, most accounts of Sudanese history written today focus on the nineteenth century, the colonial period, and the struggle for independence, before picking up again with the wars of the 1980s and 1990s. As historians we must be aware of the extent to which certain master narratives, which are often formed in real trauma, are constantly reinforced in social discourse and then filtered into our narratives at the same time that they are then reinforced by the very histories that we are writing.[69]

Seeking to disrupt the master narratives about Sudan, which explain much of Sudanese postcolonial history through the lens of identity-based conflict or alternatively as a result of inevitable center-periphery dynamics, I sought out neglected types of sources and traced the infrastructures of the bureaucracy to reconstruct how the decision-making process functioned.[70] This project was explicitly constructed around budgets, plans, financial documents, and the memos and notes that senior officials wrote to one another within the financial offices of the state. My original hypothesis was that it would be possible to use these neglected files to reveal what Leigh Gardner, quoting the sociologist Rudolph Goldscheid, asserted: that "the budget is the skeleton of the state, stripped of all misleading ideologies."[71] Following in the footsteps of Morten

[67] Alden Young, "Measuring the Sudanese Economy: A Focus on National Growth Rates and Regional Inequality, 1959–1964," *Canadian Journal of Development Studies* 35:1 (2014): 45.

[68] Malika Rahal, "Comment faire l'histoire de l'Algérie indépendante?," *La Vie des Idees.fr* (March 13, 2012), www.laviedesidees.fr/Comment-faire-l-histoire-de-l-Algerie-independante [accessed July 16, 2017], and "Fused Together and Torn Apart: Stories and Violence in Contemporary Algeria," *History and Memory* 24:1 (Spring/Summer 2012): 118–151; Jeffrey Byrne, *Mecca of Revolution: Algeria, Decolonization, and the Third World Order* (Oxford: Oxford University Press, 2016).

[69] O'Fahey, *The Sultanate of Darfur*, pp. 133–137; Aparne Pande, *Explaining Pakistan's Foreign Policy: Escaping India* (Abingdon: Routledge, 2011); C. Christine Fair, *Fighting to the End: The Pakistani Army's Way of War* (Oxford: Oxford University Press, 2014).

[70] Star, "The Ethnography of Infrastructure."

[71] Leigh A. Gardner, *Taxing Colonial Africa: The Political Economy of British Imperialism* (Oxford: Oxford University Press, 2012), p. 1–2.

Jerven, Mary Morgan, and Daniel Speich I applied a science of technology studies approach to the economic tools of the state.[72] This approach has revealed that, rather than budgets being stripped of ideology, they are chock full of ideology – framing questions of who, what, and where are worthy of receiving the resources of the state.

The book is based on eight months of research conducted in the National Records Office in Khartoum. During that trip and on repeated visits to Khartoum since 2008–2009, I have spent hours talking about, observing, and discussing Sudanese politics. I was fortunate to be surrounded by a large group of well-informed and patient Sudanese friends who were willing to open up to me about their society. While direct quotations rarely make it into the body of this text, their insights have informed my views of Sudan and influenced this work. Archival research in Sudan was significantly aided by additional research in the United Kingdom, particularly at the Sudan Archives in Durham, where the personal papers of John Carmichael, the last British permanent undersecretary of finance and later financial advisor to the three governments directly following independence, are located. His papers provide a significant narrative guide for the story that unfolds in the following chapters. The internal decision-making process of the Department of Finance, which later became the Ministry of Finance and Economics, has been amplified by drawing on US and British diplomatic reports and the Arabic and English historiography on Sudan. I also studied records from international organizations, such as the International Monetary Fund, the World Bank, and the International Bank for Reconstruction and Development (IBRD), to explore questions about the international nature of development theory and practices. Finally, I consulted a number of Arabic manuscripts written by Egyptian and Sudanese economists from the 1930s to the 1950s drawn from the Cairene bookseller Mustafa Sadiq.[73] In addition, I was also able to access, at the Hoover Archive of Stanford University issues of the *Sudanese Economist* from the 1960s.

Each type of source material has its own strengths and weaknesses, and writing a history that straddles the end of colonialism and the beginning of the postcolonial state has required me to shift the weight I gave to particular types of sources as the narrative progressed chronologically. The files classified under *Finance* within the National Records Office in Khartoum offer a wide view into the practical problems of selling cotton and the management of individual

[72] Jerven, *Poor Numbers;* Morgan, "'On a Mission' with Mutable Mobiles," pp. 6–7; Morgan, "Seeking Parts, Looking for Wholes," pp. 303–325; Daniel Speich, "Travelling with the GDP through Early Development Economics' History," Working Paper on The Nature of Evidence: How Well Do "Facts" Travel? No. 33/8 (London: London School of Economics, September 2008).

[73] I would like to thank Raphael Cormack for his help in bringing these sources to my attention. See Raphael Cormack, "The Legendary Bookseller of Cairo," *Apollo: The International Art Magazine* (March 29, 2016), www.apollo-magazine.com/the-legendary-bookseller-of-cairo/ [accessed January 2, 2017].

schemes for the entire period of my study; however, these files contained only scattered details about the plans, ambitions, and frustrations of senior colonial or postcolonial officials. In Durham, I was fortunate to find ample personal files in which senior colonial officials describe their decision-making process. While there were many overlapping sources for the period up to 1953, after that point, I was forced to rely primarily on the account of a single source, John Carmichael, for the types of discussions taking place at the most senior level within the Ministry of Finance, particularly from 1954 to 1958. However, from Carmichael's correspondence, it was possible to reconstruct in part, if not completely, policy debates between him and other leading officials within the department, particularly Hamza Mirghani Hamza. One of the sources I regret most not possessing are the personal papers of Sayyid Hamza Mirghani Hamza, who throughout – often reading between the lines of Carmichael's frustrated replies – comes across as a creative economic policy maker.

The danger posed by a reliance on personal records, particularly when those of only a few individuals are available, is that the writer becomes hostage to the interests and access of particular individuals. For the period from 1954–1958, I tried to counter this dependence by relying heavily on the Arabic and English historiography and notes of the British Foreign Office. The administrative, political, and economic history of the first few years of self-rule and independence in many ways remains the hardest to tell.

However, after the initial disorientation of independence subsided and the new bureaucracy began to orient itself, the record becomes clearer. International organizations became increasingly involved in Sudan after 1958, and their archives provide a revealing source of information about the decision-making process of senior Sudanese officials. The records of the World Bank Group Archive contain vital exchanges with a wide variety of senior Sudanese economic officials, capturing their thoughts and demonstrating the kinds of constraints that they faced as they attempted to attract the funding needed for development schemes. After 1961, the IBRD files become an increasingly useful place to find both Sudanese voices and assessments of Sudanese projects.

Outline of the Book

The chapters of this book tell the story of Sudanese economic policy making chronologically from the 1930s until 1966. Chapter 1 situates the Sudanese case within the history of development and then asks how Sudan was imagined economically before 1956. The story begins with grain markets in nineteenth-century Sudan and continues through the Anglo-Egyptian colonization and the shift in the economic focus of the country from the Red Sea to Cairo. It concludes with the role of economic expertise in the Anglo-Egyptian dispute over Sudan and how that dispute contributed to the language of Sudanese nationalism. In Chapter 2, the story picks up after World War II as Sudanese nationalists ask how Britain will repay Sudan for its contribution to the Allied victory. The

British administrators of Sudan settle on development as a goal that will allow them to continue in their role as the administrators of the country while promising the Sudanese a better future. Simple in theory, in practice this policy opened up a host of questions, perhaps the most unsettling of which was what object was in need of development. This led officials to develop "the territorial perspective" defining the goal of development with the Sudanese state. Chapters 3 and 4 begin with the transition to independence. Now that Sudan was the object of development, Sudanese finance officials were charged with creating the conditions for the Sudanese economy to grow. Despite struggling to find an independent Sudan's place in the world economy now free of Britain and Egypt, Sudanese policy makers decide to continue growing cotton, the main staple of the colonial economy: they believed that economic growth could be achieved simply by growing a lot more of it. Chapter 5 continues with the creation of an economic plan based on national income accounting that aimed to legitimate the state's development spending on the basis of a future of rising per capita growth rates. Yet, in very important ways this plan failed to take into consideration the political consequences of regional instability. Finally, Chapter 6 argues that rather than admit their limited legitimacy to allocate state spending across the country, Sudanese officials embraced the rhetoric of austerity and consequentially began to talk about the need for transparency and accountability in government budgets, signaling the end of the first Sudanese development project. The conclusion reflects on the Sudanese case and thinks about new approaches to African economic history.

1

From Colonial Economics to Political Economy, 1820–1940

Is it possible to write a global history of economic development?[1] To make this question more specific, let me modify it slightly. Can the global history of mid-twentieth-century economic development be told as the story of the proliferation of five- or ten-year plans and programs, of project management and assessment, of growth targets, and of national income accounting?[2] In other words is the history of development during the middle decades of the twentieth century the story of its elements that spread and became globalized, or is it the story of those concepts that remained local, resisted globalization, and became intelligible only when situated in local contexts?[3] If one focuses on technical elements without examining the social imaginations that were embedded inside the development discourse, one might assume that the answer to the question of whether a global history is possible is an emphatic yes; indeed, a generation of scholars writing about the history of development and its ideological companions such as modernization theory have used a model of diffusion to write about how technical concepts and tool kits emanated outward from one or at most a few locations, such as MIT, the London School of Economics, ECLA (the Economic Committee for Latin America), or the Soviet offices of planning.[4] Yet what if the diffusion narrative is incorrect?[5]

1 Sebastian Conrad, *What is Global History*? (Princeton, NJ: Princeton University Press, 2016); and Samuel Moyn and Andrew Sartori, eds., *Global Intellectual History* (New York: Columbia University Press, 2013).

2 Hirschman and Berman, "Do Economists Make Policies?" pp. 779–811.

3 Moyn, "On the Nonglobalization of Ideas," pp. 187–205; also see Rothschild, "Isolation and Economic Development in Eighteenth Century France," pp. 1055–1082.

4 See Joseph Morgan Hodge, "Writing the History of Development (Part 1: The First Wave)," *Humanity* 6:3 (2016), 429–463, http://humanityjournal.org/issue6–3/writing-the-history-of-development-part-1-the-first-wave [accessed July 17, 2017]. This discussion is informed by conversations with Nils Gilman.

5 Sivasundaram, "Sciences and the Global: On Methods, Questions, and Theory," pp. 146–158.

Sure, the technical vocabulary of economic science spread across the globe like wildfire in the service of development during the middle decades of the twentieth century. The intrepid research of postcolonial scholars such as Timothy Mitchell has shown us the extent to which the colonial world served as a living laboratory. In addition, we now know that even the experts whom historians of science ordinarily assume to be the most firmly ensconced in elite networks of theoretical knowledge developed their breakthroughs in Africa, Asia, and the Middle East.[6] While expanding the geography of where the concept of development was developed as both a discourse and a technical phenomenon has been a significant contribution to the literature – making possible the new field of the global history of development – it still falls short precisely because it propagates the idea that a single development discourse was adopted globally.[7] Although there was a shared technical vocabulary of development, that vocabulary was set to divergent ideas of what it meant to be developed. How do we explain these divergent ideas?

For an example of this divergence in the Sudanese case, just look at the writings of the Oxford-educated Mekki Abbas in 1952. Mekki was the first Sudanese director of the Gezira Scheme, the largest financial investment in the country at the time, when he wrote, "Indeed, should the civilizations which rose in the Mesopotamia of Iraq and other parts of the Fertile Crescent have any future parallel in the Sudan, it will be mainly due to the prosperity contributed by this Mesopotamia when its cultivable 2 million acres are fully developed."[8]

To the Anglo-American reader at first glance, what is striking about Mekki's statement is the connection he draws between Mesopotamia and civilization, though here we equate civilization with development, a concept frequently associated with the future. Materialist explanations grounded purely in national, social, or economic disparities cannot explain the oddness of the reference. To understand its oddity, we must use the concept of sociotechnical imaginaries, which are "collectively held, institutionally stabilized, and publically performed visions of a desirable future, animated by shared understandings of forms of social life and social order attainable through, and supportive of, advances in science and technology."[9]

Mekki's reference to Mesopotamia is a gateway to understanding the social world that he and his peers – the rulers of the independent Sudanese state – believed was good from a normative perspective. And while they were completely fluent in the language of economic rationalism and manipulated the tool kits of development with dexterity, only a partial understanding of the

6 Mitchell, *Rule of Experts*; Prakash, *Another Reason: Science and the Imagination of Modern India*; Morgan, "On a Mission' with Mutable Mobiles" and "Seeking Parts, Looking for Wholes," pp. 303–325.

7 Frederick Cooper, "Writing the History of Development," pp. 5–23; Frey and Kunkel, "Writing the History of Development: A Review of Recent Literature," pp. 215–232; Immerwahr, "Modernization and Development in U.S. Foreign Policy," pp. 22–25.

8 Abbas, *The Sudan Question*, p. 8.

9 Jasanoff, "Future Imperfect," pp. 4–5.

developmental project in postcolonial Sudan can be achieved without paying careful attention to the specificity of the Sudanese imagination of what defined a civilized or developed society during the decades after World War II.

In the years before Sudan became independent on January 1, 1956, Sudanese intellectuals took ownership of the concepts and vocabulary associated with development and transformed those concepts into their own distinctive Sudanese tradition. Traditions, however, do not emerge out of thin air. The rest of this chapter is dedicated to tracing the influences that made Sudanese economic policy making during the 1950s and 1960s unique. In accordance with the theory of sociotechnical imaginaries, the preoccupations of the Sudanese policy elite were not privately held, but rather reflected the hopes and anxieties of the politically, socially, and culturally dominant class. The focus on this class is justified by its control of the apparatus of the state at independence and its ability to use this control to transform its vision for society into a national development project. This is not to say that their projects were successful or that they become equally hegemonic throughout all strata of society, but that for a period of time the different development projects that this class put forward captured the energy of the state apparatus. The men who made up this class overwhelmingly came from the major cities such as Khartoum, Omdurman, Wad Medini, Atbara, and Port Sudan. Fluent in English and Arabic, they inherited from the Egyptians and the British a vision of development that equated mastery over nature, particularly in the form of large-scale irrigation projects and centralized control over the Nile, with modernity.[10]

Before proceeding, it may be helpful to address one more potential caveat; namely, that here we are talking about economic policy making, rather than economic science. Robert Merton defined the attributes of a science as universalism, communism, disinterestedness, and organized skepticism.[11] But he fretted about "the abuse of expert authority and the creation of pseudo-sciences [which] are called into play when the structure of control exercised by qualified compeers is rendered ineffectual." He then went on to state what is a very apt warning for the student of colonial economics: "The presumably scientific pronouncements of totalitarian spokesmen on race or economy or history are for the uninstructed laity of the same order as newspaper reports of an expanded

10 Harry Verhoeven, Water, Civilization and Power in Sudan, 36–83; also see Terje Tvedt, *The River Nile in the Age of the British: Political Ecology and the Quest for Economic Power* (New York: American University in Cairo Press, 2004), pp. 110, 212–215; for a discussion of the fact that centralized control of Nile irrigation was very much a product of the nineteenth and twentieth centuries, see the work of Alan Mikhail, *Nature and Empire in Ottoman Egypt: An Environmental History* (New York: Cambridge University Press, 2012), pp. 124–201. For a discussion of the concept of mastery in the Nile Valley, see E. T. Powell, *A Different Shade of Colonialism: Egypt, Britain, and the Mastery of Sudan* (Berkeley: University of California Press, 2003), pp. 1–26; Mitchell, *Colonising Egypt*, pp. 1–34, and *Rule of Experts*, pp. 1–19.

11 Robert K. Merton, "The Normative Structure of Science," in Norman W. Storer, ed., *The Sociology of Science: Theoretical and Empirical Investigations* (Chicago: University of Chicago Press, 1973), pp. 267–278.

universe or wave mechanics. In both instances, they cannot be checked by the man in the street and in both instances they run counter to common sense."[12]

This chapter discusses precisely what happens when science engages with large and unbounded questions about the nature of society; that is, when science becomes public reason. Economics, beginning in the 1930s, became the preeminent way in which governments demonstrated their reasonableness, thereby justifying their ability to make law and policy. Tracking the evolution of the economic imaginaries that became popular among the postcolonial elite reveals the ideologies of reasonable governance that undergirded the postcolonial state-making project. One of the central arguments in my book is that, during moments of crisis in Sudan – a society where until the 1980s violence between members of the national elite was largely restricted, though large-scale violence was frequently and unapologetically deployed against non-elite subjects – legitimacy was demonstrated in policy-making circles using the languages of finance and economics.[13]

The history of economics as a discipline in Sudan and Sudanese economic history must be told simultaneously. The economic imaginaries, a type of sociotechnical imaginary that I explore in this chapter and those that follow, were made possible or constrained by the different ways in which the physical infrastructure of Anglo-Egyptian Sudan was built, the networks of commodity production in which Sudan was situated, and the arrangements of people, finance, expertise, and violence that ultimately determined how wealth was distributed and controlled.[14]

The colonial administrators of the late 1940s and early 1950s in Anglo-Egyptian Sudan and their Sudanese successors were conversant in the economic debates of the 1920s and 1930s. These debates between British and Egyptian bureaucrats and economists focused on how to renew the development project in the Nile Valley. By the end of World War I, the economic program of the Egyptian monarchy and its British overlords had exhausted itself. Essentially, the nineteenth-century development miracle in Egypt – a miracle accelerated by the global crisis of cotton brought on by the US Civil War in the 1860s – was premised on hydraulic reforms along the Nile and the continuous expansion of cotton cultivation.[15] The introduction of new varieties of cotton, the infusion of European capital, the enclosure of privately owned lands, and new types of surveillance – particularly in fields such as public health – fueled the

12 Ibid., 277.

13 Sheila Jasanoff, "Reason in Practice," in *Science and Public Reason* (New York: Routledge, 2012), pp. 1–23. Edward Thomas, *South Sudan: A Slow Liberation* (New York: Zed Books, 2015).

14 Timothy Mitchell, *Carbon Democracy: Political Power in the Age of Oil* (New York: Verso Press, 2011), p. 8.

15 Sven Beckert, "Emancipation and Empire: Reconstructing the Worldwide Web of Cotton Production in the Age of the American Civil War," *American Historical Review* 109 (2004): 1405–1438.

nineteenth-century growth in Egypt's wealth and population.[16] Yet, the success of that era's development model depended on the acquisition of additional land, the intensification of its exploitation, and the displacement of the population into overcrowded urban slums, and it eventually collapsed, leaving yawning inequality in its wake.[17]

It is commonplace to equate the economy with the national economy – the ultimate signifier of the economy in our collective imagination being the gross domestic product (GDP), which is calculated based on national income accounts.[18] Calculating the rate of change in GDP across time produces growth rates, which politicians, as well as economists, then use to claim that this or that country is governed well.[19]

Yet for the historian, this easy equivalence obscures as much as it reveals. In the case of modern Sudan, the categories of the national and the economy are hardly stable. The historian Steven Serels has recently proposed that, rather than thinking about the "national economy," during most of Sudan's history it is more useful to speak about the gradual expansion of an integrated market for staple commodities such as grains. For Serels, grains are a particularly promising category to investigate, because communities depend on grains for their very livelihoods. The exchange of cash for basic food staples demonstrates that a community is integrated and dependent on a market. The expansions and contractions of the Sudanese grain market therefore stand in as useful proxies for the idea of Sudan as an economic unit throughout the nineteenth century.[20]

This method allows a distinction to be made between the huge size of Sudan as a political entity – either the Ottoman-Egyptian Sudan, created by Mehmet Ali's armies in the 1820s, or the Anglo-Egyptian Sudan, created by the Anglo-Egyptian armies of Lord Kitchener starting in the 1890s (see Maps 2 and 3) – and the idea of Sudan as a unit within which economic exchange occurred. A brief discussion of the difference between these two concepts historically will help illuminate what was at stake in discussions beginning in the 1930s and 1940s between Egyptian, British, and Sudanese elites about the future of the Sudanese economy.

At different times, governments in Cairo, London, and Khartoum claimed to have control of a territory that varied in size from 1821 until 1956, but that was roughly two-thirds the size of India. From north to south, the country stretched

16 Robert L. Tignor, *Modernization and British Colonial Rule in Egypt, 1882–1914* (Princeton, NJ: Princeton University Press, 1966).

17 Robert Tignor, "Equity in Egypt's Recent Past: 1945–1952," in Gouda Abdel-Khalek and Robert Tignor, eds., *The Political Economy of Income Distribution in Egypt* (New York: Holmes and Meier, 1982), p. 36.

18 Jerven, *Poor Numbers*.

19 Jerven, "Users and Producers of African Income," pp. 169–190; Speich, "The Use of Global Abstractions," pp. 7–28.

20 Steven Serels, *Starvation and the State: Famine, Slavery, and Power in Sudan, 1883–1956* (New York: Palgrave Macmillan, 2013), pp. 1–13.

MAP 2 Ottoman-Egyptian Sudan

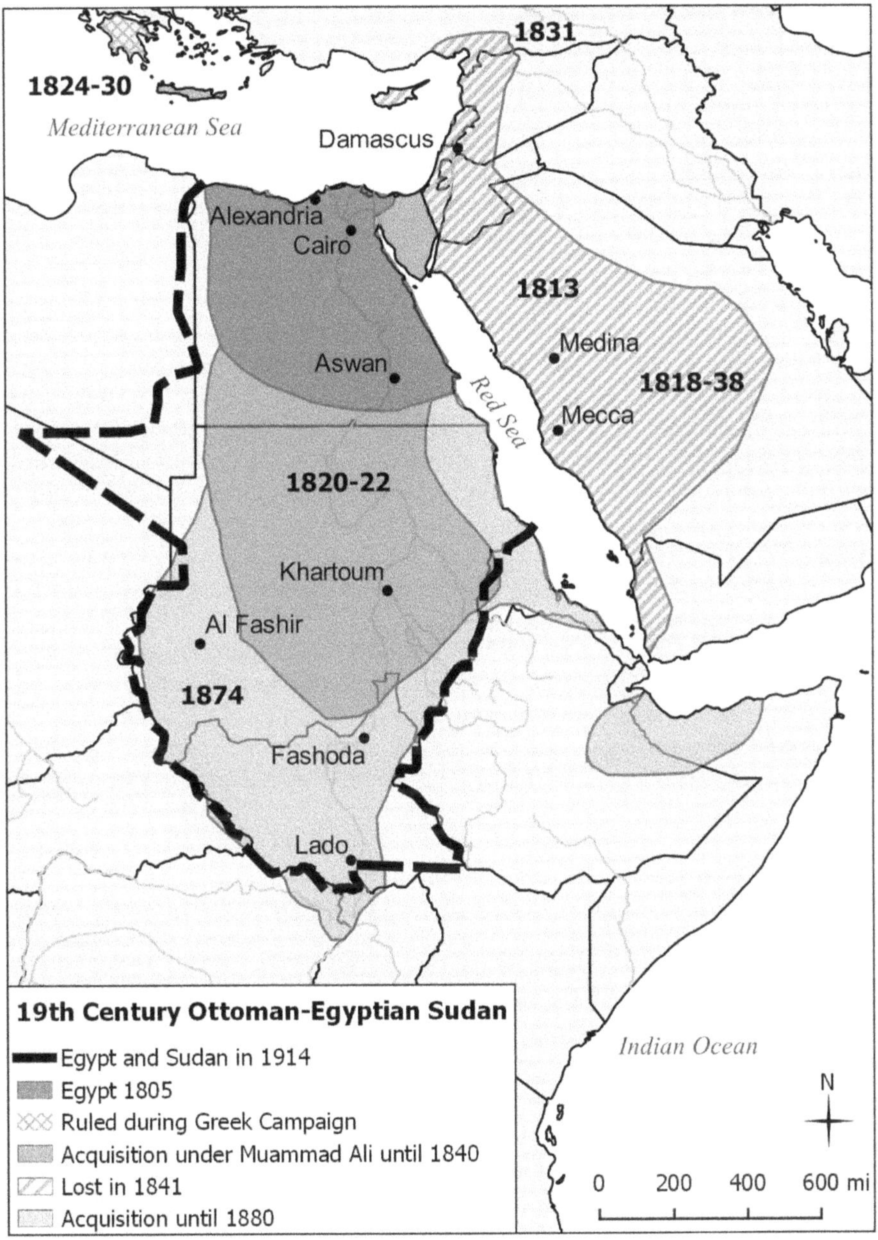

MAP 3 Anglo-Egyptian Sudan

more than 1,168 miles from Wadi Halfa and the harsh northern deserts to the tropical Imatong Mountains along the border with Uganda. The administrative unity of this vast territory came about as a result of the nineteenth-century imperial ambitions of Egypt.[21]

Yet, when thinking about the territory of Sudan as an economic unit, imperial claims represented on political maps as colored blotches have only limited analytical utility. Though Egypt's rulers beginning in the nineteenth century often asserted that there were economic, political, and cultural connections between the two regions dating back to time immemorial, before the nineteenth century, the connections between Egypt and Sudan were rather limited.[22] At the start of the nineteenth century the Funj Sultanate of Sennar – which nominally ruled the area along the Nile River from the third cataract stretching southward until the Shilluk Kingdom, the Gezira Plain, Kassala, and westward into southern Kordofan – had begun to fall apart. The northern territories stretching toward Ottoman-controlled Nubia were ruled by the Shayqiyya Federation, and internally the merchant and clerical classes had gained greater autonomy; yet most importantly for this study the rulers of Sennar during the classical period believed in administrative trade. The principal feature of administrative trade is that the sultan exercised tight regulation of the market for long-distance trade, the principal market being his court.[23] Yet, the vast majority of the population was fed locally in family-based productive units, often making use of Roman-era technology, such as the *saqiya* or Roman water wheel. For our purposes, it is worth noting that during the early decades of the nineteenth century, the central region, which became the most economically and politically advanced region of the future Sudanese state, was organized politically and economically around distinct local economies.[24] Counterintuitively, the Nile, which both nineteenth-century British and Egyptian writers often imagined as the unifying feature of *Bilad al-Sudan* and Egypt, was not the imagined or actual connection for the Sudanese kingdoms such as Sennar or Darfur to the outside world: instead, Sennar looked to the Red Sea, while Darfur turned toward the old desert routes.

Ottoman Egypt's growing power during the nineteenth century reoriented much of the trade and political authority in Sudan toward the expanding empire. However, it is vital to remember that nineteenth-century Ottoman Egypt was not only an empire of the Nile Valley but was also a Red Sea power. Thus while Mehment Ali and his successors' armies strengthened the connections between northern riverain Sudan, Egyptian Nubia, Cairo, and the Nile

[21] Anders Bjorkelo, *Prelude to the Mahdiyya: Peasants and Traders in the Shendi Region, 1821–1885* (Cambridge: Cambridge University Press, 1989); Richard Hill, *Egypt in the Sudan, 1820–1881* (Oxford: Oxford University Press, 1959).

[22] Terence Walz, *The Trade between Egypt and Bilad as-Sudan, 1700–1820* (Cairo: Institut français d'archéologie orientale du Caire, 1978).

[23] Jay Spaulding, *The Heroic Age in Sinnar* (Trenton, NJ: Red Sea Press, 2007).

[24] Serels, *Starvation and the State*, pp. 13–72.

Delta, they also strengthened the existing tendencies of central and eastern Sudan to look toward the Red Sea and Arabia. It was during this period that the Mirghani family migrated from the Hijaz region of Arabia and became both a political and religious force in the eastern region of Sudan and an area stretching into present-day Eritrea. They consolidated their power in Sudan in close connection with the rulers of Ottoman Egypt.[25] However, their influence on both sides of the Red Sea shows the ways in which even during the mid-nineteenth century when Cairo was formally in control of much of riverain Sudan, Sudanese society in political, economic, and cultural terms looked eastward as much as it did northward. Serels argues that eastern Sudan depended on Indian grain delivered to Red Sea ports, which tied the livelihoods of the vast majority of the Sudanese people to long-distance trade in the second half of the nineteenth century.[26]

Naturally, the rulers of Ottoman Egypt occupied the territory of Sudan along the Nile closest to its own borders with the most intensity. There Mehment Ali's forces brutally conquered the Shayqiyya Federation, subjugated the Danagla, and finally defeated al-Makk Nimr's forces at Shandi, scattering the Ja'alin and destroying the last remains of the Kingdom of Sennar in the process. The initial conquests focused on the northern riverain areas of Sudan extending southward into the Gezira Plain.[27] These three ethnic groups – the Shagiya, Danagla, and Ja'alin – came to dominate the future incarnations of the Sudanese state centered on the Nile Valley below the first cataract, which marked the traditional border with Egypt.

In 1999, in the midst of a split within the ruling Islamist government in Khartoum – the National Congress Party – a number of disaffected party officials under the name of "Seekers of Truth and Justice" published the now-infamous *Black Book of Sudan*, which detailed "the level of injustice practiced by successive governments, secular and theocratic, democratic or autocratic, from the independence of the country in 1956 to this day." Their main complaint was that the northern region, home to the Shagiya, Danagla and Ja'alin, made up only 5.4 percent of Sudan's population, but its residents held 79.5 percent of the positions in the central government.[28] The processes that allowed these groups to dominate the Sudanese state were set in place during the nineteenth century, when as Mehmet Ali's army conquered the northern and central regions of Sudan's Nile Basin, it began to look farther and farther afield for resources and

[25] Ahmad al-Shahi, "Noah's Ark: The Continuity of the Khatmiyya Order in Northern Sudan," pp. 13–29.

[26] Steven Serels. "Famines of War: The Red Sea Grain Market and Famine in Eastern Sudan, 1889–1891," *Northeast African Studies* 12:1 (2012): 73–94.

[27] Hill, *Egypt in the Sudan*, pp. 8–13.

[28] Abdullahi Osman El Tom and M. A. Mohamed Salih. "Reviewed Book: The Black Book of Sudan," *Review of African Political Economy* 30:97 (2003): 511–514; Julie Flint and Alex De Waal. *Darfur: A New History of a Long War* (London: Zed Books, 2008); Osman El-Tom, *Darfur, JEM and the Khalil Ibrahim Story*.

slaves, eventually pushing as far south as present-day Uganda, westward into Darfur and the border regions of the present-day Central African Republic, and eastward toward the Ethiopian highlands. As Mehmet Ali's armies advanced, and in the face of rapidly increasing taxation of the land along the northern banks of the Nile, the Shagiya, Danagla, and Ja'alin merchants, known as Jallabs, spread out and came to dominate other regions of the country as merchants, slave traders, missionaries, and political leaders.[29] As a result, just as the Egyptian Army extracted labor and resources from the peripheries, so too would the Sudanese communities that were displaced into the periphery by the initial Egyptian conquest.

As a consequence the agricultural regions along the Nile southward to Khartoum, where the Nile branches out into the Blue and the White Nile – and particularly along the Blue Nile extending to the border with Ethiopia – came to be understood by the Egyptians, British, and the Sudanese elite themselves as the most productive regions of the country. This region, along with land in southern Kordofan along the White Nile, became the basis of a self-sustaining grain market. In the process, political authorities of the new state imagined this region as an economic core. To maximize the economic returns from this region, labor was pulled from the areas of Sudan that were not incorporated into this grain market. Once in the core, these workers made up the agricultural labor force, extracting the raw materials that sustained the markets on which the growing city of Khartoum relied. The elites of Khartoum then sold goods abroad in order to pay for the luxuries they coveted, which became the markers of wealth.[30]

The end of Ottoman Egypt's control over its Sudanese provinces – brought about by the rise of the Mahdist state during the 1880s and the escalating battles for control of the Nile Valley with the Ansar, the followers of the Mahdi – further entrenched the economic role of the core of the country as a grain basket, even as areas such as Darfur, the Beja regions near the Red Sea, and the Nilotic regions south of the *Sudd* were integrated into a whole. Yet even after Anglo-Egyptian Sudan came into being in 1899, with the signing of the Condominium Treaty that enshrined the dual sovereignty of both Egypt and Great Britain, the problem of feeding the local population remained paramount. In part, this was because British rule and the presence of the Egyptian army in the territory failed to bring peace as wars of conquest and resistance in the western and southern provinces of the country continued to rage until the 1920s.[31]

[29] Mahmoud, *The Sudanese Bourgeoisie: Vanguard of Development?* and Jok, *War and Slavery in Sudan*. An explicit statement of the thesis that the Arab elite has sought to keep Africans underdeveloped can be found in Yongo-Bure, *Economic Development of Southern Sudan*.

[30] Ahmed Sikainga, *Slaves into Workers: Emancipation and Labor in Colonial Sudan* (Austin: University of Texas Press, 1996).

[31] Eifatih Shaaeldin, *The Evolution and Transformation of the Sudanese Economy up to 1950* (Khartoum: Monograph Series of Khartoum University Press, 1984), p. 16.

The sharp distinction between an economic center and a periphery in the mind of Sudan's governing elite persists to this day. In September 2005, the senior officials of the ruling National Congress Party (NCP) began to think about how to preserve their hegemony. They asked the regime ideologue Abdelrahim Hamdi to write a working paper with the title, "The Economic Paper for the Ruling National Congress: The Future of Foreign Investment in Sudan." This paper was designed to clarify the regime's priorities after the signing of the Comprehensive Peace Agreement with the Southern People's Liberation Movement/Army as both parties prepared for national elections in 2010 and a vote on southern secession in 2011. In "The Economic Paper," Hamdi declared that the NCP's priorities were clear, writing,

> The decisive voting bloc in the coming election resides in the geographical North – at least 25 million – in the Northern states, down to Sennar/Gezira and Blue Nile areas. Voters in this area are election oriented, more educated and can be influenced. Due to their high levels of education, they also have higher demands for services and employment opportunities. We must focus on this zone. Fortunately, this zone is nearer and well connected with transport networks – tarmac roads, communication facilities, etc. It is easier and faster to manage election campaigns in this zone ... The geopolitical body which I referred to earlier as the North, and which I call henceforth Dongola – Sinnar + Kordofan Axis or the Northern Axis is very homogeneous ... It is to be noted that this Northern Axis financed the Sudan throughout its Turkish, colonial and Independence eras. Even if the others have separated, this Axis can continue as a viable state. This is true in case of the separation of the South and it is equally so though in a different way in case of separation of Darfur.[32]

This policy paper demonstrates the extent to which the North that came into being during the nineteenth century has continued to be the economic core in the imagination of Sudanese politicians and intellectuals, despite the many political transformations that have changed Sudan's political economy.

This antagonism between the core and the periphery has led some historians of Sudan such as Douglas Johnson and Jok Madut Jok to focus on the persistence of patterns of exploitation between the northern riverain communities and the rest of Sudan.[33] Others have chosen to focus on the period of the Anglo-Egyptian colonial conquest of Sudan in 1898 until the present, examining how the investment decisions of the colonial state created patterns of investment that persisted after independence and established a bias toward the riverain territories. The colonial "inheritance included a bias towards big 'productive schemes,' not incidentally in the center, because these promised the returns needed to finance social services, communications, and other

[32] Abdelrahim Hamdi, "Al-Waraqa Al-Iqtisadiyya li'l-mutamar al-watani al-hakim bi'l-Sudan," Manuscript, 2005 quoted in Verhoeven, *Water, Civilization and Power in Sudan*, p. 136.

[33] Johnson, *The Root Causes of Sudan's Civil Wars*, pp. 1–9.

development."[34] Patterns of investment have remained quite stable, and patterns of inequality persist until today.[35]

In emphasizing this continuity, scholars have deemphasized the distinctiveness of the late colonial and early postcolonial state.[36] In particular they have ignored the contingency around ideas such as the state, the nation, and the economy on the eve of decolonization in favor of a nationalist teleology.[37] Certainly, for the last 200 years structural inequalities have existed between an economic periphery and the core in the territory that we now call Sudan. The rest of this chapter focuses on the debate over competing ideas of how to orient this economic core in the two decades before Sudan's independence in 1956. I also sketch out the emergence of a cotton complex in Sudan involving both the colonial state and the patrons of the nationalist movement, which prioritized the sociotechnical imaginary of the future Sudanese state that became dominant in the 1950s and 1960s.

The Interwar British Economic Imaginary of Sudan

Before 1924 Anglo-Egyptian Sudan was a colony largely tolerated by Britain as a debt that could be shifted onto the Egyptian taxpayer. However, Egypt's involvement in Sudan dramatically decreased after the murder of the colony's governor-general, Sir Lee Stacks, in 1924. The British interpreted the murder and the subsequent unrest in Khartoum as signs that the rising nationalism plaguing Egypt might prove to be infectious and spread to Sudan. Therefore the aim of British policy shifted, focusing on means to increasingly quarantine Sudan from Egypt; its relationship with Sudan was already a contentious issue in Egyptian politics and became even more so as Egyptian nationalists argued that their countrymen were being unfairly denied access to their patrimony of water, land, and economic opportunity.[38]

After the removal of Egyptian administrators from Sudan, the British-staffed Sudanese Political Service began to implement a project of colonial self-sufficiency that, at the behest of the British Treasury, was being put into place across all of British Africa. The goal of this policy was for colonial officials "to find ways of paying their local expenses without help from the British

34 "That elite was drawn mainly from the riverain north and had succeeded to the perquisites and priorities of the colonial regime." Daly, *Darfur's Sorrow*, pp. 162–163, 185–189.

35 "Economic policy over the period from 1956–1969 was geared mainly towards expansion within the framework established prior to 1956." Niblock, *Class and Power in Sudan*, p. 231.

36 Low and Lonsdale, "Introduction: Towards the New Order, 1945–1963," pp. 1–63. For a discussion of how the symbols, institutions, and metaphors of the colonial state lived on into the postcolonial state, see Young and Turner, *The Rise and Decline of the Zairian State*.

37 Frederick Cooper, "Possibility and Constraint: African Independence in Historical Perspective," *Journal of African History* 49:2 (2008): 167–196; *Citizenship between Empire and Nation*.

38 David E. Mills, *Dividing the Nile: Egypt's Economic Nationalists in the Sudan 1918–1956* (New York: American University of Cairo Press, 2014), pp. 37–42.

Treasury."[39] The need to limit local expenditures became one of the primary drivers of the bifurcated state in Sudan: a bureaucratized state in the economic core and indirect rule in the vast parts of the country that were deemed to be less productive, if not unproductive.[40]

Perhaps the most consequential economic impact of "indirect rule" was the creation of "the closed door policy." These "closed districts," which were established between 1922 and 1930, were areas that northern Arab merchants and Islamic missionaries were forbidden from entering. The justification for this policy was that certain regions and peoples in Sudan were less civilized than the predominantly Arab population of the central riverain territories and therefore required specific protections for their way of life to be preserved. These policies largely separated southern from northern Sudan and created prominent closed districts in the Nuba Mountains, the Beja Mountains, Blue Nile State, and parts of Darfur. Often an area was designated as a "closed district" if British authorities considered it African, rather than Arab.[41] One of the primary consequences of this policy was to formalize a vision of the country as an economic core surrounded by semi-autonomous regional economies that, when they interacted with the core at all, served primarily as labor reserves. In regions as far removed from Khartoum as Equatoria in the far south of Sudan, the closed door policy fed the belief – among Egyptian, British, and Sudanese officials from both the north and south – that perhaps Equatoria and the other southern provinces fit in better with British East Africa than with the rest of Sudan.[42]

If indirect rule and the closed door policy were the result of an economic imaginary of Sudan as a fragmented group of regional economies, the creation of the gigantic Gezira Scheme was the product of an imperial imaginary. The decision to grow cotton in Sudan was not an obvious one from the perspective of either the Sudanese or the Egyptians. While British administrators in Sudan felt the same need to earn foreign exchange to pay for the administration as was felt in other colonies, growing cotton was not obviously economically superior to producing food or exporting livestock, for instance. Both solutions, as we will see, were preferred by Egyptian elites. Thus the construction of the largest irrigated scheme in Africa in the Gezira Plain can only be explained in the context of British imperial ambitions of control of the Nile as insurance against an increasingly restive Egypt.

Before the mobilization for war that began in the mid-1930s, British investors implemented the Gezira Scheme, located southeast of Khartoum,

39 Gardner, *Taxing Colonial Africa*, p. 3.

40 For a discussion of the legacies of the policies of indirect rule on politics in Sudan see Mamdani, *Saviors and Survivors*.

41 M. Abdel Rahim. "The Development of British Policy in Southern Sudan," *Middle Eastern Studies* 2:3 (1966): 231.

42 Mills, *Dividing the Nile*, pp. 14–16 and 111.

as a potential second Nile Valley, providing an explicit alternative to the Lancashire's mills dependence on Egypt. The Gezira Scheme was conceived before World War I, but only became fully operational following the construction of the Sennar Dam and its main irrigation canals in 1926. The irrigation engineers who originally championed this initiative considered its construction and continued expansion as only one phase in a massive program to control the entire Nile basin. Its economic and strategic purpose was closely tied to Britain's larger imperial objectives in Egypt and East Africa[43]: British interwar planners conceived of investment in Sudan as part of a larger project to develop the Nile river system as a regional complex, while largely acquiescing to the neglect of the vast majority of Sudanese territory. The project was originally limited to 300,000 feddans, as part of the Allenby negotiations with Egypt in 1920.[44] The eventual signing of the Nile Waters Agreement between Egypt and Britain in 1929 allowed for expansion of the Gezira Scheme to 500,000 feddans.[45] The average annual acreage under cotton cultivation expanded from roughly 100,000 feddan in 1927 to approximately 205,000 feddan in 1939 (see Map 4).[46]

The full ambitions of this project and its place within larger British schemes to integrate the entire Nile basin by constructing an interlocking and mutually complementary system of hydrological works were partially revealed by the comments of the British irrigation advisor, Murdoch MacDonald, to Egyptian government officials. At a meeting convened by the British Board of Trade of the Committee on the Growth of Cotton in the British Empire in 1917, he claimed that the ultimate capacity of the Gezira Scheme might be three million feddans and that it should be thought of as a second Nile delta.[47]

A focus on plantation agriculture created a tendency for the central government to view Sudan's economic potential as consisting of little more than an archipelago of schemes, divided into a scattered, but to state officials legible, modern sector, and a series of vast, lightly administered, and scarcely improved territories. The government tried from almost the beginning of the condominium to create plantation-style estates that would employ uniform types of production on a large scale, instead of small-scale peasant production.[48] The fear was that profits would disappear if the Government of Sudan or its

43 Tvedt, *The River Nile in the Age of the British*, p. 110.

44 1 feddan= 4,200 square meters (m^2) = 1,038 acres.

45 Tvedt, *The River Nile in the Age of the British*, p. 110.

46 Daly, *Imperial Sudan*, p. 96.

47 Tvedt, *The River Nile in the Age of the British*, p. 94.

48 It must be noted that these terms are anachronistic, but they express a crucial analytical distinction noted by later scholars between two different types of capitalist production encouraged by the colonial state. The plantation mode of production separated the owners of capital and the land from labor, whereas the peasant mode of production did not enforce a strict distinction between labor and the means of production. In the production of crops such as gum Arabic and sesame nuts – traditionally described as products created by the peasant mode of production – small land holders were principally responsible for gathering or cultivating crops; most

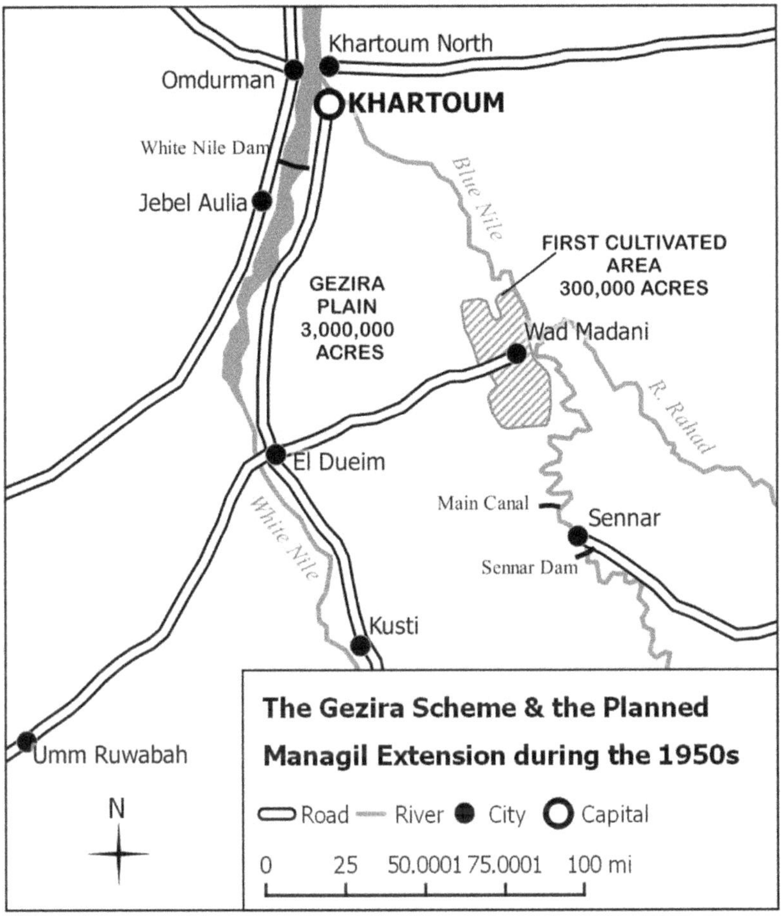

MAP 4 The Gezira Scheme

foreign investors became embroiled in an endless series of negotiations with local landlords and peasant producers. In place of small-scale production on family-owned land, the condominium government envisioned centrally managed and easily taxable estates within defined spatial boundaries. The large size of these estates would ensure that both the government and the outside investors received a reasonable return on their investments. Focusing on the building of a few estates and agricultural schemes, the government was content to neglect the economic potential of vast portions of the country.[49]

accumulated capital was subsequently invested in wholesale trading, transportation, or distribution. Henry Bernstein, "Notes on Capital and Peasantry," *Review of African Political Economy* 4:10 (1977): 60–73.

[49] Tim Niblock. *Class and Power*, p. 13.

It was during the 1920s and 1930s that cotton, grown using irrigated water from the Nile, became the centerpiece of the government's economic strategy, even as the expansion of cotton production was slowed by low prices and weak demand, particularly in Britain. Before World War II, finance officials within the Sudan Political Service were notable for their insistence that the government should possess a small economic footprint because "socialism" was to be avoided at all cost. Thus, government officials discouraged both Sudanese and foreign capital from undertaking manufacturing or other industrial activities. Except for the ever-expanding cotton schemes that they began to pursue in the 1920s, they were very hostile to any increase in the number of industrial or agricultural schemes. There was a fear among Sudanese officials, even those in the Finance Department, most of whom had begun their careers in rural administration, that capitalist development would create "new centers of non-government influence and power," and inevitably new administrative problems.[50]

Economic Debates about Sudan on the Eve of World War II

The economic autonomy that Sudan experienced during the interwar period was reduced sharply as the British Empire began to mobilize for war. The formalization of an imperial trading bloc and the attendant mobilization for war demanded increased coordination between the bodies that set imperial economic policy and the various parts of the empire.[51] This reduced the ability of individual parts of the empire to negotiate their own trade and economic policies. The Offices of the War Supply Board and the Board of Economics and Trade handled the increased coordination between the government in Khartoum and British decision makers in London and Cairo. These agencies attempted to supervise economic activity within Sudan to ensure that the colony contributed financially to the upkeep of military forces stationed throughout East and North Africa; raised the revenue necessary to contribute directly to the war effort (Anglo-Egyptian Sudan made a 5 million GBP gift to Britain); increased its production of high-quality cotton, which was vital to the war effort; and expanded food production, all the while containing inflation.[52] Sudan was relatively fortunate in facing few hardships as it adjusted its

[50] G. N. Sanderson, "The Ghost of Adam Smith: Ideology, Bureaucracy, and the Frustration of Economic Development in the Sudan, 1934–1940," in M. W. Daly, ed., *Modernization in the Sudan: Essays in Honor of Richard Hill* (New York: Lillian Barber Press, 1985), pp. 101–104.

[51] John Darwin, *The Empire Project: The Rise and Fall of the British World-System, 1830–1970* (Cambridge: Cambridge University Press, 2009), pp. 418–509; Harold James, *The End of Globalization: Lessons from the Great Depression* (Cambridge, MA: Harvard University Press, 2001).

[52] Note, John Cummins. "War Inflation," Finance Department. June 20, 1943. SAD J. W. Cummins 635/12/1–44.

economy to wartime conditions. The demands that the United Kingdom placed on Sudan remained fairly stable throughout the war, and even though the colony was asked to increase its production of foodstuffs, cotton – the country's main export – continued to find ready markets. Sudan's success in selling cotton, particularly certain types of high-quality cotton, meant that the damage done to the economy as a result of its adjustment to the needs of war was more limited than in many other countries.[53]

The British conception of portfolio investment dotted across potentially profitable sites in the Nile region or, alternatively, Africa in general could not survive either the escalating tensions between Britain and its primary client in the region, Egypt, or the growing demand for the resources necessary to sustain a war against the Axis powers. British officials' desire for tighter coordination of their possessions in preparation for the war encountered immediate resistance in Egypt, where the political class resented the new pressures placed on their economy. One of the issues on which Britain and Egypt fought was the status of Sudan.

The origins of Sudan's economy as an international rather than an imperial unit of economic analysis lay in the interwar struggle between Britain and the Egyptian monarchy to define Egypt's sovereignty. This struggle burst into the world of high politics between 1919 and 1936, when the League of Nations ratified the Anglo-Egyptian Treaty, reaffirming Egypt's sovereignty with reservations. One of those reservations concerned Sudan, which remained under the protection of both the British and Egyptian crowns. However with Egypt's privileges in Sudan now adjudicated by the League, the Egyptian crown was allowed to send an economic expert to Khartoum in 1938. British officials had debated almost from the moment they inherited the condominium how to make it a productive part of the empire, but what was new about the efforts of the Egyptian economic expert Abdullah Fakri, was his determination to make the debate about Sudan's economic potential public, a determination that sprang from Egypt's relative weakness in relation to Britain.

By making public the question of Sudan's economic potential, Abdullah was transforming what had previously been technical discussions about public finance into a discourse of political economy that colonial officials stationed in Sudan and nationalist leaders later took up. The idea of Sudan as an economic region evolved as it entered public discussion in Arabic. In the 1930s, Egyptian officials and intellectuals first treated Sudan as a special region of the Egyptian customs and tariff zone, but one that was improperly harmonized with Egypt because of counterproductive British regulations. This became the basis for the argument made by an emerging circle of Sudanese nationalists that British rules were hindering Sudan's agricultural productivity and potential income.

[53] Note, "Sudan Cotton in Wartime. Financial Secretary's Office." SAD J. W. Cummins 635/12/1–44.

As a consequence of the 1936 Anglo-Egyptian Treaty, Abdullah Fikri Abaza wrote his *Buhuth Iqtisadiya 'an al-Sudan* (Economic Researches on Sudan), which began,

> I was fortunate to be the first to occupy the position of Egyptian economic expert in Sudan, which was stipulated according to the *Treaty of Alliance and Friendship between Egypt and Britain* (*The Treaty of Alliance Between His Majesty, in Respect of the United Kingdom, and His Majesty, the King of Egypt*), in accordance with the agreed upon minutes in regards to the detailed questions connected to the second paragraph of the 11th article of the treaty.
>
> I saw from the first that my duty upon arriving in the city of Khartoum on the 22nd of January 1939 was that I become acquainted with the capabilities of Sudan in all its economic and social aspects, and that I get on top of the official reports and statistics which the different institutes of Sudan issued to the end of 1938, so I sought to summarize from them what information would concern the sons of the nation with special care and I supervised that first review under my own personal watch in that period which I remained there for the first time.[54]

Sudan was of interest to Egyptian policy makers because of its potential resource base and its ability to serve as a market for Egyptian goods. Unlike colonial economists such as S. Herbert Frankel, who doubted the efficacy of government intervention in bringing about the development of backward regions, for the Egyptians what made economic cooperation and investment in Sudan difficult was the need to harmonize laws and regulations between the British and Egyptian economic regions. They believed that such harmonization was made all the more difficult because Britain did not promote in Sudan an understanding of the needs of the Egyptian economy. A stronger reading of the Egyptian position was that British officials imposed laws on Sudan that actively retarded its development.

The solution that the Egyptian Office of the Economic Expert in Sudan adopted was to design an active program to promote Egyptian economic interests in Sudan. This program centered on information gathering and advocacy. The economic expert also took an active role in trying to match potential Sudanese and Egyptian customers. Abdullah Fikri Abaza felt that the difficulty in understanding Sudanese economic activity and its lack of organization were two of the major obstacles to increased investment:

> Among the most important questions which confronts the researcher is the lack of a fixed system of agriculture, in particular in the rainy areas the way followed currently is the way of shifting agriculture including the injury of burning which is inescapable in order to clear the wild grass and wild trees which enrich the earth anew. And so on this surface the population is distributed without order and equally there are lacking any instruments of irrigation in order to obtain agriculture in a semi-permanent manner for them.[55]

54 Abdullah Fakri Abaza, *Buhuth al-Iqtisadiya 'an al-Sudan* (Cairo: Dar al-Taba 'at al-Masriya, 1940), 5 [author's translation].

55 Ibid., p. 34.

While Sudan was seen as potentially rich, large areas of the territory were described as wastelands. Writing about the natural wealth of the Sudanese periphery, particularly the southern provinces, Abdullah Fakri wrote, "Bananas, papaya, pineapples and mangos grow in abundance with ample quantity in the southern region, [but] the people there don't exploit this wealth due to a lack of laborers and roadblocks to transportation and that the southern regions were closed to the northern population."[56] Yet despite the often pejorative nature of Abdullah's comments, what separated them from those made by the earlier generation of imperial intellectuals such as Frankel was the belief that investment could make a difference if the government had the correct data and regulations were modified.

The Egyptian officials' renewed interest in Sudan was partly due to their desire to guarantee that Sudan not be turned into a site for smuggling, from which traders or the British could seek to undermine the Egyptian government's ability to control its economy and direct its rate of industrialization. This fear stemmed from the fact that, even as increasingly nationalist governments came to power in Cairo during the interwar period, because of the Condominium Treaty of 1899, tariffs could not be charged on goods that originated in either Egypt or Sudan, but were sold in the other country. However, tariffs and taxes could be charged on foreign goods that were merely transiting through either country on their way to the other[57]:

> The rising quantity of coffee imports from Sudan in the year 1937 was noticeable from these statistics and Sudan's increase in the quantity of crops grown and the real production in Sudan – and indeed the vision of the first superintendent in the Egyptian government was turned towards this phenomenon and this phenomenon clarified for them that some traders indeed sought refuge to import coffee by means of Sudan in order to escape from paying the custom tax imposed on imports of coffee.[58]

As the threat of war loomed over Egypt, trade from the South emerged not only as as a threat but also as a potential lifeline. Abdullah reported,

> In March 1939, there occurred research on the subject of food provisioning in the case of an emergency, which clarified that it is among the most important subjects which the Government of Egypt needs to study and research in order to obtain the interest of Egypt and Sudan, particularly the extent to which each of the two countries can depend on the harvest of the other in the case of an emergency in order to provision its agricultural, food and manufacturing needs taking into consideration the means of transport and communication between the two countries, creating facilitates at the border according to their needs and capabilities.[59]

The 254-page report that Abdullah Fakri Abaza finished in 1940 was primarily a survey of Sudan's natural resources and the ways in which they could fit into the national development strategy of Egypt and be dedicated to the Egyptian crown. Therefore, while it included a large number of sections on the resource

[56] Ibid., p. 51. [57] Ibid., p. 194. [58] Ibid., p. 49. [59] Ibid., p. 167.

base of Sudan, it ended with a long discussion of commercial regulations in Sudan and, more specifically, the rights and obligations of Egyptian traders and government officials negotiated in treaties and through bilateral agreements with the British authority in Khartoum.

Gathering trade statistics and cataloging natural resources were not by themselves novel in 1940; the colonial apparatus had already been engaged in similar projects for a long time. What was novel was that the Egyptians, because of their position as the subordinate power, engaged in public diplomacy. Therefore the first part of Abdullah's report is dedicated to describing how to design the apparatus necessary for this public diplomacy. From the opening of an office for the Egyptian economic expert in Khartoum to the formation of a permanent council in Egypt dedicated to reviewing Sudanese economic affairs, its lasting impact was to accelerate the introduction of economic information into the public sphere. This economic information, while biased toward the Egyptian point of view, was collected in such a manner that it highlighted the shortcomings of British policy.

The Growth of Economic Nationalism in Sudan

During the 1930s, nationalist sentiment within the senior ranks of the civil service began to grow for several reasons. The first cause was the increase in the stature of the governor-general and his cabinet in Khartoum. This was manifest in the Government of Sudan's assumption of more responsibility for running its affairs without reference to either Cairo or London. The Anglo-Egyptian Treaty of 1936 and the complete absence of any Sudanese participation in its negotiations, however, came as a shock both to the British officials who staffed the upper ranks of the Sudanese government and the Sudanese urban and professional classes, many of whom also worked in government positions. While Governor-General George Stewart Symes was kept abreast of the negotiations, informed Sudanese opinion was ignored, as were the opinions of the members of the Sudanese Political Service.[60] To the British and Egyptian negotiators who signed the treaty, however, this exclusion was to be expected because the treaty primarily concerned Britain's continuing relationship with a sovereign Egypt.

The treaty of 1936 enabled Egypt to become a member of the League of Nations, and in 1945, it became one of the original members of the United Nations. However, the prospect of direct negotiations between Egypt and Britain over the fate of Sudan and the reintroduction of Egyptian administrators in the Anglo-Egyptian Sudanese government threatened both the British officials who were making their careers in Sudan's administration and many members of the Sudanese educated class. The latter feared that their expected easy access to promotions and other responsible positions within the

[60] Daly, *Imperial Sudan*, pp. 57–58.

government would be hindered by the presence of Egyptian administrators.[61] As for the British members of the Sudan Political Service, their response to being ignored during the 1936 treaty negotiations was to quickly realize that the only way to secure their position as the legitimate authority presiding over Sudanese affairs was to argue that they spoke for the Sudanese people.

Therefore, senior members of the Political Service, such as Civil Secretary Sir Douglas Newbold,[62] began to advocate, if reluctantly at times, for an Anglo-Sudanese Sudan to replace the existing Anglo-Egyptian Sudan.[63] The administration first supported the formation in 1938 of a nonsectarian caucus to represent the Sudanese intelligentsia, the Graduates' General Congress. The Congress, which included a large number of Sudanese government officials, was initially to limit its activities to those of a cultural association. However, by 1942 it produced a memorandum that it delivered to the government demanding that the Congress be recognized as having the right to speak for the Sudanese people.[64] Even though the British administrators in Sudan were searching for Sudanese organizations that could legitimize their presence in the international arena, they were unwilling to cede, or even share, the right to speak for the Sudanese people with another authority. The administration in Khartoum rejected the Congress' demands, signaling that the British-staffed administration would not smoothly transfer its authority to another group.

This rejection ushered in a period of division within the nationalist movement and among British administrators, as both groups attempted to figure out how to proceed. Egypt challenged Britain's legal right to govern Sudan during the years 1946–1947, even going so far as to take the issue to the United Nations

61 It should be noted that the Anglo-Egyptian Sudan was not administered by the British Colonial Office, but was under the auspices of the Foreign Office. The administrators were members of the Sudan Political Service, not of the various technical services in the Anglo-Egyptian Sudan, the Foreign Office, or the Colonial Office. These officials did not rotate between Sudan and other colonies, but spent their entire careers within Sudan. Their pensions were guaranteed not by the British government, but by the Government of Sudan.

62 Like many of the British officials who held senior positions in Sudan during the 1940s, Newbold began his career in the Anglo-Egyptian Sudan in the 1920s, and was governor of Kordofan from 1932–1938 and then civil secretary, perhaps the highest-ranking position within the civil service, from 1939 until 1945.

63 Regarding the rise of nationalism in both the Ottoman Empire and the Russian Empire at the end of the nineteenth century, Michael Reynolds has the following to say, which also holds true of the manner in which interstate competition between Britain and Egypt gave rise to nationalism among both Anglo-Sudanese administrators and Sudanese civil servants: "The rise of nationalism in these borderlands at this time is better seen as a byproduct of interstate competition than as the stimulus of that competition." See Michael Reynolds, *Shattering Empires: The Clash and Collapse of the Ottoman and Russian Empires, 1908–1918* (Cambridge: Cambridge University Press, 2011), p. 18.

64 Peter Woodward, *Condominium and Sudanese Nationalism* (London: Rex Collings, 1979), pp. 23–24; Daly, *Imperial Sudan*, p. 73; also see Sharkey, *Living with Colonialism*, for an in-depth discussion of the cultural milieu from which most of the members of the Graduates' General Congress came and also of the emergence of *Sudani* as a category of self-identification.

Security Council. The presence of Egypt as a willing ally for Sudanese factions that wished to push for faster changes to the political landscape in Sudan created a situation where there were few incentives for squabbling factions to cooperate. Consequently the six years between the end of World War II and the Egyptian decision in 1951 to renounce its claim to sovereignty over Sudan were marked by political stagnation. Neither Sudanese politicians nor British administrators knew how to proceed in order to create a new political equilibrium, one in which Khartoum's voice could be heard and accorded more independence.

The Anglo-Egyptian debate about whether or not the Government of Sudan was correctly stewarding the resources of the country became the basis of the economic nationalism espoused by the early independence leaders and officials of Sudan. Its underlying current was that, through the control of the Nile waters, as Mekki Abbas said, Sudan could be transformed into a second Mesopotamia.[65] To the despair of the Egyptians, Sudanese leaders accepted that they were being held back by British regulations, but they did not come to see their fate as tied to providing Cairo with sustenance. As World War II drew to a close, the Department of Irrigation began to contemplate the future of development in Sudan. One of its striking conclusions was that Sudan needed more water than it currently had at its disposal. Even though in 1945 Sudan was unable to consume all of the water to which the country was entitled as a result of the 1929 Nile Waters Agreement, despite the Gezira Scheme expanding to more than 875,000 feddan, the department's internal projections were that Sudan would exhaust its supplies of water in the next five years. This impending shortage of water was interpreted as having the potential to halt Sudan's continuing development of irrigation schemes.[66] The department promised that expanding the amount of land under irrigation would increase the amount of food grown internally, promoting food security and increasing Sudan's exports of cotton, thereby allowing the country to purchase ever more goods from abroad. However, all proposals to significantly expand the amount of land under irrigation within Sudan were indefinitely stalled awaiting a clarification of Egypt's rights to the Nile waters.[67]

The Political Environment before Postwar Development

However, as the political future of Anglo-Egyptian Sudan remained mired in the ambiguity and the uncertainty of negotiations among multiple factions of Egyptian, Sudanese, and British politicians, questions about its economic future could no longer be put off. Britain was deeply indebted to its imperial possessions, owing Egypt (the money that it owed Sudan was included in this

65 Abbas, *The Sudan Question*, p. 8.

66 Draft Transcript of Broadcast. "Irrigation in the Sudan Now and the Next Five Years," October 1, 1945 SAD R. J. Smith 498/6/1–66/.

67 Ibid.

sum) approximately 425 million pounds sterling. Egypt, along with Sudan, was Britain's third largest creditor after the United States and India, and Egypt and the broader Middle East figured prominently in postwar British economic planners' visions of a restored imperial economy.[68]

After World War I, the Sudanese government sought to assure the loyalty of prominent Islamic religious leaders by making them large landowners, thereby creating the major constituency for Sudanese water nationalism as the struggle for independence escalated during the 1940s. The religious sheikhs and native authorities were encouraged to participate in exporting cotton and were often given privileged access to land and finance to do so. They developed their own private estates and obtained dominant positions in tenant schemes in which the government was a significant partner.[69] Although all of the major religious sheikhs were granted lands by the condominium government and encouraged to participate in commercial agriculture, Sayyid 'Abdul Rahman's enthusiasm for cotton made him known by the early 1950s as the richest man in Sudan.[70]

The following chapters tell the story of how colonial Sudanese officials and the first Sudanese men to staff the bureaucracy came to understand the development of an independent Sudan.

[68] Tignor, *Capitalism and Nationalism*, pp. 27–62.

[69] The Gezira Scheme, which became a model for other schemes throughout Sudan, was based on a tenant system in which profits were allocated at a ratio of 25:35:40 between the government, the syndicate, and the tenants. Individual tenancies were to be limited to forty feddan, but large landowners, who were often tribal leaders, could accumulate tenancies of several hundred feddan. Niblock, *Class and Power in Sudan*, pp. 14–15.

[70] M. Abu Salim, *Buhuth fi Tarikh al-Sudan: al-Aradi, al-'Ulama', al-Khilafah, Barbar, 'Ali al-Mirghani* (Beirut: Dar al-Jil, 1992), p. 184.

2

Planning and the Territorial Perspective, 1945–1951

Whether to unite the territory of Sudan as a single political and economic unit or to allow it to function as several largely independent parts was a decision that those who sought to rule Sudan wrestled with constantly. The political and economic orientation of the territory of Sudan had changed frequently in the century and a half leading up to Sudan's independence in 1956. At the beginning of the nineteenth century, it was made up of a number of political and economic entities, most of which did not look northward along the course of the Nile to Cairo. Therefore the Ottoman-Egyptian empire of Mehmet Ali and his successors tried to orient Sudan along the Nile, founding Khartoum as a new capital at the crossroads of the White and Blue Nile. Later, as political rulers in Khartoum gained more autonomy, they frequently tried to limit the economic and political influence of Cairo in Sudanese affairs. During the interwar period of the 1920s and 1930s, questions about the political and economic orientation of the Anglo-Egyptian Sudan came to the forefront again.

Rival constituencies, imperial officials in London, Egyptian nationalists in Cairo, British officers in the Sudanese Political Service, Sudanese nationalists in Khartoum, and intellectuals in the provinces of Sudan all imagined different political futures for the territory of Sudan and therefore envisioned orienting their imagined economy differently. Ultimately, however, the mundane tasks of creating budgets and dealing with the preexisting financial infrastructure of the state determined how Sudanese independence was formulated.

With the shape and structure of a Sudanese state suddenly in flux, the end of World War II and the breakup of the British Empire added urgency to planning for Sudan's future. The new fragility of the umbrella of empire freed intellectuals, officials, and politicians to imagine a wide variety of competing political and economic geographies. During the decade and a half that followed World War II, imperial officials and nationalist political leaders in colonial territories developed a variety of ideas about how to promote political and economic development. Just how the national economy became the primary unit of economic management in the case of the Anglo-Egyptian Sudan, a territory with two sovereigns, is one of the major themes of this chapter. To answer this question, it is necessary to examine the economic decision-making process during the years immediately following the conclusion of World War II.

The overlapping and entangled British and Egyptian colonial legacies of the Anglo-Egyptian Sudan made the territorial unit simply one of many competing economic or political units that could have emerged from the process of decolonization.[1] The most compelling alternatives, in competition with that of an independent national economy, were economic unification with Egypt, closer economic ties to Britain, or even a loose federated state with high degrees of economic autonomy at the regional or local level. That the national economy eventually became the dominant way in which officials understood the economy, even in a country with as weak a political or economic legacy of unity as Sudan, demonstrates the power of that concept in the decades after World War II.

Historians studying the process of decolonization have tended to focus on the political grievances that led to the end of empire and the creation of independent states.[2] However in doing so, scholars have failed to adequately take into account how shifts in the ways in which the role of government was conceptualized as an economic actor and in how the economy was visualized altered official understandings of where political and economic authority should be located.[3] In this chapter, I focus on how the thinking of finance officials and their political position within the government were altered by their embrace of national economic planning and the constant budgeting and reprioritizing such a process entailed. The planning process both strengthened the conviction of finance officials in a unified Sudanese economy and bolstered their ability to convincingly advocate for it. The decision to economically prioritize a

1 "If the last fifty years have made it seem as if the territorial nation-state is both 'modern' and inevitable, in 1958 it did not appear to some to be either." Cooper, "Possibility and Constraint: African Independence in Historical Perspective," p. 168.

2 See, for instance, Prosser Gifford and William Roger Louis (eds.), *The Transfer of Power in Africa: Decolonization, 1940–1960* (New Haven, CT: Yale University Press, 1982).

3 For a global history of the different ways in which national income accounts made economies visible, see Paul Studenski, *The Income of Nations: Theory, Measurement, and Analysis: Past and Present: A Study in Applied Economics and Statistics* (New York: New York University Press, 1958). The theory of diffusion suggests that these representations then spread across the world, inspiring their emulation. See the work of Mitchell, *Rule of Experts*. For the diffusion of modernization theory, see Nils Gilman, *Mandarins of the Future: Modernization Theory in Cold War America* (Baltimore: Johns Hopkins University Press, 2007), and Michael Latham, *Modernization as Ideology: American Social Science and "Nation-Building" in the Kennedy Era* (Chapel Hill: University of North Carolina Press, 2000). However, while a theory of intellectual diffusion exists, no in-depth case study has yet tested the relationship among the diffusion of the idea of the economy, the end of empire, and the rise of nation-states nor examined to what extent and in which ways they are related to one another.

unified Sudan over economically autonomous territorially defined regions such as the southern and the western provinces or ethnically defined units such as the Nuba or Azande derived in part from the financial arguments made by finance officials during the planning process. The blueprint for the Sudanese national economy was created in the Department of Finance during routine and repeated discussions about prioritizing and implementing various projects included in the centralized financial decision-making system created as a result of the planning process. The need to centralize funding for individual projects and to develop a means of prioritizing them followed directly from the logic of the national planning process itself. Planning, as practiced in Khartoum from 1946–1951, demanded a centralized system of budgeting, even as it encouraged various parts of the government to design development projects in a decentralized manner. Reconciling these two processes centralized budgeting, localized project design, and prompted finance officials to create an evaluative framework. This framework was shaped by the planners' territorial perspective in which those projects that benefited the Sudanese economy as a whole – in practice those that made the largest contribution to the central budget – were prioritized over projects that focused on local development or imperial strategic interests.

This specific territorial perspective unfolded over several years. At war's end, when officials in Khartoum, London, and Cairo sought to clarify the boundaries of their respective economic responsibilities and Sudan's political and economic ties, the senior members of the Sudan Political Service felt an imperative to define the extent to which Sudan should be managed as a single economic unit. Britain's and Egypt's dual sovereignty over the territory of Sudan left it with a legacy of overlapping economic ties to to them.[4] The main issue that decision makers in Sudan confronted was whether to favor policies that focused on the economy of the Anglo-Egyptian Sudan as a whole, or on local and regional economies within Sudan, or on a Nile Valley economy, or on the wider imperial economy.

Sudan's Department of Finance was the agency primarily concerned with planning the economy and hence is the focus of this study. Before World War II, however, its role was confined to developing the budget and supervising and auditing other parts of the bureaucracy, rather than formulating long-range national policy objectives. In addition, because Sudan was an Anglo-Egyptian colonial responsibility the Sudanese financial secretary was stationed in Cairo where he coordinated fiscal decisions with the British resident in Cairo, the Egyptian Ministry of Finance, and the governor-general in Khartoum. For the first decades of the condominium, the stationing of the finance secretary outside

[4] The legacy of the Anglo-Egyptian Condominium intensified the dilemmas faced by officials in Sudan, even though planners in other colonies, who were also trying to transform their colonies into unified and autonomous units of political and economic governance, dealt with similar problems. For a discussion of the Indian experience, see Manu Goswami, *Producing India: From Colonial Economy to National Space* (Chicago: University of Chicago Press, 2004), pp. 8–9.

the boundaries of Sudan only further weakened tendencies within the bureaucracy to think of the Anglo-Egyptian Sudan as a coherent unit whose economic interests should be privileged. The Sudanese bureaucracy's autonomy increased greatly when the Sudanese governor-general's council became a more important policy-making institution during the 1930s and the office of the finance secretary moved to Khartoum. But by then Sudan's financial prerogatives were constrained by the demands of the Great Depression and the subsequent mobilization for World War II. Moreover, for much of the history of the British presence in Sudan, imperial officials saw Sudan alternatively as a province of Egypt, a department within the Egyptian government, or an integral part of the imperial trading and war-fighting machine. Rarely did they see it as an independent economic entity.[5]

During the late 1940s and 1950s, however, Sudan's Department of Finance increasingly began to focus on the formulation of "national" economic policy. Senior officials began to ask what was "good for the national economy" in policy debates, and they came to expect that these questions should be accorded as high a priority as the ones that had previously guided policy formation, such as how to maintain political order while guaranteeing good governance. Because cotton was the principal source of the state's revenue and therefore occupied the majority of finance officials' time, understanding the vast shifts in the Sudanese cotton industry is critical to understanding the emergence of the modern Sudanese state.

Cotton and the Sudanese Economy during the 1940s

By 1945, economic growth in Egypt had plummeted. Per capita GDP had declined precipitously during the war years, and in 1945 it may have been 20 percent lower than it had been in 1900.[6] For Egyptians who understood this economic stagnation largely as the result of the exhaustion of their cultivable land, the prospect of incorporating Sudan with all of its agricultural potential into their economic sphere of influence was immensely attractive.[7] At the same time, British officials saw Sudan as a potential hedge against losing Egypt and as a bargaining chip they could leverage in negotiations to maintain their military and economic position in the Middle East.[8]

[5] M. W. Daly, "The Development of the Governor-Generalship of the Sudan, 1899–1934," *Journal of African History* 24:1 (1983): 77–96.

[6] Tignor, *Capitalism and Nationalism*, pp. 29, 36.

[7] In 1967, it was estimated that, in Sudan, only 8 million acres of a potential 100 million acres of land that could be cultivated were actively being developed. See Adel Amin Beshai, *Export Performance and Economic Development in Sudan, 1900–1967* (London: Ithaca Press, 1976), 2.

[8] In many ways Britain's desire to maintain its massive bases within the Suez Canal was even more significant than its desire to expand its economic activities within Egypt. Tignor, *Capitalism and Nationalism*, pp. 27–62.

One of the reasons why officials in Khartoum felt the pressures of imperial economic weakness so acutely was that Sudan, though its economic activity was growing rapidly, remained a frontier of the two divergent economies of Britain and Egypt. Internally, the territory of Sudan included numerous autonomous, local economies within its borders.[9] Even as the value of Sudan's exports increased more than tenfold from LS (Sudanese pounds) 5.6 million in 1936 to LS 61 million in 1951, Sudan remained more of an economic frontier of other countries than a distinct and autonomous economic space.[10] For example, the territory, like many other African possessions, had an underdeveloped transportation network. At the same time, a vast array of hydrological and irrigation works were scattered across the territory, which, moreover, were designed to function as part of a transnational Nile river basin, rather than as an infrastructure system defining the Anglo-Egyptian Sudan. The economic and financial unity of the country was also limited by the use of Egyptian currency and an overlapping banking network that was alternately centered in Cairo and in London: although the National Bank of Egypt served as the bank of the government in Khartoum, government officials were eager to use British banks, such as Barclays DCO, in order to separate their financial transactions from those of Egypt.[11] Tensions over the international orientation of Khartoum's monetary policy were further exacerbated by Egypt's announcement that it would leave the Sterling Convertibility Zone in 1947.[12] This move put Sudan into two distinct monetary spheres as Sudanese officials strove to preserve their place within the sterling zone.

Senior British officials within the Department of Finance in Khartoum were among the first to contest Sudan's position as a mere economic frontier of Egypt or of the British Empire and to argue instead that the territory constituted its own economic space. Development planning played a key role in this transformation. Before 1946, the Sudanese government conceptualized development planning as the process of creating a series of individual projects and paid little attention to the need to coordinate agricultural or development schemes. The planning process initiated in 1946 changed this focus.[13] The conceptualization of the Sudanese economy as an independent object of planning was a gradual

9 Goswami, *Producing India*, 8–9.

10 These figures were derived from the Sudan government's Annual Foreign Trade Reports in Beshai, *Export Performance and Economic Development*, pp. 11–12. The rate was USD 2.87 for one Sudanese pound in 1957.

11 A. L. Chick, letter to C. G. Davis on Sudan Sterling Balances, November 14, 1951, SAD, G. D. Lampen Collection 732/8/1–162/.

12 Tignor, *Capitalism and Nationalism*, p. 36.

13 The three main planned schemes before 1945 were the Gezira Scheme, the Alternative Livelihood Scheme, and the Gash Delta Project. The Alternative Livelihood Scheme was designed for the resettlement of 70,000 families whose land was flooded by the construction of the Jebel Aulia Dam on the White Nile. The Gash Delta Project was a 35,000-acre scheme with 7,000 tenants. It was primarily a cotton-exporting project. Beshai, *Export Performance and Economic Development*, pp. 15, 29 n. 18. See Chapter 1 for a description of the Gezira Scheme.

process that developed over the next twenty years as the planning process itself matured.

Before the war, agricultural schemes had been developed and managed individually, each scheme possessing its own independent board of supervisors. The principal departments such as the Departments of Agriculture, Public Works, Finance, and Irrigation and the Board of Trade and Economics typically had representatives on the oversight boards of each scheme. But supervision was limited and confined to the infrequent meetings of those boards. The ad hoc nature of governance and oversight meant that individual agricultural schemes were able to pursue divergent aims and ambitions, with some devoted to local development and others simply producing raw commodities for the imperial economy.

The 1930s were marked by administrative conservatism and a general sense of malaise throughout the bureaucracy. The Department of Finance was not closely involved in the management of the individual agricultural schemes, confining itself to sending accountants and auditors to help with bookkeeping and the creation of operational budgets.[14] And even though British officials made many proposals for economic development in this decade, poor economic conditions meant that the majority of them were never carried out. However, mobilizing for war in the late 1930s propelled the Sudanese bureaucracy into action, even as it further diminished the ability of individual parts of the empire to negotiate their own trade and economic policies. The formalization of an imperial trading bloc and the attendant preparations for war demanded greatly increased coordination between the bodies that set imperial economic policy within the various parts of the empire.[15]

During the war years, the greatest economic disruptions were caused by wartime inflation and the artificial suppression of agricultural prices. Export prices were kept low through purchasing agreements with Britain that enabled it to pay far below market prices for commodities like cotton. In exchange Britain agreed to buy fixed quantities of cotton. In addition, tenant farmers working on and selling to state-run agricultural schemes were often forced to participate in price-stabilization funds, which promised to reimburse them when market prices for commodities were low with savings accumulated when prices were high. The strict nature of the colonial government's price controls allowed the price-stabilization funds to grow to a size that was unimaginable

14 Like much of the Government of Sudan, the Finance Department grew out of the Egyptian Army's Intelligence Branch, which took over administrative duties as early as 1896 in Dongola in northern Sudan. As late as 1914, the financial secretary remained in Cairo attached to the Sudan Agency, which was charged with representing Sudan's interests to the Egyptian government and the British representative in Cairo. He was thus beyond the direct control of the Sudanese governor-general. All budgets had to be passed first by the Egyptian Council of Ministers. Matters having to do with the Nile Waters were also reserved for Cairo. Daly, "The Development of the Governor-Generalship of the Sudan, 1899–1934," pp. 77–96.

15 Darwin, *The Empire Project*, pp. 418–509; James, *The End of Globalization*.

before the outbreak of the war. The size of the fund at the conclusion of the war in 1945 meant that colonial finance officials could no longer justify restricting its use solely to providing insurance to farmers against low prices. Questions about how to equitably spend the funds accumulated within the price-stabilization funds became the impetus for postwar planners in Sudan and throughout much of British Africa to conceptualize development.[16]

Forced savings particularly galled farmers, because they were suffering as a result of the impact of inflation. Finance officials also noted that unprecedented sums of money had begun to circulate within the economy. Before 1939, the amount of currency typically in circulation in Sudan was LE 1.75 million, while by 1943 that figure had risen to LE 4.25 million.[17] The war made imported consumer goods increasingly scarce, causing inflation in the major cities. The impact of price rises in the major cities was intensely felt by the colonial government, because the urban population was the most politically restless. The nightmare scenario playing out in the minds of colonial officials was a continuous sequence of "rising wages and rising returns to cultivators and cattle owners followed by a tendency towards a general rise in prices and then wages."[18] Officials believed that inflation would undermine the legitimacy of the colonial government.

As the war came to an end, finance officials recognized that economic activity in Sudan would not immediately revert to its prewar pattern. Therefore, economic controls could not be abandoned in the near term, and inflation continued to be seen as a problem that demanded constant attention. Yet on the positive side of the ledger, the six years of austerity budgets prior to 1946 that British officials had drafted facilitated the accumulation of fiscal surpluses earned from the rising price of cotton on international markets.[19]

The wider public's acute awareness of rising cotton prices put added pressure on the British officials managing financial policy to find a means of either returning a share of the profits to the farmers, who had earned them, or to reinvest the profits in ways that mitigated rising public outrage. Yet officials within the Department of Finance remained cautious about committing themselves to large expenditures, citing the difficulty of determining with precision the size of the market for cotton. They knew that they lacked the expertise to reliably forecast the future of the international cotton market, so the International Cotton Advisory Committee was enlisted to help the Government of Sudan interpret

16 Tignor, *Capitalism and Nationalism*, pp. 195–293.

17 LE stands for Egyptian pound. Until 1957 the Egyptian pound was the legal tender in Sudan. From World War I until 1962, it was pegged to the British pound at almost 1=1 parity or 0.975 Egyptian pounds to 1 British pound. The exchange rate with the US dollar was 0.25 Egyptian pounds to 1 US dollar.

18 John Cummins, "War Inflation," note, June 20, 1943, Finance Department, SAD, J. W. Cummins Collection, 635/12/1–44/.

19 "Statement by Financial Secretary, Sudan Government, Post-War Development," (1945) SAD, J. W. Cummins Collection, 635/14/1–7/.

general trends.[20] The association represented the interests of the major cotton-producing countries, and it aimed to provide data about future patterns of both consumption and production.

The caution of senior officials seeking to embark on large development projects reflected the reality that the international market for cotton was unstable. Even as the demand for cotton rapidly rebounded following the conclusion of World War II, the supply of cotton continued to lag. It was this lag that created the conditions in which cotton prices appeared destined to rise indefinitely. As of July 31, 1947, worldwide consumption was approximately 27.5 million bales, which was close to 95 percent of the prewar totals. At the same time, production was only 70 percent of its prewar average of 31 million bales. Stores of cotton that had been built up in the cotton-consuming countries during the war years were used to cover the difference between the amount of cotton consumed and the amount of cotton available after the war finished; it was thus difficult for market participants to calculate the extent of these stores. The estimated production of the 1946–7 season was barely 21.5 million bales, and although production levels were slowly increasing, there were serious constraints on how quickly they could rise. Many countries, including India, the USSR, and Egypt, were placing limits on the production of cotton, because they needed to prioritize the production of food crops. The price of cotton traded on markets in the United States was at least three times the prewar level.[21]

Another reason that the international cotton market remained volatile was its extremely fragmented and opaque nature. This fragmentation resulted from a "world of import and exchange controls, of floors and ceilings, of large-scale contracts, sales tied to credits, of free and official currencies, of export taxes, and of barter." For policy makers trying to understand the future, "prices lost some of their meaning and comparisons [were] difficult."[22] Uncertainty counseled caution. In these circumstances, officials were hesitant to commit capital to new investments that might take a long time to pay back their initial capital.

Despite the uncertainty involved in spending the accumulated revenues from cotton, the very size of those revenues meant that finance officials felt compelled to respond to surpluses with new development plans. One way of illustrating the changed circumstances of the Government of Sudan is to note that in the 1951–2 fiscal year, government revenue was ten times its prewar level and more than five times what it had been only three years earlier. Government revenue stood at LE 8.3 million in 1946, compared to LE 41.87 million in 1950–1951.

[20] The International Cotton Association was created on September 9, 1939, with its headquarters based in Washington, DC. Its original members were the governments of India, Egypt, Brazil, USSR, Peru, Mexico, Sudan, and the United States; the British Cotton Exporting Colonies; and the French Cotton Exporting Colonies.

[21] Cotton, Statistics and International Cotton Association, International Cotton Executive Committee, Minutes of the Fifth Meeting of the Executive Committee of the ICAC, Washington, DC, April 30, 1947, NRO Finance 3-A/28/8/30.

[22] Ibid.

The rise in revenue was a product of the high price of cotton in international markets.[23]

The First Five-Year Plan for Postwar Development

Getting to the point where a colonial or postcolonial official in Sudan would even ask what was good for the Sudanese economy was a long process. The impetus for this transformation in thinking was that the Anglo-Egyptian Sudan was ineligible to receive official British development aid since it was technically not a British colony, but a condominium government managed by the Foreign Office, rather than the Colonial Office. Still British officials in Sudan asserted frequently that the Anglo-Egyptian Sudan was an imperial responsibility. After sustained official and popular protests in 1946, the British Treasury granted Sudan two million sterling pounds in appreciation of the country's commitment to the wartime struggle. One result of this grant was that Sudan began a process of long-term development planning, designed to emulate the planning processes mandated for Britain's official colonies under the Colonial Development and Welfare Act of 1940.[24]

The writing of the first plan, a thirteen-page aggregate of Sudan's development priorities, was undertaken by Finance Secretary Sir Eddington Miller, Deputy Financial Secretary A. L. Chick, and Assistant Financial Secretary John Carmichael.[25] This document, titled *The Five Year Plan for Postwar Development in Sudan: 1946–1951* was a hodgepodge of projects, reflecting

[23] Daly, *Imperial Sudan*, p. 303.

[24] Wm. Roger Louis, *The British Empire in the Middle East, 1945–1951: Arab Nationalism, The United States, and Postwar Imperialism* (Oxford: Clarendon Press, 1984), p. 181; Daly, *Imperial Sudan*, pp. 304–305; Monica M. van Beusekom and Dorothy L. Hodgson, "Lessons Learned? Development Experience during the Late Colonial Period," *Journal of African History* 41:1 (2000): 31.

[25] J. W. E. Miller, "1945/46 Development Budget," letter to Secretary General's Council, May 3, 1946, SAD, J. W. Cummins Collection, 636/1/1–42/. Miller had arrived in Sudan in 1920; Chick and Carmichael came in the 1930s. In 1948, on Miller's retirement, Chick would become the finance secretary and Carmichael would get promoted to deputy finance secretary from assistant finance secretary. The Sudan Political Service, created in 1901, operated independently of the other British civil services, such as the Colonial Service, the Home Service, and the Indian Civil Service. The vast majority of its members were recruited from a narrow demographic base of the lower gentry, trained at elite British schools such as Eton and Harrow, and earned their undergraduate degrees from Oxford and Cambridge. The narrowness of the social base from which these officials were recruited, combined with the Sudan Political Service's autonomy from other administrative orders, allowed the Sudanese Political Service to develop its own autonomous administrative culture, which marked its administrators and the administration in the Anglo-Egyptian Sudan as distinct from that in other parts of the British empire. See Robert O. Collins, "The Sudan Political Service: A Portrait of the 'Imperialists,'" *African Affairs* 71: 284 (July 1972.): 293–303. See, also, Daly, *Imperial Sudan*, p. 26. Daly suggests that, even during the 1930s, Sudanese officials were divorced from larger debates about colonial governance, despite struggling with similar challenges.

many different desires and priorities.[26] The Development Priorities Committee, which comprised the financial secretary, the civil secretary, the comptroller-general of war supply, and the general manager of the Sudan Railways, was charged with prioritizing what would be included in the plan. To allocate funds for development and reconstruction, a General Development Account was created, which was managed by officials within the Supplies (Expenditure Branch) of the Department of Finance. This branch was also charged with formulating ordinary budgets.[27]

The *Five-Year Plan* allocated LE 11,480,470 to a wide variety of schemes suggested by the governors of various provinces and the heads of departments.[28] On the first page it explicitly stated that its goal was to create "a store of development plans out of which projects could be selected from time to time," provided that the government possessed the resources and inclination necessary to invest in these capital improvements.[29] Since the planning process was so ad hoc, the plan itself possessed very little coherence. It included ample warnings that development should not be allowed to proceed too quickly and that increased government spending would spur inflation either domestically or internationally, in conjunction with reconstruction spending occurring simultaneously in other parts of the empire. The discussion of inflation was a way to remind Sudanese officials that they would not be permitted to prioritize the economic development of Sudanese territory over broader imperial objectives. Despite persistent worries about inflation, the planners believed that a cautious increase in spending was justified by the rapid increase in revenues throughout the 1940s.[30]

The plan was heavily skewed in favor of productive (revenue-generating) schemes. Because it gathered up projects promoted by imperial and Sudanese bureaucrats, it attempted to blend local development projects, aimed at regional self-sufficiency and increasing the governability of local populations, with territory-wide programs and supraterritorial programs, notably the further expansion of major irrigation schemes, which were tied to the management of the entire Nile Basin. Nonetheless, the first five-year plan did not primarily pursue development goals that were focused on the territorial unit of the Anglo-Egyptian Sudan, for the planners did not regard Sudan as the primary unit of economic development. Instead, the plan addressed economic units that were both much larger and smaller than the administrative unit of the Anglo-Egyptian Sudan.

26 Sudan Government, *Five Year Plan for Post-War Development* (Khartoum: Department of Finance, 1946).

27 Mirghani, *Development Planning in the Sudan in the Sixties*, pp. 8–9; Daly, *Imperial Sudan*, p. 304.

28 In today's US dollars, the funds allocated by the Government of Sudan for development equal $526,257,670 (2010).

29 Sudan Government, *Five Year Plan for Post-War Development*, p. 1.

30 Ibid.; "Statement by Financial Secretary, Sudan Government, Post-War Development."

The planning process involved interdepartmental meetings, budgeting, oversight of specific project plans, project modifications, and re-budgeting.[31] Budgeting and re-budgeting are central to this story, because it was in the process of allocating and managing funds that Sudan came to be defined as the primary economic unit. The planning process was centralized through the creation of the General Development Account, and those managing it found themselves in a position to coordinate the funding of new capital investments. In the budgets of the Finance Department capital expenditures were kept distinct from recurring expenses covered by allocations from the ordinary budget. Deputy Financial Secretary A. L. Chick and his assistant John Carmichael were constantly being asked to supervise and comment on the priority of particular schemes and projects and whether they were worthy of being funded. Altering the purpose of particular projects was not within the original mandate of the Department of Finance; after all, it was supposed to confine itself to prioritizing and coordinating the implementation of various projects designed by other branches of government. However, finance officials soon found themselves involved in the details of designing projects and setting actual development policy. And once Chick and Carmichael became involved in development policy, because they then had to advocate certain positions in the midst of bureaucratic competition, they were inexorably led to promoting a national territorial perspective. As the officials in the Finance Department reviewed development projects and plans, they saw their influence grow, and they increasingly based their funding choices on whether or not individual projects contributed to the territory's overall development.[32] By the 1950s, the "national" territorial perspective had won out over the concepts of imperial and local economic management that had had the upper hand in the 1940s.[33]

As mentioned, officials within the Department of Finance before the war confined themselves to aggregating and supervising proposals designed in other parts of the government. The process was designed to allow development proposals to flow smoothly from the local level to the central government, based on the premise that development was to originate with those who knew the local conditions best. It was a commonly held belief within the Sudan Political Service that in designing development projects "local knowledge must

[31] Morgan, "On a Mission' with Mutable Mobiles," pp. 6–7.

[32] Helen Tilley, *African as a Living Laboratory: Empire, Development, and the Problem of Scientific Knowledge, 1870–1950* (Chicago: University of Chicago Press, 2011), p. 6. See also the frequent use of the terms "territorial" and "territory" in Low and Lonsdale, "Introduction: Towards the New Order 1945–1963," pp. 1–64.

[33] The idea that different groups of officials and departments within the same government can simultaneously be working toward divergent conceptions of the state and even mutually competing policies within the same bureaucracy has been explored by Boaventura de Sousa Santos: "The Heterogeneous State and Legal Pluralism in Mozambique," *Law and Society Review* 40:1 (March 2006): 42–44; and *Toward a New Common Sense-Law, Science, and Politics in the Paradigmatic Transition* (New York: Routledge, 1995).

prevail."[34] However, this division of labor required a system of fluid communication between the different branches of government that rarely existed. Officials within the Finance Department acknowledged that the process of developing proposals at the local level and then sending the information up the chain of command so that the proposals could be prioritized was failing badly.

Problems of information management persisted throughout the entire period of experimenting with planning in practice and went to the heart of debates about planning in theory. Dissatisfaction was rampant. John Carmichael's frustration with the governor of Kordofan's attempts to expand cotton cultivation in the Nuba Mountains stemmed partly from the poorly functioning communication system. He wrote that the governor of Kordofan was "groping for some scheme but wants someone to think it out for him." At the same time, the governor wrote to the civil secretary that he wanted "those who settle policy" to come and see the conditions locally before they started the process of detailed planning.[35]

The development projects that finance officials evaluated originated not only in regional or local authorities but also in functional departments such as the Departments of Irrigation and of Agriculture. The irrigation department was principally concerned with large-scale engineering works and was responsible for their design, construction, and operation.[36] In the 1940s, the most important projects over which it had oversight powers were the Sennar Dam, the Gezira Canalization System, and various other works in support of the Gezira Scheme; it also supervised smaller irrigation works in the Gash Delta and in the Northern Province.[37] The Department of Irrigation saw itself as the "water treasurer of the country."[38] A key principle under which it operated at the end of World War II was that water was an asset that belonged to the country as a whole. Therefore even as they encouraged private enterprise, irrigation officials argued that development had to be managed in a centralized fashion.[39]

[34] John Carmichael, comment to A. L. Chick, the Financial Secretary, December 23 1949, Economic Development, Nuba Mountains, Delami Conference, The National Records Office, Khartoum, Sudan NRO Finance 3-A/42/1/2/.

Contrary to the idea of development as a universalist discourse imposed from the outside conveyed in Arturo Escobar, *Encountering Development: The Making and Unmaking of the Third World* (Princeton, NJ: Princeton University Press, 1995), finance officials acknowledged that local knowledge was important. Their primary challenge was gaining access to the knowledge of farmers and even of local colonial officials: local knowledge was often not incorporated into the planning of development schemes because of a lack of access, rather than outright bias.

[35] John Carmichael, comment to A. L. Chick, the Financial Secretary, December 23, 1949. Economic Development, Nuba Mountains, Delami Conference, NRO Finance 3-A/42/1/2/; and Comment, From F. S. to D. F. S., "Governor Kordofan to C.S. re. proposed meeting to consider Nuba Mountain Cotton industry," December 22, 1949, Economic Development, Nuba Mountains, Delami Conference, NRO Finance 3-A/42/1/2/.

[36] Transcript of Broadcast by Mr. A. E. Griffin, April 5, 1943, SAD, R. J. Smith Collection, 498/6/1–66/.

[37] Ibid. [38] Ibid.

[39] Draft Transcript of Broadcast, "Irrigation in the Sudan Now and the Next Five Years," October 1, 1945, SAD, R. J. Smith Collection, 498/6/1–66/.

After 1946 finance officials charged with implementing the planning process began to throw their weight behind the perspective that the appropriate spatial unit for planning was the territory of Sudan. The concept of Sudan as a distinct economic unit was adapted from officials in the Sudan Irrigation Department, who developed this argument while negotiating with Egypt over water rights. The competition over which agency, the Egypt Ministry of Public Works or the Sudan Department of Irrigation, had the right to manage the territory's water resources began in the 1930s. A distinctly nationalist view developed in the irrigation department as a result of its competition with Egypt over the right to manage the Nile water flowing through Sudan's borders on its way to Egypt.[40] The adoption of the territorial perspective by finance officials, as the planning process matured, allowed the water nationalism of irrigation experts to be imposed on agricultural schemes, transportation, and the budgets of the Anglo-Egyptian Sudan. While most members of the condominium bureaucracy saw themselves as either local officials or as imperial civil servants, the competition between members of the Sudanese Irrigation Department and their Egyptian counterparts in the Ministry of Public Works over managing the Nile waters led Sudanese irrigation officials to think in terms of Sudan's territorial prerogatives.

When drafting the first five-year plan in 1946, finance officials as well as many other members of the bureaucracy, unlike their colleagues in the Department of Irrigation, were still trying to define their positions as imperial, local, or Anglo-Sudanese officials and therefore were unable to offer a definite set of criteria about which projects should be funded. However, between 1946 and 1951 when the second national plan was put forward, the department gradually developed a set of criteria about what types of projects it would support. Finance officials prioritized development projects that maximized the potential financial contribution to the central budget. One of the primary consequences of this approach was a growing intolerance within the Department of Finance for projects that focused on regional or local development without attempting to increase economic activity throughout the territory or to maximize the contribution to the central government in Khartoum. Naturally, finance officials had always been concerned with earning a profit. But whereas earlier they would have found their views subordinated to other interests within the government, the increasing importance of planning strengthened both their voice within the government and their autonomy. Gradually, the position of the senior members of the Department of Finance hardened as they came to see Sudan as an economic unit in itself, distinct from both the smaller units of its subregions and the Egyptian and British imperial

40 See discussion in Chapter 3 and in Robert O. Collins, *The Waters of the Nile: Hydropolitics and the Jonglei Canal, 1900–1988* (Princeton, NJ: Markus Wiener Publishers, 1996), pp. 247–249. See also Letter from Secretariat to African Department, FO, February 25, 1950, FO 371/97019; Letter from African Department, FO to Secretariat, February 17, 1950, FO 371/80531; Letter from Secretariat to African Department, FO, February 25, 1950, FO 371/80531.

economies.[41] By 1949, the newly promoted Financial Secretary Arthur Chick was heard complaining, "Development planning in Kordofan must fit in with central planning for the country as a whole and we have yet to decide what is the best machinery to set up for the latter."[42] Chick was articulating a planning perspective that defined the territory of Sudan as the most relevant unit of planning.

During the 1940s, the development of a territorial perspective as an evaluative lens can be traced by examining how economic policy was made in three cases: the Nuba Mountain Cotton Cultivation Scheme, the Equatoria Projects Board, and the regulation of river traffic on the southern stretches of the Nile. Each of these cases embroiled large parts of the Sudanese government in debates about the purpose of economic development. By examining each of these controversies, it is possible to uncover the positions of senior officials within the Sudanese government on the main aims of economic policy. Some officials advocated trusteeship over specific peoples, and others, particularly within the Finance Department, argued that economic policies should be designed to maximize revenue generation.[43] Finance officials gradually came to believe that the costs and inefficiencies associated with local government and indirect rule should not be inserted into the design of economic development programs.

Implementing *The Five Year Plan for Postwar Reconstruction*

The Nuba Mountains Cotton Cultivation Scheme, the Equatoria Projects Board, and the debate that arose over regulating river traffic on the southern stretches of the Nile illustrate some of the major controversies about the objectives of development; they also demonstrate that officials within the Department of Finance were successful in arguing that development should support

41 For a discussion of how changes in the relevant unit in which questions such as poverty, economic growth, or development generally were discussed affected the types of answers that experts and other officials formulated, see James Ferguson, *Global Shadows: Africa in the Neoliberal World Order* (Durham, NC: Duke University Press, 2006), pp. 60–61.

42 A. L. Chick, comment to John Carmichael, June 12, 1949, Economic Development, Nuba Mountains, Delami Conference, NRO Finance 3-A/42/1/2/. As Monica M. Van Beusekom describes in her article on the Office du Niger, it was difficult to impose a unified vision of how to manage development schemes or particular projects (when such a vision existed) because not only did "African settlers at the scheme often fail to follow project directives" but "also significant were the struggles among Office personnel, colonial officials of Soudan, the government general of French West Africa and ultimately the metropolitan policy makers." Monica M. Van Beusekom, "Disjunctures in Theory and Practice: Making Sense of Change in Agricultural Development at the Office du Niger, 1920–60," *Journal of African History* 41:1 (2000): 80–81.

43 "A related development was the newfound belief in the organizational and administrative abilities of bureaucracies to manage such large projects; the days of itinerant district officers haphazardly implementing small projects was long gone." Beusekom and Hodgson, "Lessons Learned?" p. 31.

the expansion of economic activity at the scale of the territory of Sudan, rather than at more local levels, regions, provinces, or ethnically defined districts.

By insisting that the economic success of government policies be measured primarily at the level of the condominium as surpluses accumulated in the central development and ordinary budgets, finance officials were indirectly demanding significant changes in the ways in which the condominium ruled its people. In particular, these shifts meant abandoning two long-standing administrative objectives developed in the 1920s and carried out in various ways until after World War II. The first policy was the devolution of administrative authority to localities responsible for ruling specific groups of people in Sudan.[44] The second policy was the establishment between 1922 and 1930 of "closed districts," areas in which northern Arab merchants and Islamic missionaries were forbidden from entering. The policy of closed districts allowed administrators to argue that certain development projects should be designed to benefit particular groups primarily or exclusively, because those groups were economically or politically less advanced.[45]

The Nuba Mountains Cotton Scheme

The Nuba Mountains are located in the southern part of Kordofan, a large province directly west of Khartoum and east of Darfur. The province stretches from the deserts in the far north of the country down into the grasslands and swamps that marked much of the boundary with southern Sudan. The British considered Kordofan an Arab province. But living near the agro-pastoralist Dinkas among the southern regions bordering the Upper Nile Province was a substantial African population, whose origins the British considered obscure. These people living in a series of hills in the southeast of the province were often referred to as the Nuba. The British ethnographic literature acknowledged that the Nuba were not a single people, but the remnants of several distinct peoples eventually pushed into the hills and off the clay plains that dominated the landscape of Kordofan. Based on this ethnographic perspective, British officials

44 For a discussion of the legacies of the policies of indirect rule on politics in Sudan, see Mamdani, *Saviors and Survivors*; Justin Willis, "Violence, Authority and the State in the Nuba Mountains of Condominium Sudan," *Historical Journal* 46:1 (2003): 89–114; Cherry Leonardi, *Knowing Authority: Colonial Authority and Local Community in Equatoria Province, Sudan, 1900–1956* (PhD diss., Durham University UK, 2005); and Chris Vaughan, *Negotiating the State at its Margins: Colonial Authority in Condominium Darfur, 1916–1956* (PhD diss., Durham University UK, 2011). For an explanation of the liberal underpinnings of good governance and indirect rule as a "form of rule that would work towards the improvement of the subject races," see Karuna Mantena, "The Crisis of Liberal Imperialism," in Duncan Bell, ed., *Victorian Visions of Global Order: Empire and International Relations in Nineteenth-Century Political Thought* (New York: Cambridge University Press, 2007), pp. 118, 124.

45 M. Abdel Rahim, "The Development of British Policy in Southern Sudan," *Middle Eastern Studies* 2:3 (April 1966): 231. See also Veena Das and Deborah Poole, "State and Its Margins: Comparative Ethnographies," in Veena Das and Deborah Poole (eds.), *Anthropology at the Margins of the State* (Oxford: James Currey Press, 2004), pp. 3–35.

created policies to treat the Nuba as distinct from the Arabs; this differential treatment became the basis of ongoing debates about how the Nuba Mountains should be developed.[46]

Cotton was cultivated in the Nuba Mountains beginning in the interwar period. Although it was not the most prominent crop grown at the time, cotton was considered to be the crop that would most efficiently propel the future economic growth of the region.[47] Administratively, the Nuba Mountains Development Area was created in 1939 as an autonomous region focused on the production of cotton. It included the Tegale and Jebels Districts and some parts of western Kordofan.[48] In the ten years after 1939, the price of cotton increased fivefold.[49] Yet, despite repeated attempts to make the cultivation of cotton attractive, government officials remained concerned about their ability to incentivize the Nuba to grow more cotton. Cotton production continued to increase with the involvement of Arab groups, such as the Hawazma and the Misseriya, but those groups posed a persistent challenge to authority at the district level, and district officers advocated for the need to exercise trusteeship over the Nuba.[50] Trusteeship would allow district officers greater authority to intervene directly in the local communities of the Nuba.

Amid growing doubts about the purpose of development efforts centered on the Nuba Mountains in particular and the province of Kordofan in general, D. C. Cummings, the governor of Kordofan, began a series of conversations with high officials throughout the government. He pleaded for the reconstitution of the Nuba Mountain Economic Development Conference, which had gone into abeyance during the war; the government agreed to reconvene it to include the director of the Department of Agriculture, the financial secretary, the civil secretary, the director of the Department of Economics and Trade, and various deputies.[51] These senior government officials began to meet in order to determine the development strategy that the government should pursue in the Nuba Mountains.

46 Willis, "Violence, Authority, and the State in the Nuba Mountains of Condominium Sudan," pp. 89–114. See also Martha Saavedra, "Ethnicity, Resources and the Central State: Politics in the Nuba Mountains, 1950s to 1990s," in Endre Stiansen and Michael Kevane (eds.), *Kordafan Invaded: Peripheral Incorporation and Social Transformation in Islamic Africa* (Boston, Brill, 1998), pp. 224–225.

47 The Nuba Mountains were one of Kordofan's most reliable sources of grain. Sesame, groundnuts, and gum Arabic were also extremely profitable crops grown primarily in the adjacent plains.

48 D. C. Cumming, letter to Civil Secretary, December 27, 1949, NRO Finance 3-A/42/1/2/.

49 Ibid.

50 Saavedra, "Ethnicity, Resources and the Central State," 227–230; Abdel Basit Saeed, "Merchant Capital, The State and Peasant Farmers in Southern Kordofan," in Norman O'Neill and Jay O'Brien (eds.), *Economy and Class in Sudan* (Brookfield, VT: Avebury, 1988), pp. 186–211.

51 D. C. Cumming, circular to Civil Secretary, December 27, 1949, NRO Finance 3-A/42/1/2/.

The discussions initiated in the reconvened 1949 Economic Development Conference addressed the slow pace at which cotton cultivation was expanding in the Nuba Mountains. In the face of extraordinarily high cotton prices, there was a renewed push by Jallaba merchants, often of Ja 'aliyyin and Danagla origins, to assert their right to increase their investment in cotton cultivation.[52] However, local administrators remained committed to limiting Arab merchants' access to Nuba communities and Nuba lands.

One topic under debate was whether the clay plains immediately adjacent to the hills where the Nuba resided should be considered an area reserved for exclusive Nuba cultivation. This concern soon gave way to questions about whether development funds collected from Nuba farmers could be spent to improve lands that would not be tended by members of the Nuba community. At stake was whether certain lands should be reserved for the development of particular communities and whether funds collected from particular communities could only be spent on them or if they could be redirected to the general improvement of the country's infrastructure. This question fed into a larger debate about whether the Nuba were a special community or if Nuba farmers should be treated as individual economic actors just like their Arab neighbors, and therefore equally prone to respond to economic incentives; these issues played out together. The spatial debate about where to measure the benefits of development overlapped with questions about whether the basic economic unit was the individual or the community.[53] A related question concerned the extent of the state's responsibility to protect its subjects from market forces, either as members of a group or as individuals.[54] The conference also debated whether to allow Arab investment in agriculture in the Nuba areas.

The differing positions grafted easily onto competing ideas about whether the state should support the creation of a distinct Nuba Mountain economy

52 Jallaba was a generalized term used for merchants from the central riverain areas along the Nile between Khartoum and Dongola. For a discussion of these groups and their relationship with the rest of Sudan under the *Turkiyya* and later under the Anglo-Egyptian Condominium, see Gabriel Warburg, *Sudan: Islam, Sectarianism, and Politics in Sudan since the Mahdiyya* (Madison: University of Wisconsin, 2003), p. 13.

53 In discussing the limits of applying Foucault's ideas of "bio-power" to colonial African psychiatric medicine, Meghan Vaughan has highlighted the contradictions inherent in a colonial state that wished to create individuals who would enter the market as rational actors, yet remained committed to preserving its European officials' right to rule by emphasizing the pathology of different groups of Africans and their distance from the European ideal. Megan Vaughan, *Curing Their Ills: Colonial Power and African Illness* (Stanford: Stanford University Press, 1991), pp. 9–12.

54 Letter from Governor of Kordofan to Senior Inspector of Agriculture, El Obeid, "Minutes of the 7th Annual Economic Conference Held at Delami, February 24, 1940," March 12, 1940, NRO Finance 3-A/42/1/2; D. C. Cumming, letter to Director of Agriculture, November 20, 1949, NRO Finance 3-A/42/1/2; John Carmichael, comments to Financial Secretary, "Developments in Kordofan," November 29, 1949, Economic Development, Nuba Mountains, Delami Conference, NRO Finance 3-A/42/1/2.

or if that region should be imagined as an integrated part of the Kordofanian or Sudanese economy. Some officials remained committed to the idea of a distinct Nuba Mountains entity, considering it a distinct region from Kordofan and reasoning that it therefore needed to be developed separately. Others, particularly those within the provincial government, wanted to develop Kordofan as a single, autonomous unit. Provincial officials were able to make common cause with officials within the Department of Finance, who had increasingly come to see the economy as composed of individual actors and transactions taking place within territorial subunits, rather than as collectives of different social groups. Still, while officials in El-Obeid, the capital of the province of Kordofan, might have found it convenient to aggregate economic activity primarily at the level of the province, other officials, particularly those within the Finance Department, had begun to see the territory of Sudan as a whole as the preferred unit.[55]

The immediate provocation for these debates was how to justify the ever-increasing sums of money accumulating in the Nuba Mountains Cultivators' Equalization Fund.[56] Profits in the Equalization Fund began to rise so rapidly in the latter years of the 1940s that the official rationale that the fund was designed to provide price stability to individual growers during periods of low prices could hardly be sustained. When during the interwar period, the Cultivators' Equalization Fund was set up for the Nuba Mountains, asking tenants to take part in cotton schemes was seen to be akin to encouraging them to take part in a fixed investment. At a 1936 meeting on the future of cotton schemes in the Nuba Mountains, the general consensus among government officials was that if the government were suddenly unable to sell sufficient future contracts for the next season's cotton crop, reducing the price of cotton for the coming season would be preferable to changing the price of cotton mid-season. The fear was that if the price of cotton fluctuated freely, farmers would rush to enter cotton farming when prices were high and abandon cotton production recklessly when prices were low.[57]

Forced savings extracted from cultivators had traditionally been justified as a means of insurance. However, as in much of Africa, by the end of World War II, the sums collected had grown so large as to make untenable the idea that they were to be used only for insurance. This put the state in an awkward position, because it neither wanted to cease collecting surplus funds, nor did it want

55 John Carmichael, comments to Financial Secretary, "Developments in Kordofan," November 29, 1949.

56 Most cultivators who were tenant farmers on public or quasi-public estates paid a portion of their income, beyond that taken by the government and management in exchange for their use of the land and other services, into a fund meant to guarantee price stability in case of low market prices for their crop.

57 Letter from Governor of Kordofan to Senior Inspector of Agriculture, El Obeid, "Minutes of the 7th Annual Economic Conference Held at Delami, February 24, 1940."

to return the funds to individual cultivators. It thus came up with a new justification for both continuously paying below-market prices to cultivators and keeping those surplus funds: spending the saved funds on development.[58] Once the purpose of the fund had shifted from insurance to development, questions about how to develop the region were brought to the fore. The first issue concerned the extent to which the benefits and costs of development had to be tied together. If the benefits of development and its cost should be conjoined, this led to a second question about whether the contributors to the fund, and therefore the preferred beneficiaries of its largess, should be thought of as individuals or as communities. The geography of the Nuba Mountains, where agricultural undertakings were relatively spread out, made a resolution to the problem of aligning the cost of development with its beneficiaries particularly vexing.

Some of the ways in which the state's responsibility to individual cultivators was debated are reflected in the writings of John Carmichael, the deputy financial secretary. His comment – "Each existing cultivator has a stake in these funds. If they are to be used for development then they must be applied to projects which are of direct benefit to all existing cultivators"– reflected his commitment to ensuring that those who contributed to development should benefit from it. However, because cultivators lived and worked in a highly dispersed manner across great distances, finance officials believed that it would be impossible to ensure that spending on site-specific infrastructure such as clinics, schools, or even wells would equally benefit all the farmers who had contributed to it. The Finance Department found it difficult to even determine the identity of the "existing cultivators" who had contributed to the Equalization Fund. One argument was that if it was so difficult for the government to allocate funds from the reserve account in an equitable manner, cultivators should no longer be forced to contribute to it. Instead they should be free to spend their own money as they wished.[59] Another idea floated briefly was to allow cultivators to levy their own voluntary taxes on future cotton crops to fund development.[60]

Officials working in the administration of the province of Kordofan made a counterargument that, instead of despairing about the inability of the state to make investments that would meaningfully improve the economic fortunes of the Nuba farmers, the farmers should be encouraged to resettle in the plains. The mountainous area only permitted the development of dispersed and hard-to-reach settlements, whereas the plains could be developed in a more systematic manner. Money from the Equalization Fund could then be spent on creating an infrastructure for cotton growing throughout southern Kordofan – to build roads, excavate and bore for water, and purchase well-digging machinery. After the Nuba migrated to the clay plains, they would be encouraged to expand their

58 D. C. Cumming, letter to Director of Agriculture, November 20, 1949.
59 Ibid. 60 Ibid.

land holdings using new mechanized techniques.[61] The clay plains were more attractive as a site of investment in infrastructure because attempts to create the deep boreholes necessary for drinking water had poor results in the mountains; on the plains the use of mechanical excavators to create *hafirs* (underground reservoirs designed to store rainwater) made it relatively inexpensive to open up additional land.[62]

However, it was not easy to convince Nuba farmers to relocate to the clay plains, where cotton cultivation among the Arab tribes already settled there was not deemed attractive. Therefore, it was perhaps inevitable that, after proposals to develop the clay plains were adopted, the governor of Kordofan put forward the idea that revenue from the Cultivators Equalization Fund did not need to be spent only in the villages and towns directly associated with the Nuba Mountains cotton-growing schemes. He argued that these resources should be allocated for development throughout western Sudan and among other disadvantaged populations, not the Nuba alone.[63] Settling Arab tribes among the Nuba meant potentially overturning decades of government policy, which was premised on the idea that the Nuba were backward relations of the Arabs and, as a consequence, needed to be shielded from direct competition with them.

Subsequently, government officials within the Department of Finance began to question the policy of segregation. Their concerns were supported by a 1949 report, which described the Nuba Mountains as "a settled area with administrative, educational and medical services comparable with other rural areas in Sudan."[64] These finance officials' willingness to abandon the idea of trusteeship and separate development for the Nuba peoples was also related to the exodus of young Nuba to work for wages in cities such as Khartoum.[65] As mentioned, even with development of the clay plains, it proved to be extremely difficult to get Nuba to move from their hills into the plains to work that land. Indeed, Arab farmers instead of Nuba farmers owned much of the land under cotton cultivation in the plains.[66] Fading concerns among colonial officials about the ability of the Nuba to compete if put into direct competition with Arabs justified a relaxation in government regulations about which populations could occupy land that had previously been reserved for the Nuba.

Meanwhile, the financial secretary had made his belief explicit that it would be economically advantageous to the country if the Nuba Mountains were to grow as much cotton as possible. The goal was eventually to expand production

61 D.C. Cumming, letter to Director of Agriculture, November 20, 1949.

62 D.C. Cumming, letter to Civil Secretary, December 27, 1949, NRO Finance 3-A/42/1/2/.

63 D.C. Cumming, letter to Director of Agriculture, November 20, 1949.

64 "Minutes of Nuba Mountains Economic Development Conference at Delami," January 30 and 31, 1950, NRO Finance 3-A/42/1/2/.

65 Previous attempts to control the movement of Nuba, particularly those from the Tira and Nima groups, had failed during the 1930s. See Ahmed Alawad Sikainga, *Slaves into Workers: Emancipation and Labor in Colonial Sudan* (Austin: University of Texas Press, 1996), pp. 123–126.

66 D. C. Cumming, letter to Director of Agriculture, November 20, 1949.

to upward of 500,000 kantars (45.02 kg) of cotton annually. In 1950, only half that amount was being produced. As anxieties increased about meeting target levels, so did calls to expand the development of the clay plains, even if that meant diverting resources from the Nuba Mountains and the Nuba people.

The pressure that finance officials in Khartoum, and province-level officials located in El-Obeid, felt to increase the total amount of cotton that the Anglo-Egyptian Sudan produced each year led them to demand increased productivity from the agricultural schemes. The result was that, despite a lingering belief among colonial authorities that even crudely defined ethnic groups such as the Nuba or the Arabs possessed different attributes and were therefore differently attuned to market forces, finance officials increasingly demanded that local officials surrender the legitimacy they derived from their trusteeship of "backwards people" and allow Arab immigration into Nuba lands, even encouraging them to enter into direct economic competition as cultivators.

The Equatoria Projects Board (Zande Scheme)

In March 1946, the members of the Equatoria Projects Working Committee met for three days at Yambio, a small town and provincial center in what is today western Equatoria, near the border with the Belgian Congo. They met inside a girls' school of the Church Mission Society. Their task was to assess the potential of what was at the time considered to be the most ambitious development project ever undertaken in southern Sudan: the Zande Scheme. The meeting was remarkable for two reasons. First, it included a wide variety of Sudan's senior officials concerned with development. Second, as the conversation progressed, government officials drew a stark line between economic development and social welfare. The director of agriculture and forestry sat directly across from the governor of Equatoria, the deputy civil secretary, the director of the Board of Economics and Trade, and the assistant financial secretary, along with the district commissioner of Zande. These men met to clarify whether investment in the Zande Scheme was meant to create a self-contained and self-sufficient economy or to contribute to the overall economic growth of the Sudanese territory.[67]

The immediate question was where to locate the headquarters of the Equatoria Projects Board. Yet that question quickly gave way to new ones about the purpose of the Equatoria Projects Scheme and the functions that it should fulfill. The consideration of possible locations for the headquarters became enmeshed in discussions about the scheme's function. For instance, Lingasi, near the port of Adok, was seen as particularly well suited for industry. Yambio, in contrast, was close to the regional administrative center and therefore could be supervised easily, even if exports would be more costly because they would have to

[67] J. Smith, circular, "Minutes of Provisional Working Committee," April 1, 1946, NRO Fin 3-A/42/2/5/.

be transported over a longer distance. Finally, Anzara, which was where the majority of Azande resettlement had taken place, was considered to be an ideal place for the cultivation of cotton. Anzara was eventually chosen as the site of the scheme's headquarters. The original plans for the site included spinning and ginning factories, a soap factory, and possibly an oil mill. Yet a debate about whether the Zande Scheme should produce finished textiles or simply export raw cotton persisted. There was also an unresolved debate about the extent to which the project should emphasize cotton as a monocrop or if agricultural diversification should be encouraged. After all, the Zande Scheme already included small experiments with sugar, oil palms, tung, coffee, and tobacco cultivation.[68]

By the second day of the Equatoria Projects Working Committee the battle lines were clearly drawn. Deputy Financial Secretary Chick claimed that the idea of setting up spinning and weaving operations was outlandish and economically foolish. Given the prices prevailing in 1946, he argued that the scheme should focus instead on exporting raw cotton, which would generate the greatest amount of revenue. By taking this stand, Chick, the representative from the Department of Finance, found himself in direct conflict with Marwood, the governor of Equatoria; Hancock, the deputy civil secretary; and Foley, the director of the Board of Economics and Trade. They argued that the "financial aspect was being stressed too strongly," that the main goal of the project was not financial profit; rather "the whole concept of the scheme was one of social emergence." The phenomenon of social emergence tied together advances in education, economics, and medicine. The extent to which those interested in the "self-sufficiency" of regions and peoples were opposed to tying the Zande to the international or national commodity market can be seen in the governor of Equatoria's comments that, without a commitment to process cloth locally, he would not support intensive cotton cultivation.[69]

The underlying issue was whether or not the development scheme was intended to develop the Azande people as a self-contained unit or whether the Zande Scheme should contribute to the development of a larger unit, such as the territory of Sudan or even Britain's imperial system. Dr. John Douglas Tothill, a prominent colonial agricultural expert, argued that communities at different stages of economic development should be allowed to progress in isolation. Tothill made his case in a policy note with the title "Social Emergence of Indigenous Races in Remote Areas." Highlighting the importance of an industrial component to the Zande Scheme, Tothill argued that the goal of development should be to "make these areas very nearly self-contained and to enable them to market sufficient manufactured products in the 1000 mile coastal belt to enable them to obtain the comparatively small amounts of sterling funds required for

[68] For a history of the Zande Scheme from its inception in 1945 until the mid-1950s, see Conrad C. Reining, *The Zande Scheme* (Evanston, IL: Northwestern University Press, 1966).

[69] J. Smith, circular, "Minutes of Provisional Working Committee," April 1, 1946.

financial self-sufficiency."[70] Spinning and weaving factories would create clothing for approximately 150,000 Azande and would allow them to earn a small surplus that would cover the cost of the capital invested in the factories and needed imports. His belief was that "this policy would render the community largely immune to the vagaries of world markets." Much of the Sudan Political Service subscribed to the idea that, without protecting particular populations from the market, "social emergence" was impossible.[71]

Yet, such a policy cut directly against the interest of officials like Chick and his assistant Carmichael in the Department of Finance, who were beginning to see themselves as responsible for formulating both regular and development budgets at the territorial level. Even if they did not have a fully worked-out idea of a territorial economy, they were at least beginning to plan and to envision aggregates at the level of the territory. Given the end goal of combining disparate revenue streams into a single series of aggregates, the idea of focusing on the social emergence of individual groups as opposed to the social and economic development of the territory of Sudan as a whole began to appear irrational.

Regulating Nile Water Traffic

Not all development questions revolved around the management of specific agricultural schemes. Finance officials were also vexed by questions about how to regulate the Sudanese transportation network. Traditionally, senior officers within the civil service believed that the state had an obligation to develop and maintain the transportation infrastructure and ensure that it directed development to specific regions.[72] The core of the Sudanese state's transportation network was the railroad system. Until the 1960s, the capital-intensive requirements of creating an alternative to the railroad network prevented the emergence of alternative long-distance transportation systems. Since extensive networks of roads suitable for long-distance travel were absent, the only means of connecting disparate regions of the country, besides the railways, were the various branches of the Nile River and its tributaries.[73] The Sudan Railways Corporation (SRC) was not merely a railway operator; it also operated other

70 J. Smith, circular, "Appendix B: Note by Major Wyld on the Necessity of Spinning and Weaving," April 1, 1946, NRO Fin 3-A/42/2/5/.

71 Ibid.

72 For a discussion of the role of transportation in "colonial economics," see Frankel, *Capital Investment in Africa*. While Frankel questioned the utility of investing in railroads as the economist participating in Lord Hailey's *African Survey*, he also presented railroads and increased investment in transportation as the best means of spurring economic development in the African interior. For a discussion of the ways in which the expansion of the Sudan Railways to southern Sudan, particularly the extension to Wau, also facilitated death and destruction, see Ushari Ahmed Mahmud and Suleyman Ali Baldo, *The Dhein Massacre: Slavery in the Sudan* (London: Sudan Relief and Rehabilitation Association, 1987), pp. 16–20.

73 With the emergence of increased foreign aid in the late 1950s and the early 1960s, the Sudan Railways Corporation began to face increased challenges from advisors, particularly those in the US government, who believed that the Sudanese government should shift its allocation of

installations vital for transporting people and goods throughout Sudan.[74] It was allowed to monopolize steamship traffic along the Nile, particularly the stretch from Juba to Khartoum. However, this route also attracted the interest of private operators, who challenged the justification of SRC's internal waterway shipping monopoly.[75]

By examining the regulation of riverboat traffic in the 1940s, it is possible to identify two key debates about the state's role in facilitating economic development: (1) the extent to which the government should intervene in the market and seek to regulate private economic activities and (2) whether the state should seek to alleviate the inequality between different regions of Sudan. SRC managers argued that the railway played a key role in both government intervention and the state role in reducing inequality. They justified SRC's monopoly privileges as necessary to its larger mission, which was not just to be a profitable state enterprise but also to extend transportation at reasonable prices to the different regions of the country. These managers claimed that the scope of the railway's transportation network, and its differential pricing schemes for the transportation of certain types of products along particular routes, enabled the government to stimulate economic growth in specific regions.

Beginning in 1941, private companies began to request permits to run steamships not only on short routes between different points in southern Sudan but also along the 745 miles of the Nile from Juba in Equatoria Province to Khartoum. Mikhail Hajjar, a prominent businessman of Syrian descent,[76] submitted a petition in 1941 to develop a steamer service between Khartoum and Juba and to dock at government-sanctioned facilities. Immediately after the conclusion of World War II in 1945, the request by Hajjar's firm was followed by similar requests from other concessionary companies – the African Trading Company of Khartoum, the Southern Sudan Trading Company, and the Societé du Haut Uele et du Nil operating from the Belgian Congo.[77]

development funds from railways toward the construction of a road network, but that was still in the distant future in the mid-1940s.

74 John Carmichael, assistant financial secretary between 1946 and 1948, described the ideal situation from the government's perspective as the railways handling long-distance traffic, whether by road, river, or rail, particularly for export items, while private enterprises handled regional and short-distance traffic.

John Carmichael, note, "Individual Bases, Navigation on Southern Reaches by Commercial Firms," August 21, 1946, NRO Finance 3-A/25/1/2/.

75 Minute 195, "Application to Run Private Steamer and Barges on Southern Nile Route," April 22, 1941, NRO Finance 3-A/25/1/2/.

76 For up-to-date information on the Hajjar family's business holdings and for biographical information about the Hajjar family, particularly Mikhail's son George, see "George Mikhail Hajjar, 1915–1996: Eighty Years of Contribution," www.haggarholding.com/haggarbook/hhcjpegs/haggarbook1.htm [accessed February 22, 2011].

77 D. Newbold, letter to President, Resource Board, April 22, 1941, NRO Finance 3-A/25/1/2/; J. R. Shaw, letter to G. R. Foley, December 4, 1945, NRO Finance 3-A/25/1/2/; Office of Supply, Khartoum, "Note for the Board of Economics and Trade," August 27, 1945, NRO Finance

Initially there were two separate aspects to this controversy. The first issue was the legal question of whether the Nile River was an international waterway on which riverboat traffic could not be restricted. The second concern was whether SRC's monopoly was indeed in the best interests of the country. The legal secretary of the Anglo-Egyptian Sudan quickly ruled that the Government of Sudan did not have the right to block concessionary companies from plying the Nile waters outright because treaty obligations guaranteed freedom of navigation on the river.[78]

The debate next shifted to the conditions under which commercial firms would be permitted to profit from carrying goods along the river. E. C. Chandler, the acting traffic manager of the Sudan Railways Corporation, argued that all carriers along the river should be forced to operate as "common carriers," which carried an obligation to transport a full range of goods at published rates broken down according to different classes of goods. In particular, SRC officials argued that a highly differentiated system of rates allowed the railway to subsidize the transport of vital commodities to the south without earning a substantial profit and that, if allowed, private operators would simply continue to carry the most profitable goods without transporting a vast array of loss-making items.[79] The transportation of commodities such as dura, salt and cement was then being heavily subsidized, just as transporting many of southern Sudan's goods to northern Sudan was subsidized. The implication of the railway officials' argument was that without the continued transport of highly subsidized goods to vast regions of the south, living standards would decline, and already marginal economic activities would be adversely affected. They claimed that a substantial modification of the rate system would be extremely disadvantageous. Abandoning a differentiated scale would reduce the amount of revenue earned on high-value goods, goods whose resale price would not be substantially affected by changes in the rate charged for transportation. In addition, the price of transportation would rise for bulk goods; as a consequence these goods might not travel, retarding development.[80]

Beginning in 1946, railway officials began demanding extensions of their monopoly rights to cover not only the long haul between Khartoum and Juba but also shorter hauls between Juba and Kosti; by 1949 they demanded a monopoly on routes covering all the navigable reaches of the Nile.[81] Around the

3-A/25/1/2/; L. Bossaers, letter to Governor, Equatorial Province, December 14, 1945, NRO Finance 3-A/25/1/2/.

78 Minutes, "G. M. S. R. to L. S. re. Competition on the Southern Reaches and Making Suggestions for Regulations," August 19, 1946, NRO Finance 3-A/25/1/2/.

79 E. C. Chandler, letter to General Manager, "Subject: Barges Privately Owned Plying Southern Reaches of Nile in Competition with S. R. Services," August 6, 1946, NRO Finance 3-A/25/1/2/.

80 Ibid.

81 S. H. Brookfield, letter to GM, Sudan Railways, September 30, 1946, NRO Finance 3-A/25/1/2/; J. G. Mavrogordato, letter to Advocate General to Director of Economics and Trade, "Competition with Sudan Railways River Craft on Southern Reaches," May 11, 1949, NRO Finance 3-A/25/1/2/.

same time, those privileges were coming under increased scrutiny by the bodies responsible for determining national economic policy, such as the Finance Department and the Board of Economics and Trade. In 1946, Deputy Financial Secretary Arthur Chick took this issue up with the Board of Economics and Trade. He framed it as a question of whether it made sense to continue a monopoly in order to "carry certain goods at uneconomical rates." The broader question was whether or not it was desirable to subsidize certain goods coming from and to the south with low freight charges.[82]

There was growing unease within the financial, legal, and civil secretariats in Khartoum about SRC's demands for monopoly, control, and inspection in the name of directing economic growth: should the government allow a state-run monopoly to create price incentives for certain types of cargo? The fear among finance officials was that the drive for regulation would eventually prove to be insatiable, potentially ending with the regulation of the transport of all private cargo.[83] It was generally acknowledged within senior government circles that the result of SRC's monopoly over cargo coming from southern Sudan was not cheaper goods in Khartoum, but more expensive goods (especially those consumer goods imported from the south). This insight only added to the general unease within the Finance Department about the continuation of these privileges.[84] The prospect of dramatically cheaper consumer goods and lower rates on frequently carried items resonated with officials in the Finance Department, who quietly began to argue that less government involvement in riverboat traffic might actually stimulate increased economic activity. Paradoxically, even as finance officials began to think of a unified market in which goods could be traded freely, their commitment to ensuring that "underdeveloped" areas of the country received adequate supplies receded as a focus of government policy. The central government gradually became more concerned with increasing the total amount of cotton grown in the Anglo-Egyptian Sudan than with fostering projects that focused on the self-sufficiency of local areas.

Three Case Studies: Conclusion

These three cases reveal how finance officials used the new authority granted to them by the planning process to alter the purpose of development projects and to shift economic policy in ways that prioritized Sudan as an economic unit. Despite the Sudanese government's drafting of a five-year plan in 1946, the objectives of economic development remained muddled. In part this confusion

82 S. H. Brookfield, letter to GM, Sudan Railways, September 30 1946.

83 From J. G. Mavrogordato, letter to Advocate General to Director of Economics and Trade, "Competition with Sudan Railways River Craft on Southern Reaches," May 11, 1949

84 "Railroad pricing policies made goods transported north considerably more expensive even without taking into account the possibility of allowing private companies to transport scarce consumer goods like soap or coffee from the Belgian Congo to Khartoum." G. F. Foley, Director, Department of Economics and Trade to Civil Secretary, Khartoum, letter, March 12, 1946, NRO Finance 3-A/25/1/2/.

can be attributed to continuing questions about the constituencies to whom different members of the bureaucracy were responsible. Officials in southern Sudan and in the other historically closed districts, such as the Nuba Mountains, continued to think of their primary responsibility as the governance of distinct communities rather than the improvement of the Sudanese territory as a whole. In addition, unlike Department of Irrigation officials, officials from the Department of Agriculture tended to focus on the management of individual schemes. Many of the senior officials within that department had previously served in other territories within British East Africa. As a consequence, they were committed to the idea that development projects should provide welfare to specific underprivileged communities.[85] Sudanese railway officials argued that their monopoly over river traffic served to promote development in parts of the country that might not otherwise be reached, even though they were very conscious of their role as a revenue-generating department and were anxious to protect their privileged position. At the same time, officials stationed in Khartoum were increasingly anxious to assert their authority to speak on behalf of the Sudanese people as the future fate of Sudan was negotiated between Britain, Egypt and the various nationalist parties within Sudan itself. Senior officials within the Department of Finance strove to exercise their power over the direction of Sudan's economy with a greater degree of autonomy. Consequently, while their policies continued to reflect a commitment to the imperial project, they were sensitive to the need to direct policies in ways that would assert the primacy of the "national" territorial unit as the main object of economic policy.

Conclusion

The practices of economic planning fostered the emergence of a genuine territorial economy. At the end of World War II, there was a widespread consensus among policy makers that the government had to foster development. The problem was that there were widely divergent views about the unit that needed to be developed and about the role and responsibilities of the state in carrying out development policies. Nonetheless, the period from 1945 to 1951 should be considered the beginning of the development of Sudan as a territorially defined economy. The effort to create a unified economic plan for the Anglo-Egyptian Sudan meant that development could now be conceived of as a territorial project. Yet, in the absence of a Sudanese apparatus of economic control and management, the colony of Sudan remained only one of several competing ideas about the unit at which development should be located. The

[85] Tilley, *Africa as a Living Laboratory*, pp. 115–169, and Joseph Hodge, *Triumph of the Experts: Agrarian Doctrines of Development and the Legacies of British Colonialism* (Athens: Ohio University Press, 2007).

competition between imperial, territorial, regional, and local ideas of development was clearly visible in the first national economic plan. As Sudan began to move inexorably toward independence, the government in Khartoum increasingly asserted its autonomy from Egypt and Britain and its control over local authorities. These changes allowed finance officials to make the logic of territorial development dominant.

The spatial locus of development was never the only question. Equally relevant was the need for policy makers to define what it meant to be developed. Some policy makers thought that the state's primary responsibility was to control inflation and to ensure price stability. Other officials within the Department of Finance wanted to ensure that Sudan's development did not interfere with larger imperial goals by competing for scarce resources and raising prices. These officials wanted to prevent Sudan from suffering from urban unrest, which was seen as one potential consequence of swiftly rising prices. In contrast, there were those parties who supported the idea of trusteeship and who thought that development should be local and intensive in order to protect individual groups and address "social issues," allowing distinct communities to be maintained in the face of economic competition from other communities. Finally, some finance officials argued that the whole territory should be developed as a unit. As a result they pushed for prioritizing policies promoting the fastest increases in economic activity without regard to the impact of those policies on imperial reconstruction efforts or on underprivileged regional or local interest groups.

The debate over how to increase cotton cultivation in the Nuba Mountains demonstrates the extent to which finance officials' vision of economic management shifted from an emphasis on concerns about local development and welfare to prioritizing development and profitability at the national level. The immediate concern was how to increase the amount of cotton grown in the Nuba Mountains. The obvious answer was to expand cotton cultivation to the clay plains that bordered the mountains. This strategy would ensure that cotton cultivation increased as rapidly as possible, while still making use of proven technology, such as the digging of *hafirs* on clay, to expand the amount of land that could be exploited by settled populations. However, this strategy would not ensure that money spent on development would continue to support the Nuba people, thereby fostering their "social development," rather than that of their Arab neighbors. The question that emerged was to what extent the Government of Sudan was responsible for the development of distinct communities. Should the government aim for policies that increased economic activity in particular regions or support national development without regard for the special circumstances of different groups?

The Equatoria Projects Board was at the center of a second debate about the same basic question. Should the Equatoria Projects Board develop projects, such as the Zande Scheme, that would support the creation of a separate "self-sufficient" economy among the Azande people in western Equatoria? A third debate that highlights how planning theory and practices focused more and more on the territory of Sudan as a whole rather than on subregions centered on whether to regulate riverboat traffic on the Nile River. Should the government guarantee that all types of cargo be transported on the Nile at set prices, or should it allow private operators to set their own prices? Competition would permit some goods to be carried at much lower prices, but might make certain goods needed in the south or other difficult-to-access places much more expensive or even inaccessible.

As senior officials ensconced in their offices in Khartoum from the period 1946 until 1951 debated these key issues about the spatial locus of economic planning, they increased their power, particularly over the country's financial and economic matters. One of the distinctive features of this period was the strengthening of the position of the financial secretariat within the Sudanese government. While development had always been a major concern of the Anglo-Egyptian Sudanese state, it was in the postwar period that the idea of territorial development began to compete vigorously with concepts related to the development of specific schemes or even regional development projects. One manifestation was that officials within the Finance Department embraced an increasingly centralized logic of the state. This emphasized the importance of the Anglo-Egyptian Sudan as a single economic unit, even as officials within the Department of Agriculture or those in charge of the boards and schemes focused on localized development and imagined a decentralized state made up largely of autonomous regions and economic units. What it meant to spur development increasingly became an issue of contention. As the decade came to a close, the stakes involved in settling these disputes only increased as a result of rising political pressure to define the political contours of the Sudanese state.

By 1951, Sudanese officials were still struggling to resolve fundamental questions about the purpose of development and how much and what type of independence the Sudanese economy should strive to achieve. During the 1940s, finance officials were able to bring about a decisive shift in economic policy, which made thinking of the Anglo-Egyptian Sudan as a territorial whole a priority. Questions about who could participate in the Sudanese economy and on what terms, as well as how the Sudanese economy should relate to other economies, would have to be decided during the first years of the 1950s, against the backdrop of the country's swift move toward independence. The struggle to decide on the terms of participation in the Sudanese economy continued to add to the instability of Sudan well into the 1960s.

However the rush to create an independent economy was only beginning. While officials were hesitant about defining the contours of an independent economy during the 1950s, by the 1960s, economists and national statistic officials using econometric tools such as national income accounts were quantifying economic exchange. Using new macroeconomic tools, it was possible to calculate a nation's GDP or per capita income.[86] The diffusion of new ideas

[86] Speich, "Travelling with the GDP through Early Development Economics' History."

and economic techniques enabled officials on the ground to practice their jobs in new ways. Still, the mere introduction of concepts such as national development planning did not shift the ways in which officials understood the economy; shifts in how the economy was understood arose from encountering the practical problems of prioritizing the various projects and schemes included in the five-year economic plan.

3

Calculable Development, 1951–1954

In the two previous chapters, I showed that the prioritization of the territorial – that is, the territory of what became the modern Sudan – over the local, over the regional, and over the supranational in policy-making circles was by no means inevitable.[1] The economic planning of Sudan operated in a reflexive manner with the political planning of Sudan. The British Empire increased its grip on the Nile Valley and its wider Middle Eastern and African colonial holdings as it mobilized for World War II. Pressure from the metrople pushed finance officials in Sudan to to think in terms of an imperial economy. However, after 1945, as a deeply indebted Britain turned increasingly inward and acrimony spread between Britain and Egypt when the latter demanded both more political and economic autonomy, officials in Sudan defined their territory for planning purposes as the land between the Imatong Mountains along the southern border with Uganda to Wadi Halfa at the crossing with Egypt in the north. This territory became the primary reference point for government policy.[2] Sudanese anticolonial leaders, much like their peers in Egypt, began to ask British colonial rulers to make an accounting for how they had stewarded the resources of Sudan. Colonial officials responded to these questions by drawing up plans, budgets, and surveys that could demonstrate that they were prudent guardians of the territory's resources.

In this chapter, I demonstrate that developing a single vision of how the Sudanese economy should be governed involved a number of conflicts about

[1] Supranational ideas that were current among thinkers in Anglo-Egyptian Sudan at the time included a new federation with Egypt or perhaps a federation of at least part of Sudan with British East Africa.

[2] Tilley, *African as a Living Laboratory*, p. 6. See also the frequent use of the terms "territorial" and "territory" in Low and Lonsdale, "Introduction: Towards the New Order, 1945–1963," pp. 1–64.

how to represent progress; for example, the debate about the purpose of the Jongeli Investigation Team. In particular, I focus on arguments within the colonial government on whether planning should be done in prose or through numbers. While this might appear to be a simple methodological debate about how to plan, I argue that it was really a key moment in the quest to define the purpose of development. Those who favored planning in prose believed that the purpose of the development process was to imagine potentially different futures, while those who favored planning with numbers believed that the function of planning was to use past historical data to develop linear projections into the future about how to spend the government's finances in a prudent manner. Those who wished to plan in prose were willing to tackle charged political questions, such as the autonomy of the various regions of the country, particularly the culturally distinct southern provinces, and to ask questions about which voices should be included in official plans. In contrast, planning in numbers tended to enforce an economizing logic that privileged futures that lacked a clear break with the past.

To understand the economic decision-making processes of colonial and Sudanese officials, it must be put into the context of past patterns of extraction, dating back to the Egyptian conquest of Sudan in 1821. That conquest established a legacy of a territory divided between a rural periphery, which provided factors such as raw commodities and labor, and a productive, export-oriented core based in and around Khartoum.[3] Historical patterns of extraction deeply shaped how finance officials manipulated and interpreted their economic tools and figures during the 1950s.

In 1951, it was still a novelty for economic policy makers in Khartoum like the Finance Secretary Arthur L Chick to confront questions about Sudan's political future and identity. After all, Sudan's political and economic destiny had been decided outside of the territory's borders for decades. But Egypt's decision in October 1951 to unilaterally abrogate the 1899 Condominium Agreement and the 1936 Anglo-Egyptian Treaty brought decades of dual British and Egyptian juridical sovereignty over the territory of Sudan to an abrupt end.[4] During the late 1940s, to counter both Egyptian demands for a greater role in the governing of Sudan and Sudanese demands for representation, British officials promised self-determination for the Sudanese. Now in 1951, Egypt formally renounced its right to govern Sudan and declared that the Sudanese had the right to determine their own future. A legacy of dual sovereignty and regional autonomy meant that the fight for self-determination was not going to

3 Steven Serels, "Political Landscaping: Land Registration, the Definition of Ownership and the Evolution of Colonial Objectives in the Anglo-Egyptian Sudan, 1899–1924," *African Economic History* 35 (2007): 60. For a discussion of labor migration to Khartoum, see Sikainga, *Slaves into Workers*, and Bjorkelo, *Prelude to the Mahdiyya*.

4 Louis, *The British Empire in the Middle East, 1945–1951*, pp. 249–253, 262–263; see also the discussion in K. D. D. Henderson, *Sudan Republic* (New York: Praeger, 1966), p. 100.

be a simple battle between the colonizers and the colonized.[5] Instead, the struggle for independence from Britain fractured into a multiparty contest between those who supported a unified Sudanese state or multiple Sudanese states, and those who believed that Sudan could best realize its independence as part of the Egyptian state. A considerable proportion of the urban and politically conscious southern population rejected the idea of a single Sudanese state, favoring instead schemes of regional autonomy or independence.[6] In addition until the 1940s, large areas of the territory of Sudan had enjoyed high degrees of regional autonomy.[7]

The rationalities of finance officials cannot easily be divorced from their politics; however, the extent to which technical discussions shaped the ways in which officials perceived the state's political and economic interests has frequently been overlooked. The focus here is on financial and economic matters, because the battle to define the correct stewardship of the territory's resources was one of the areas where international actors, local politicians, and colonial officials agreed on the custodial responsibility of the state to protect the resources of the people. In fact, much of the debate during the period of decolonization centered on questions about who would be the better steward of the people's resources. The technical nature of many of the discussions allowed debate to continue without it becoming overburdened by partisan slogans.[8]

The Second Development Program and Survey of Sudan

In this chapter, I focus on the ways that finance officials delegitimized the forecasts of development planning based on prose, and in the following chapter I discuss why finance officials gravitated toward the readily quantifiable when making decisions about unknowns.[9] The high cotton prices prevailing immediately after World War II provided the context in which development planning in Sudan began in earnest. During the war years from 1939 until 1945, high cotton prices and ready markets led to increased production for export. At the same time, chronic food shortages, even famine conditions, plagued Darfur and the southern provinces. Despite years of relative prosperity, by the conclusion of the 1940s, inequality between the core regions of the country such as Khartoum and the outer provinces had increased. As the first development plan, *The Five*

[5] Powell, *A Different Shade of Colonialism*, p. 7.

[6] Daly, *Imperial Sudan*, pp. 243–280. For more on the background of the sectional conflict within the nationalist movement, see Afaf Abdel Majid Abu Hasabu, *Factional Conflict in the Sudanese Nationalist Movement* (Khartoum: Graduate College, University of Khartoum, 1985).

[7] Jay Spaulding and Lidwien Kapteijns, *An Islamic Alliance: Ali Dinar and the Sanusiyya, 1906–1916* (Evanston, IL: Northwestern University Press, 1994), pp. 1–49.

[8] Sara Berry, "Unsettled Accounts: Stool Debts, Chieftaincy Disputes and the Question of Asante Constitutionalism," *Journal of African History* 39:1 (1998): 39–62.

[9] Mary S. Morgan, *The World in the Model: How Economist Work and Think* (New York: Cambridge University Press, 2012), p. 2.

Year Plan for Postwar Development, 1946–1951, came to a close and questions about the political legitimacy of the Sudanese state arose, finance officials came to believe that the second development plan would have to propose solutions to address regional inequality.[10]

In the early 1950s as officials began to write Sudan's second development plan, *The Sudan Development Programme 1951/56*, they proposed a series of surveys to assess the potential for undertaking new development schemes. The two major personalities within the Finance Department during the period between 1951 and 1954 were the Finance Secretary Arthur L. Chick and his principal deputy John Carmichael. In 1953 Chick retired and was replaced by Carmichael, who became the Acting Finance Secretary. He received an acting appointment in recognition of the fact that the first elections in Sudan were soon to be held, leading to self-government in 1954 and the appointment of Hammad Tawfik as the first Sudanese Minister of Finance.[11] Finance officials were especially interested in the extension of low-cost infrastructure development, such as well and bore drilling, as well as veterinary services, as a means of making development more geographically inclusive.[12] Chick, already near the end of his career in 1951 and acutely aware of the sensitivity of the negotiations about the fate of Sudan, strove to define his expertise as technical and therefore avoided decisions that might infuriate British, Egyptian, or Sudanese politicians.[13] Consequentially, there were significant reservations about whether development spending should aim to unify the country or simply to raise revenue. While discussion about the Sudanese currency centered on questions about how the Sudanese state should relate to other major international and regional economic powers, development planning and surveying focused on the issue of how the different regions of the country related to one another and to the national state.[14]

Finance officials' discussions about how to plan and survey the Sudanese economy were marked by ambivalence. Underlying these discussions was the question of whether finance officials were empowered to use development policy to unify a Sudanese economy prior to the creation of a Sudanese state. After

10 Finance Department, *Five Year Plan for Post-War Development* (Khartoum, Sudan, 1946), and Daly, *Imperial Sudan*, pp. 172–185.

11 While Carmichael initially held the senior civil service position of Permanent Undersecretary for Finance within the newly titled Ministry of Finance, his senior colleagues included many of the men who would go on to assume leading roles within the ministry during the second part of the 1950s, such as Hamza Mirghani Hamza, Mamoun Beheiry, and Mansour Maghoub. See Mamoun Beheiry, *Glimpses from the Life of a Sudanese Public Servant* (Omdurman, Sudan: M. O. Besheer Center for Sudanese Studies, 2003).

12 Finance Department, *The Sudan Development Programme 1951/56* (Khartoum, Sudan, 1953).

13 Chick was at the end of his career and could look forward to a secure retirement. Daly, *Imperial Sudan*, p. 247.

14 For a discussion of how Sudan obtained its own currency, see Alden Young, "Accounting for Decolonization: The Origins of the Sudanese Economy" (PhD diss., Princeton University 2013), pp. 84–144.

1954, as the Sudanese government became increasingly politically representative, finance officials began to worry about whether the production and dissemination of increased amounts of economic data would help or hinder policy makers. They grew particularly concerned about the extent to which new constituencies might use economic data to argue for development programs in their regions. This advocacy would obviously constrain the ability of policy makers to implement the projects they favored.

Designing an Economic Survey of Sudan: A Search for International Legitimacy, 1950–1953

Surveying was an integral part of planning, and finance officials had long recognized its importance, even though the undertaking of extensive surveys was often postponed. However, in 1950, colonial finance officials felt a new urgency to embark on the project. They believed they could improve their credibility as the legitimate spokespersons for the Sudanese people if they convinced representatives of the US government to work directly with them to carry out a survey of the latent economic potential present within the Anglo-Egyptian Sudan. Officials in Khartoum knew that an economic survey of Sudan carried out by a team of outside experts would not only bolster the international legitimacy of the government in Khartoum but also, if structured correctly, win the favor of the different regional constituencies spread throughout Sudan by confirming and offering potential remedies to the lack of development in many provinces. Overtures to the United States were made through the Economic Cooperation Administration, an agency set up as part of the Marshall Plan. These overtures reflected Khartoum's increased assertiveness in determining economic policy.[15]

Even after London's objections to what British officials perceived as a violation of their sovereignty, Civil Secretary J. Robertson and other officials in Khartoum did not give up hope of inviting outside experts to conduct an economic survey of Sudan; instead, they began to seek American expertise as part of the Point Four Program. This was a US technical assistance program created in 1949, in the context of the Cold War, to support developing countries. The concept was that a team resembling the one sent to Colombia under the direction of Lauchlin Currie of the International Bank for Reconstruction and Development (IBRD), which would later become commonly known as the World Bank, could be formed to examine the Sudanese economy, thereby granting officials in Khartoum both political and technical cover to implement their future economic plans.[16] Officials in London responded by suggesting a British-chaired team with American members.[17] As negotiations dragged on between the Foreign Office and officials in Khartoum, it became increasingly apparent that Sudan's status as a condominium made it very awkward to arrange for

[15] Letter from Mr. Mayhall to Mr. Clutton, January 16, 1950, TNA FO 371/80531/.
[16] Letter from J. W. Robertson to Mr. R. Allen, May 22, 1950, TNA FO 371/80404/.
[17] Letter from M. N. F. Stewart to Sir J. Robertson, October 10, 1950, TNA FO 371/80404/.

an independent survey of the country. IFIs (international financial institutions) considered the Anglo-Egyptian Sudan a colony, while the British characterized it as an independent protectorate. And even though Sudan was not a formal dependency of Britain or Egypt, it lacked its own currency. Thus the IBRD could not sponsor researchers to travel to the Anglo-Egyptian Sudan because the country was not and could not become a member of the bank, and if the IBRD did not sponsor American researchers, it would be difficult to arrange for another neutral institution to do so. Similarly, it was unclear if officials from international agencies such as the Food and Agricultural Organization (FAO) could be independent members of the proposed international survey or whether they would have to be sponsored by British organizations.[18] Other difficulties were that the US government was unwilling to issue Point Four aid without the approval of both condominium powers, and Egypt was unwilling to acquiesce to an agreement in which Britain took the lead.[19]

Despite the fact that British officials in Khartoum were increasingly trying to assert their control over matters of foreign policy, legally they were still subordinated to the wishes of senior officials in London and Cairo. Amidst fears in Khartoum and London about how much influence international actors such as the Americans would have over the economic survey, a decision was made to transform the survey from an exercise centered on Sudan as a whole into one that examined southern Sudan specifically. Thus the survey of the southern provinces of the Anglo-Egyptian Sudan began almost as an accident.

Limiting the geographical scope of the survey meant that the government's main development priorities, such as investing in cotton production in the central Gezira Plain, would not be analyzed. Despite the intensity of the debate on the need to spread the investment in development more equitably throughout the country, the Sudan Irrigation Department remained steadfast in its belief that development efforts should focus on the most developed regions of Sudan near Khartoum in the Gezira Plain. In 1949, the Sudanese Irrigation Department completed a study of the country's future irrigation needs, and as early as 1950, planning began for the Managil Extension, a proposed doubling of the Gezira Scheme. However, the decision to embark on the Managil Extension was not formally taken until 1954.[20]

Addressing the southern provinces initially appeared to be a convenient means of attracting international support for the colonial government and of tackling unrest both within the Sudan Political Service and among Sudanese political figures who argued that Khartoum needed to do more to reduce

18 Letter from T. E. Evans to D. Greenhill, October 10, 1950, TNA FO 371/80404/ and from F. H. Locke to Miss Waterlow, August 28, 1950, TNA FO 371/80404/.

19 Minute from Denis Greenhill to T. E. Evans, October 23, 1950, TNA FO 371/80404/.

20 Letter from R. J. Smith to Finance Secretary, April 13, 1950, SAD 499/14/1–52; Letter from R. J. Smith to Commissioner for Development, c/o Finance Department, "Development of Gezira," SAD 499/14/1–52/. Collins, *The Waters of the Nile*, pp. 247–249.

domestic inequality. London believed that it would be easier to make the case for American support of an economic survey if it was directed to "the pagan South, which, so far, has not had the benefit of capital outlays on this scale applied to the Moslem [sic] center and North."[21] Once the battle to restrict the economic survey to southern Sudan was over, a natural next step was to redirect officials who were already working on a survey of the Jonglei Canal to plan for the southern provinces as a region. The Jonglei Canal was a massive project designed to allow the tributaries of the White Nile to cut through the swamps known as the Sudd in southern Sudan, thereby increasing the amount of water flowing through to northern Sudan and Egypt. These efforts eventually culminated in the publication of a survey report titled "The Natural Resources and Development Potential in the Southern Provinces of the Sudan."[22]

From its inception, planning for a survey of the southern provinces of Sudan caused problems for the government in Khartoum. It became a lightning rod around which southern politicians such as Buth Diu advocated for southern autonomy. One of the earliest demands was for the creation of a southern development board to be administered by the Ministry for the Coordination of Southern Development. This potential administrative innovation was interpreted by northern politicians as the first step in the establishment of southern autonomy and the creation of a federal Sudan. A federation for southerners encountered strong resistance from Sudanese officials who worried that if the southern provinces were granted federal status, a similar status would be demanded by easterners and westerners. One suggestion was that the Ministry for the Coordination of Southern Development become institutionalized as a site where southerners could have a voice in determining the direction of their own development.[23]

By February 1953, the southern survey team had won widespread international recognition. Known as the Jonglei Investigation Team, it was based at Malakal and was charged with the collection of scientific facts and designing proposals for economic development. A flattering report about the team's work, which appeared in London's *The Daily Telegraph*, stated that the team's goals were not merely resolving questions of irrigation and Nile water control but also included wider issues such as communications, economic development, and the provision of alternative and improved means of earning a livelihood for the people of southern Sudan. The team was led by Dr. Paul Howell, a former southern district commissioner who had worked with the Nuer in southern Sudan.[24]

[21] Letter from R. C. Couldrey to T. Evans, July 10, 1952, TNA FO 371/80404.
[22] P.P Howell, "Jongelei Investigation Team and S.D.I.T.: 1952–53," October 5, 1952, SAD 768/8/1–101/.
[23] Letter, A. Lewis to E. H. Nightingale, December 27, 1952, SAD 768/8/1–101/.
[24] Eric Downton, "Britons Plan Economy for South Sudan, Five Year's Study," *Daily Telegraph*, February 4, 1953, SAD 768/8/1–101/.

One of the first questions raised was to what use the information gathered by the team was to be put. Would it be used to facilitiate southern Sudan's development as an independent economy or to make the southern Sudanese economy complementary with the northern economy? The choice of Howell to lead the investigative team only further encouraged this debate, because southern district commissioners were known to be supportive of special political safeguards for the southern provinces and even southern autonomy.[25] Howell openly wrote in intergovernmental communications that four federated states might produce a more stable Sudan than the current centralized state. He also openly opposed the political power of the religious sheikhs in northern Sudan and suggested that southerners should be allowed to develop their own civil service list in order to win appointments to government jobs.[26] The Sudanese politicians who came to power in 1954 swiftly rejected all of these ideas, because they were seen to violate the very principles of *Sudani-ness* as a unifying political identity and to hearken back to the division of Sudan into separate parts that nationalist politicians saw as a hallmark of the colonial project.[27]

Once appointed to a position of planning authority, Howell quickly transformed the scope of his assignment from examining the feasibility of a few capital-intensive projects, projects that would ideally attract international investments, to planning an autonomous southern Sudanese economy. Howell imagined the Jonglei Investigative Team's final written report being a "'word picture,' which might include somewhat imaginary passages here and there, of what we intend southern Sudan to look like, economically and socially, some 10 or even 20 years hence." The report he intended to write would not be made up merely of conventional and detailed cost and benefit estimates, but would instead lay out an alternative development scenario.[28] The members of the Jonglei Team saw themselves as painters drawing a picture of possible futures, rather than acting simply as the arbiters between different development schemes designed in other parts of the government. This was a direct contrast with the approach of finance officials such as Carmichael, who were increasingly striving to organize facts about the world into numbers and to make policy decisions according to budget balances.

Differences in their understanding of the aims of the government's surveying, programming, and planning efforts created tensions between Chick and Howell.[29] Chick often found the requests of the Jonglei Investigation Team extravagant and unnecessary.[30] In Khartoum, the move away from budgeting toward "word pictures" was thought to be a dangerous overstepping of the

[25] Letter from R. Stevenson to FO, January 19, 1953, TNA FO 371/102739/
[26] Letter from Howell to JSR Duncan, December 31, 1952, SAD 768/8/1–101/
[27] Abbas, *The Sudan Question.*
[28] Letter from B. A. Lewis to R. C. Wakefield, January 7, 1953, SAD 768/8/1–101/.
[29] Letter from R. C. Wakefield to Paul Howell, March 9, 1953, SAD 768/9/1–114/.
[30] Letter from P. P. Howell to R. C. Wakefield, March 13, 1953, SAD 768/9/1–114/.

role of the surveyor or planner. Howell thought, however, that Sudan's move toward independence made it necessary to plan differently. In effect, he believed that "unless a degree of self-sufficiency can be assured, plus the development of exports sufficient at least to pay for the maintenance and gradual expansion of social services, 'safeguards' for the South may well be meaningless or in any case transitory." Officials who had been stationed in the southern provinces, many of whom were used to and supported the political project of southern autonomy, brought a sense of urgency to plans for a new South in the last years of the condominium. They recognized that once independence was achieved, it was unlikely that the North would possess the money necessary to develop southern Sudan or to adequately address the deficiencies within the country in a manner that would make unity attractive.[31] Essentially, the objective of the members of the Jonglei Investigation Team was to imagine an entirely different economy, rather than finding an effective way to spend the budgetary surplus and so place the central government on a more secure financial foundation. Though never explicitly stated, the different factions involved in this debate understood and expected that economic autonomy was the basis for political autonomy.

The Assertion of Authority: A Restriction of Surveying

The terms of the southern provinces' integration with northern Sudan lay at the heart of the increasing discontent that began to roil southern Sudan in 1953 and 1954. One reason that there was so much resistance in Khartoum to conducting a survey of the economic potential of the southern provinces was that Carmichael realized that there would not be sufficient money to carry out the development projects that a survey would find feasible. He believed that the priorities should be the Roseires Dam and the expansion of the Gezira Scheme (the Managil Extension), projects long advocated by the Sudan Irrigation Department.[32]

Officials at the Department of Finance correctly foresaw that an economic survey of Sudan would greatly expand the number of proposed alternative investments and, consequently, increase the frustrations of various constituencies within Sudan whose expectations about the future remained unfulfilled. By August 1953, while morale was still high within the Department of Finance, providing sufficient clerks and supervisors to manage the financial boom caused by the record cotton crop of 1950–1951 had begun to place a severe strain on the department. The department even began to have trouble supervising the few projects it had identified as vital. Concerns about the limited capacity of officials within the Finance Department to manage the proliferation of development projects only increased as the 1950s progressed.

[31] Note, "A Few Facts about the Southern Sudan: The Upper Nile Province in Particular," March 9, 1953, SAD 768/9/1–114/.

[32] Letter from D. M. H. Riches to W. Morris, August 25, 1953, TNA FO 371/102759/.

The rising discontent of the nascent southern elites fueled unrest in the southern provinces. As independence approached, they understood that officials in the central government were content to limit economic development initially to the central riverain provinces, and they were angered by the Department of Finance's decision to focus on a narrow development agenda. The discontent in the southern provinces that followed this realization reached its most acute levels in Equatoria, which was not only the farthest province from Khartoum but also the most economically developed of the southern provinces.[33]

In many ways it makes sense that the most developed southern province felt unrest first. At the end of World War II, the rapid economic and social developments taking place in Equatoria gave rise to new social classes, whose well-being was tied to the patronage of an expanding government in the southern provinces.[34] Southerners who were employed in local government or in the military units garrisoned in Equatoria had a lot to lose if the southern provinces were unceremoniously combined with the north, without first securing adequate procedures to protect their position in the future bureaucracy.[35]

The promotion of civil servants was a highly politicized issue. Once Sudanese were allowed to join all of the civil service ranks in 1953, the enormous pent-up frustration of northern Sudanese government employees, who had long been denied promotions and were extraordinarily influential within the mainstream political parties, meant that most British officials were replaced within a year or so. The new civil servants staunchly resisted reserving official positions for southerners, who for reasons such as the Arabic-language exam administered as a requirement for entrance into the service, found themselves largely excluded.[36] One of the solutions initially proposed was to strive for parity between the salaries of southern and northern employees in the security services, rather than pursuing a strategy of increasing opportunities for southerners to work in the civil bureaucracy.[37] Even as the competition for scarce government posts within the bureaucracy rapidly increased, "a serious shortage of not only technicians, but also of book-keepers, clerks and artisans," endangered the successful execution and maintenance of development projects in the southern provinces.[38]

33 Poggo, *The First Sudanese Civil War*, pp. 21–73.

34 Development in Juba was greatly accelerated by the decision in 1947 to integrate southern Sudan with the rest of Sudan. Minute No. 27, "Mr. Riches' Tour in the Southern Sudan," March, 1953, TNA FO 407/232/. For a discussion of state formation in southern Sudan, see: Cherry Leonardi, *Dealing with Government in South Sudan: Histories of Chiefship, Community and State* (Woodbridge, Suffolk: James Currey Press, 2013).

35 Memo, A. C. Beaton, "The Effects of the Recent Anglo-Egyptian Agreement on the Southern Sudan," March 17, 1953, TNA FO 371/102753/.

36 J. Carmichael, "Self-Government and the Early Years of Independence," SAD G//S 1166/4/7/.

37 J. Carmichael, November 11, 1954, SAD G//S 1166/4/6/.

38 J. Carmichael, "Notes Relating to the Government's Policy Statement on 1st March, 1954," February 20, 1954, SAD G//S 1166/4/7/.

Anger over the unequal distribution of civil service posts fed into a general fear that the development of the southern provinces within a unified Sudan would be stalled by neglect. Many prominent southerners in Juba and the rest of Equatoria wanted to align with East Africa. Yet although G. W. Ogden, the head of the development branch within the Department of Finance, recognized the importance of working out a special plan to facilitate the economic integration of the southern provinces, he could not figure out how to harmonize the Jonglei Investigation Team's recommendations with the government's long-term planning for the development of the national unit.[39] Because the Department of Finance had originally conceived of the economic survey of the southern provinces as a means for the central government to secure international financing and legitimacy, there was very little tolerance in Khartoum for experimentation or the adoption of novel pilot projects.[40]

The reluctance of finance officials to integrate the efforts of the Jonglei Investigation Team's work reflected an operational desire to simplify and consolidate the number of development initiatives pursued by the department, rather than to expand them. Indeed, already in 1953, Carmichael was arguing that the emphasis on an extensive survey of the Sudanese economy was misplaced. Instead, Carmichael favored a focus on expanding the amount of cotton grown within the Gezira triangle. He advised his British superiors in the Treasury that expansion of the Gezira Scheme would be "an adequate shield behind which the Sudanese Council of Ministers would permit consolidation rather than a too rapid expansion" of development initiatives.[41]

Carmichael well understood that if the expansion of the Gezira Scheme were pursued aggressively there would be insufficient resources to pursue other development goals. Estimates in 1953 suggested that this expansion might cost upward of LE 30 million. While officials within the department were interested in getting outside funding for an economic survey that would bolster the state's legitimacy, they had serious reservations about pursuing economic surveys in practice. There was little enthusiasm about a Point Four survey or a potential IBRD survey of the entire Nile Valley. There was a similar hesitancy to fund surveys of particular regions of Sudan. The danger in pursuing additional economic surveys was that they would create an image of the territory's economic potential that would then necessitate a commitment by the government in Khartoum to further develop those regions.[42] Meanwhile, finance officials believed that maintaining and eventually expanding the Gezira Scheme was integral to ensuring a sound fiscal position for the Sudanese state. Carmichael thought that

39 Letter from G. W. Ogden to P.P. Howell, "Southern Development Investigation Team," June 18, 1953, SAD 768/9/1–114/

40 Letter from P. P. Howell to R. C. Wakefield, March 30, 1953, SAD 768/9/1–114/.

41 Letter from J. Carmichael to D. R. Serpell, September 24, 1953, SAD 732/8/1–162 G. D. Lampen.

42 Ibid.

economic activity and capital investment should be concentrated in a few select centers and not distributed across the country.[43]

However, even as Carmichael suggested that plantation agriculture was the preferred method of development, funding these enterprises remained a problem. Therefore, at the same time as an export economy geared toward the former imperial system found active support among finance officials, British Treasury officials were hinting that they would be unwilling to extend new development funding to Sudan, since it was outside of the Commonwealth. Officials within the Sudanese Department of Finance were more concerned with stimulating growth in state revenues than were officials within the British Treasury Department, who had begun to question the wisdom of continuing to rely on cotton as the basis for the Sudanese economy.[44] Also, by 1954, the United Kingdom was beginning to import a smaller and smaller share of Sudan's cotton exports.[45] Experiments in the adoption of new crops and the development of new products from the cotton plant were being pursued. Yet all of these schemes ran into intense resistance from the Ministry of Finance.[46]

By the beginning of 1954, the decision to concentrate the state's financial resources on expanding irrigation in the Gezira Plain had been made. The supplementary development budget for 1954–1955 clarified that the Managil Extension and the Gezira Scheme would receive the vast majority of the government's resources. The other areas to which government resources would be devoted were the expansion of education facilities and of health services and the provision of additional rural water supplies.[47] Targeting government expenditures in this manner constituted a marked change in priorities from those enumerated in the 1946–1951 and the 1951–1956 plans, neither of which earmarked more than minor planning funds for the construction of the Roseires Dam or the Managil Extension.[48]

In making this turn, finance officials remained principally concerned with balancing their budget and increasing their reserves of foreign currency. This was despite their evolution from being the expatriate officials of a wider empire

43 Note, J. Carmichael, "Financial Assistance from HMG towards Economic Development," October 19, 1953, SAD 732/8/1–162 G. D. Lampen.

44 Note, J. Carmichael, "Note on Further Discussions at the Foreign Office on Problems other than compensation," October 20, 1953, SAD 732/8/1–162 G. D. Lampen.

45 Note, John Carmichael, "Points Which Maybe Raised by the Sudan Delegation to the UK on Financial and Economic matters," October 31, 1954, SAD G//S 1166/4/7/.

46 The Department of Finance became the Ministry of Finance in 1954, the year of Sudanese self-governance. Sudan achieved complete independence in 1956. Letter from George Raby to Sayyid Hammad Tewfik, "Idea of Setting Up a Department of Supply within the Ministry of Finance," March 15, 1955, SAD G//S 1166/4/7/.

47 J. Carmichael, "Notes Relating to the Government's Policy Statement on March 1st, 1954," February 20, 1954, SAD G//S 1166/4/7/.

48 Note, J. Carmichael, "State of Government's Finances," November 3, 1954, SAD G//S 1166/4/6/.

to the servants of a self-governing state. The enormous contribution of cotton to Sudan's national revenue, in particular the size of the Scheme's contribution, meant that according to the logic of accounting, the Gezira Scheme and a few other prominent irrigated schemes could credibly stand in for the territorial economy as whole. Measuring progress by focusing on easily identifiable targets such as the size of the country's reserve of foreign currency or the amount of free capital that a particular project could contribute to the central budget justified a focus on a few large schemes, even as it obscured other political or social considerations. Evaluating the merit of projects according to their potential contribution to the central budget rationalized the decision of officials in Khartoum to ignore vast areas of the country. Officials calculated that the potential financial contributions to the central budget from those areas were negligible.

Conclusion

Traditionally, studies of the economic history of Sudan have focused on the organization and management of the country's most capital-intensive agricultural schemes.[49] Agricultural experts such as Arthur Gaitskell, the British manager of the Gezira Scheme during the 1940s, and John D. Tothill, the visionary behind the massive Zande Scheme, epitomized the development model championed by agricultural departments throughout the empire. Both men imagined the creation of massive centralized agricultural schemes.[50] These schemes were self-contained, uniform, grid-like projects whose planners strove to create homogeneous environments in which the social, political, and economic transformation of each project's target population would occur. The state would assert its authority by creating workers and citizens at the same time that it tightly regulated the production of commodities such as cotton.[51]

The assumption that the late-colonial state hoped to uniformly develop its territory is captivating, but in practice, a better metaphor for how finance officials in Khartoum imagined the development of the Sudanese economy was

[49] Tony Barnett, *The Gezira Scheme: An Illusion of Development* (New York: Routledge, 1977), and Norman O'Neill and Jay O'Brien, eds., *Economy and Class in Sudan* (Brookfield, VT: Avebury, 1988).

[50] J. D. Tothill, "Social Emergence of Indigenous Races in Remote Areas," 1943 in Circular from J. Smith, "Appendix B: Note by Major Wyld on the Necessity of Spinning and Weaving,." April 1, 1946. National Records Office in Khartoum, Sudan (NRO) Fin 3-A/42/2/5/ and Arthur Gaitskill, *Gezira: A Story of Development in the Sudan* (London, UK: Farber and Farber, 1959); see also Hodge, *Triumph of the Expert*.

[51] James C. Scott, *Seeing like a State: How Certain Schemes to Improve the Human Condition Have Failed* (New Haven: Yale University Press, 1998); Victoria Bernal, "Colonial Moral Economy and the Discipline of Development: The Gezira Scheme and 'Modern' Sudan," *Cultural Anthropology* 12:4 (1997): 449.

to see it as made up of discontinuous sites of investment, "an archipelago of schemes" surrounded by large swaths of territory that finance officials did not believe possessed the economic potential to make development worthwhile.[52] Describing a state that was at best lukewarm in its ambitions to pursue development, and not simply ineffectual in practice, contrasts with much of the literature on the "Second Colonial Occupation," which argues that a homogenizing developmental state had become archetypical by the early 1940s in colonial Africa and throughout much of the decolonizing world.[53] Instead, countervailing political and financial priorities prevented officials in Khartoum from striving to create the institutions necessary to gather economic data from throughout the Anglo-Egyptian Sudan.

While many agricultural experts advocated for the continuous expansion of the state's gaze and the increased production of economic knowledge, finance officials such as Chick and Carmichael were hesitant to invest heavily in the development of an infrastructure independent of the state's plantation agriculture schemes.[54] Accountants and auditors by training, they were primarily concerned with calculating the cost and potential return on an investment in specific projects.[55] The focus on cost and returns made them keen to wall off particular sites of investment from the rest of the country and not to spend money preparing far-flung regions of the country for economic surveillance.

With the rejection of prose, quantifiable estimates of the return on investment became the foundation of the first national budgets written by the officials of a decolonizing Sudan. Quantification allowed Sudanese finance officials to project as stable inherently unstable forecasts of future cotton sales. This allowed these officials and the Sudanese politicians to whom they reported to continue justifying the priority of the central region of Sudan in all investment decisions. Still because of large fluctuations in the international cotton market, Sudanese officials were unable to stabilize their financial projections about the

52 James Ferguson, "Seeing like an Oil Company: Space, Security, and Global Capital in Neoliberal Africa," *American Anthropologist* 107: 3107 (2005): 379; see also, Frederick Cooper, "What Is the Concept of Globalization Good For? An African Historians Perspective," *African Affairs* (2001): 100, 189–213.

53 Low and Lonsdale, "Introduction: Towards the New Order 1945–1963," pp. 1–64. Ferguson, "Seeing like an Oil Company," p. 380. Also see Cooper, "Modernizing Bureaucrats, Backward Africans, and the Development Concept," p. 70.

54 Letter rom J. Carmichael to D. R. Serpell, September 24, 1953, SAD 732/8/1–162 G. D. Lampen. See also Joseph Hodges, *Triumph of the Expert*; Joanna Lewis, *Empire State-Building: War & Welfare in Kenya, 1925–52* (Athens, Ohio: Ohio University Press, 2000); and Priya Satia, "Developing Iraq: Britain, India and the Redemption of Empire and Technology in the First World War," *Past and Present* 197 (Nov. 2007): 213.

55 When writing about Kenya, Lewis states, "The men of finance were another group of skeptics [of spending on welfare and new agricultural schemes] trained in the school of strict accounting principles." J. E. Lewis, "The Ruling Compassions of the Late Colonial State: Welfare versus Force, Kenya, 1945–1952," *Journal of Colonialism and Colonial History* 2:2 (2001).

future. The unstable view of the future, produced by the repeated failure of the financial projections encoded in Sudan's annual development budgets and exacerbated by the ongoing war in the southern provinces, undermined the ability of government officials to use the idea of development as a stabilizing force in the country's volatile politics.

4

The New Finance Officials, 1954–1958

The British officials who controlled the Anglo-Egyptian Sudan's Department of Finance between 1945 and Sudan's self-government in 1954 viewed Sudan as a single economic unit and favored the expansion of the Gezira Scheme. They also fought a series of bureaucratic battles within the government to prevent the emergence of regional development authorities. The Sudanese officials who replaced the colonial authorities inherited these bureaucratic habits of mind, taking up plans developed during the colonial period and actualizing them to establish the foundations of the newly independent state.

Senior Sudanese finance officials were privileged members of a small and intimate elite.[1] In the years after Sudan achieved self-governance in 1954, the bureaucratic elite largely overlapped with the political and economic elite, and one of the key ties between all of them was cotton. Consequentially, the government poured the vast majority of its resources into the cotton-growing sector, overwhelmingly located in the central riverain area from Kosti to Omdurman to Sennar. When expanded to include the stretches of the Nile extending from Khartoum north to the border with Egypt and along the Atbara River, this area was the homeland of the political elite. That the most economically and politically advanced regions of the country overlapped was not a coincidence.

Most of the senior Sudanese finance officials attended Gordon's Memorial College in Khartoum, as had the vast majority of Sudan's political and senior military leaders. The main difference between the first military general to become the president of Sudan, Ibrahim 'Abboud, and the first Sudanese Permanent Under-Secretary of Finance, Hamza Mirghani Hamza, was a generation:

[1] Mohamed Ahmed Mahgoub, *Democracy on Trial: Reflections on Arab and African Politics* (London: Andre Deutsch, 1974), p. 180.

their education was very similar.[2] Hamza's father Mirghani Hamza was a well-known Sudanese politician, a colleague and peer of 'Abboud, while Hamza's bureaucratic rival, Deputy Permanent Under Secretary Mamoun Beheiry, was the son of a senior military officer. Conspicuously absent from this group were southerners, who made up one-quarter of the population of Sudan at independence, who had been ruled separately from the North by the British and whose elite were sent to different schools. Only eight southerners made it into the senior bureaucracy at independence.[3] The *effendiyya* class was composed of men who saw themselves as a class for themselves, conscious of their relationship to the state.[4] Their consciousness was formed by what Benedict Anderson termed the "secular pilgrimage" of succeeding in educational and bureaucratic organizations through which cohort after cohort passed.[5] The importance of education in defining membership within the rising leadership class of schoolteachers and mid-level civil servants was inscribed even in the name of the most prominent proto-nationalist society of the 1930s, the *Graduates' General Congress*.[6]

The independence generation, a few of whom were Oxford-trained in politics, philosophy, and economy, such as Mekki Abbas and Mamoun Beheiry, served from the early 1950s until the end of the 1960s: they saw themselves as the vanguard of the still nascent Sudanese nation and state.[7] Mekki Abbas became the first Sudanese director of the Gezira Scheme after his return from Oxford in 1951. This project, which covered more than two million acres, provided more than 50 percent of the government's revenue. It was owned and operated as a partnership between the state and individual tenants. Its further expansion became the primary concern of the newly named Ministry of Finance, absorbing the lion's share of the state's development budget, until the mid-1960s.[8]

Yet, even as there was a focus on the Gezira region of Sudan in the economic imaginary of Sudanese financial policy makers, Sudan's very first economist, Sa 'ad al-Din Fawzi, understood the Sudanese economy as explicitly national, as

[2] Ghasan Rasakh, "*Hamza Mirghani Hamza: Wazir al-Malia Al-Sudan*," Sudanyat.com http://sudanyat.org/vb/showthread.php?p=569457 [accessed July 26, 2014].

[3] Daly, *Imperial Sudan*, pp. 371–374.

[4] The masterwork on this class in Sudan remains Sharkey's *Living with Colonialism*. See also Lucie Ryzova, *The Age of the Efendiyya: Passages to Modernity in National-Colonial Egypt* (Oxford: Oxford University Press, 2014).

[5] Benedict Anderson, *Imagined Communities: Reflections on the Origins and Spread of Nationalism* (New York: Verso, 2006), pp. 123.

[6] The first gatherings of the club dated back to 1911, and as a class the graduates were perceived as political moderates pushing for gradual reforms that would lead eventually to self-government. Daly, *Imperial Sudan*, p. 79.

[7] Beheiry, *Glimpses From the Life of a Sudanese Public Servant*, pp. 17–24, and Margery Perham, "Editor's Preface," in Mekki Abbas, ed., *The Sudan Question: The Dispute over the Anglo-Egyptian Condominium, 1884–1951* (London: Faber and Faber, 1952).

[8] Young, "Measuring the Sudanese Economy," pp. 44–60.

grounded in Sudan's very constitutional order. Sa 'ad opened his 1958 book composed of a series of lectures on the Sudanese economy by noting that he first needed to take a short detour in political history. He wrote,

> These chapters are about the Sudanese economy. But I am compelled to precede them with a short article on the history of modern Sudan, and with a general presentation about the Sudanese constitution. There are a number of reasons for the path I follow. Among them is the fact that the Sudanese economy did not come into existence between a day and a night and on the contrary it advanced gradually over days, until it arrived to its current stage. Certainly the present came from the past, and looks to the future in light of the present. Among the reasons also is that the economic infrastructure of any country (among the countries) is very influenced by the constitutional or political framework of that country. So supreme economic policy is being decided by the logic of the constitution, and through the means of the political and administrative apparatus, which the constitution specifies to take the necessary measures. Without doubt the nature of these institutions, especially in a country where the state plays a large role in production, is shaped by its service of the political economy.[9]

Sa 'ad' decided to begin his collection of printed lectures with an essay of political history because of his interest in demonstrating that the economy did not simply grow out of geography as a sort of natural feature, but rather was tied to political concepts and institution building. In this way, Sa 'ad sought to differentiate himself from his Egyptian colleagues who, also writing in Arabic, tended to see Sudan's economic potential as "governed by the natural factors, such as the quantity and fertility of the land."[10]

Grounding the Sudanese economy in political institutions rather than geography opened up the possibility of limitless growth. However, it also acknowledged the extent to which Sudan's economy was at the mercy of the country's fragile political institutions. For instance, the constitution in which Sa 'ad grounded his theory of Sudan's economy was actually an interim constitution. "Sudan received its complete independence and total sovereignty on the 1st of January 1956 and the Sudanese parliament signed a temporary constitution, the country has lived in its shadow since that time, and still lives in it."[11] One marker of the frailty of the new constitutional order was that it remained on

[9] Sa 'ad al-Din Fawzi, *Muhadirat 'an Juanib min al-Iqtisad al-Sudan 'ala taliba Qasim al-Darasat al-Iqtisadiya wa al-Ijtima'aiya*, (Cairo: al-Mutab 'at al- Kamalit, 1958), p. 1 [translations by the author].

[10] Muhammed Mahmoud al-Sayyad, *Iqtisadat al-Sudan muhadarat ilaqaha 'ala taliba qasm al-dirasat al-iqtisadiyya wa al-ijtima 'aiyya* (Cairo: Ma 'had al-Bahuth wa al-Dirasat al-Arabiyya, Jama't Al-Douwla Al-Arabiyya, 1957), p. 2.

[11] Another factor in the instability of the country that he noted was the fact that the impetus for Sudanese decolonization was an agreement between the two colonial powers, Britain and Egypt, for the Sudanese people to participate in a referendum on self-determination, which was signed on February 13, 1953. The large role of outside powers in Sudan's independence cast doubt on whether Sudan truly had a consolidated nationalist movement. Fawzi felt the need to emphasize that the Sudanese economy was an authentic outgrowth of Sudanese political expression, particularly because he was speaking in Cairo where many intellectuals continued to think of Sudan as a natural part of Greater Egypt. Fawzi, *Muhadirat 'an Juanib*, p. 1.

an interim basis for two more years until the military coup of General 'Abboud ended Sudan's first experiment in parliamentary democracy in November 1958.

The principal reason why Sudan's political parties were unable to agree on a permanent constitution was the unresolved question of regional autonomy. Members of the southern elite, in particular, wanted assurances that they would be able to direct a significant share of the development budget to their own provinces. Before independence, senior officials in the colonial Department of Finance had rejected regional autonomy in development spending, and after independence the senior Sudanese politicians and officials in the Ministry of Finance rejected it again.

Instead, northern Sudanese politicians expressed a politics that was centered on economic growth as the measure of development and that took for granted that the nation was a singular entity. In prioritizing economic growth over issues such as regional inequality, national policy makers in Sudan were hewing to the assumptions of a generation of growth economists such as Simon Kuznets that political and social harmony would be easier to achieve by seeking to expand the overall economic pie, rather than fighting over its pieces or debating how to implement redistribution policies.[12] The leader of the Sudanese Senate, Sayyid Ali 'Abd al-Rahman, articulated the consensus of the political class in favor of economic development and its relationship to political independence when he declared in 1958,

> As a united and responsible people we have successfully passed through the struggle stage for liberation and independence – we now begin the stage of development, construction and maintenance of our independence and this is certainly one of the most important epochs in the life of a nation.[13]

Like many prominent members of the northern elite, 'Ali 'Abd al-Rahman believed that each state would pass through stages of national realization, the first of which was political independence, quickly followed by the phase of national economic development. Therefore, for men like him, a failure to achieve economic growth and development threatened to jeopardize the independence of the nation.[14] Taking for granted the singular quality of the nation,

[12] Easterly, *The Elusive Quest for Growth*, pp. 25–45; for the belief that there is a direct connection between economic growth and social harmony, see Benjamin M. Friedman, *The Moral Consequences of Economic Growth* (New York: Vintage Press, 2006). For the classic dissenting view on modernization theory's thesis that economic growth and social and political harmony would all advance together, see Samuel Huntington, *Political Order in Changing Societies* (New Haven: Yale University Press, 1968/1986).

[13] Sayyid 'Ali Abd al-Rahman, "Weekly Digest of Proceedings in the Senate, No. 1, From 22nd March to 15th May, 1958; Summary of Proceedings, Sitting No. 2," May 12, 1958, NRO Finance 3-A/59/1/2/.

[14] For a discussion of the link between economic development and political independence in the imaginations of African independence leaders, see Frederick Cooper, *Africa since 1940: The Past of the Present* (New York: Cambridge University Press, 2002).

they believed that independence had already guaranteed political unity and that all that was necessary now was to increase the strength of the Sudanese state and the living standard of its people. In the process they neglected the role that economic development plays in forging political consensus and national unity even at the expense of economic efficiency.

The Cost-Benefit Analysis of the Zande Scheme and the Managil Extension

Sudanese politicians and officials defined their first task of economic management as finalizing and then implementing a national development strategy. British officials in the decade after 1945 had left behind plans, surveys and reports about a large number of potential development and economic schemes scattered across the country.[15] Therefore, Sudanese officials were not struggling to imagine new development schemes as much as they were trying to select which to expend the state's limited resources pursuing. Sudanese officials firmly believed that the state was the most capable driver of economic development.[16] Consequentially, they largely ignored the dynamic potential of the private sector, particularly the ranching industry with its exports of cattle, sheep, and camels; the transportation industry; commercial services; peasant farming; and even private commercial farming outside of state-owned projects.[17] Although finance officials discussed the potential of small-scale food processing and of diversifying away from cotton in favor of other crops, these plans remained exploratory.[18] Aside from the state monopolies on services such as railway transportation and duties on the importation of consumer goods such as sugar, the main revenue generator for the government remained the country's cotton cultivation schemes.[19]

The government partially owned a number of tenant estates devoted to producing raw cotton for export, located along the Nile and in the Tokar and Gash Delta, as well as in the Nuba Mountains. But the two projects that occupied the vast majority of finance officials' energy between 1956 and 1958 were the Managil Extension Scheme, which if completed would double the acreage of irrigated land cultivatable in the Gezira Plain, and the Zande Scheme for

15 See discussion in Chapter 2; Letter from George Raby to Sayyid Hammad Tewfik, "A Verbatim Report of Mr. C. W. Raby's Recorded Speech," Khartoum, SAD G//S 1166/4/7/; and Yongo-Bure, *Economic Development in Southern Sudan*.

16 Memo, J. Carmichael, "Movements in Sudan's Foreign Exchange Reserves in the Period 1952–1955 Leading to a General Financial Review and Suggestions as to Future Policy," May 22, 1956, SAD G//S 1166/3/1/.

17 R. L. Tignor, "The Sudanese Private Sector: An Historical Overview," *Journal of Modern African Studies* 25.2 (1987): 179–212, and Mahmoud, *The Sudanese Bourgeoisie*.

18 Ali Mohammed al-Hassan, ed., *An Introduction to the Sudan Economy* (Khartoum: Khartoum University Press, 1976).

19 Ibid.

growing cotton, tea, tobacco, and other crops and manufacturing textiles operated by the Equatoria Projects Board, which its advocates hoped would spur the economic development of the southern provinces.[20]

In 1956 most senior Sudanese officials believed that exporting primary agricultural commodities was the economic model Sudan should pursue for development. Minister of Finance Ibrahim Ahmed stated in 1956, "We rely on the export of our commodities for the funds with which we pay for the imports and other services which are essential not only for maintaining our existing standard of living but also for new development, and the raising of our standard of living."[21]

The ideal of an export-oriented economy was firmly rooted in the minds of many Sudanese officials and politicians. The immediate goal of economic development was not to change the structure of the economy, but rather to increase the amount of revenue that the state was capable of collecting by increasing its exports. During World War II, the Sudan Irrigation Department and the Department of Agriculture had already begun to draw up plans for expanding agricultural exports by constructing what eventually became the Managil Extension.[22]

While the Sudanese economy was complex, from the perspective of the accountants' ledgers it was simple. The income earned from the country's exports of cotton needed to match or surpass the costs of its imports (of capital and consumer goods.) Any surplus, which accrued to the state, could be devoted to increasing the country's production of cotton (thereby enabling even larger gains in the future) or building up and improving the bureaucratic apparatus. Finance officials were inclined to think of Sudan's economy as a reflection of its cotton production, in part because the revenue derived from cotton could be measured with such ease. Consequentially, it was easy for finance officials to associate the success or failure of economic policies with the amount of revenue earned from cotton each year.

In 1954, following the publication of the 1954–1955 development budget, finance officials defined their national development priority as the construction

20 Reining, *The Zande Scheme*, and H. Ferguson, *The Zande Scheme* (Khartoum: Agricultural Publications Committee, 1954).

21 Minister of Finance and Economics Ibrahim Ahmed, "The 1956/57 Budget Speech," June 7, 1956, SAD G//S 1166/3/5/.

22 Questions about how much water Sudan could make use of were intimately tied up with its relationship to Egypt, and the "water nationalism" of the Sudan Irrigation Department during the 1940s was a direct response to their perceived position of subordination to Egyptian officials. Letter from Secretariat to African Department, FO [The Foreign Office, National Archives, Kew, UK], February 25 1950, FO 371/97019; Letter from African Department, FO to Secretariat, February 17 1950, FO 371/80531; Letter from Secretariat to African Department, FO, February 25 1950, FO 371/80531; Deparment of Finance, *Five Year Plan for Post-War Development*, p. 13.

of the initial phases of the Managil Extension Scheme.[23] The decision to invest in Managil sidelined alternative investment possibilities aimed at agricultural diversification in long-neglected regions, including the Jonglei Canal project, the proposals of the Equatorial Projects Board in the southern provinces of Sudan, and the Jebel Marrah Scheme in Darfur.

Examining the rationale that finance officials provided for favoring the Managil Scheme over development of the Zande Scheme reveals their approach to financial planning and stewardship. Between 1954 and 1958, finance officials gave priority to the Managil Scheme for two reasons. First, it was familiar. Managil was essentially an expansion of the Gezira Scheme, the most successful of Sudan's major agricultural estates. Second, the potential cost of Managil and the future revenue that could be earned from it were easily calculable. In contrast, while finance officials understood the potential of the Equatorial Projects Board's projects, they were not sure how to align that potential with the central state's economic aims. Where Managil was clearly envisioned as a scheme for the export of raw cotton, the Zande Scheme project was sometimes interpreted as an exporter of raw cotton, an incipient industrial complex, or even as a series of experimental farms hoping to introduce new crops either for the domestic or international market into Sudan. As a result, it was difficult to integrate the Zande Scheme into the Ministry of Finance's planning aims.

While finance officials knew in theory that the reliance of the Sudanese economy on a single commodity represented a strategic vulnerability, in practice policies designed to foster economic diversification were difficult to implement. Sudanese officials, for example, believed that the country already produced as much gum arabic (Sudan's second largest export commodity after cotton) as the world economy could absorb. In fact, Sudanese dominance of the gum arabic market was so complete that by World War I production increases in Sudan led directly to a reduction in its price in world markets.[24] Other projects to produce alternative cash crops such as sugar, soap, tobacco, rice, citrus, and palm oils all remained in an experimental phase: the quantities harvested were too small for an accurate evaluation of their potential. The most promising sites for agricultural diversification were in southern Sudan on the experimental farms in Equatoria Province and around Jebel Marrah, in the far west of Sudan. Jebel Marrah, while surveyed for its economic potential by the British during the early 1950s, had never been developed. At the same time, the Equatoria Projects Board, which by 1956 had developed into a complex industrial agricultural establishment, was hindered by the political unrest centered in Equatoria Province. After the announcement in 1954 that the southern provinces of Sudan would be

[23] J. Carmichael, "Notes Relating to the Government's Policy Statement on March 1st, 1954," February 20, 1954, SAD G//S 1166/4/7/, and Note, J. Carmichael, "State of Government's Finances," November 3, 1954, SAD G//S 1166/4/6/.

[24] Serels, "Political Landscaping," p. 64.

integrated into a unified political entity with the North without the benefit of any real regional political, administrative, or cultural autonomy, violence erupted in Torit and quickly spread throughout Equatoria. Key demands of the protestors were for some form of integration with British East Africa, as well as political and economic autonomy.[25]

The development of the Equatoria Projects Board, which was often portrayed by both northern officials in Khartoum and southern politicians as a general development agency for southern Sudan, pointed to the possibility of an autonomous southern economy. The impracticality of shipping goods from the south all the way to Port Sudan in the far north gave additional credence to the fears of policy makers in Khartoum that the development of a separate industrial capacity in the southern provinces would eventually facilitate greater integration between the south and neighboring countries such as Uganda or Kenya. Even the northern officials running the Equatoria Projects Board felt compelled to suggest that Mombasa might make a better outlet for southern goods than Port Sudan.[26] Khalifa Mahjoub, general manager of the Equatorial Projects Board (EPB), which managed the Zande Scheme, found himself unable to define the true purpose of the scheme. He wrote a letter to the EPB's directors, expressing his concerns:

> I look upon the Board as a project which has "eaten" much money and must pay a dividend, and as a scheme which has possibilities to share in building up a national economy or, to say the least, in making this country partly self-sustaining. To do so it must expand. Should the expansion be agricultural? Industrial? Both? In what order?[27]

What was clear was that as an exporter of raw cotton the Equatoria Projects Scheme was failing. It produced only enough raw materials in 1956 to supply its own mills, and the cloth that these mills produced was of such poor quality that only government customers such as the prison system were willing to buy it. To the extent that officials in Khartoum considered the Equatoria Projects Board financially beneficial, it was primarily as a way to produce agricultural substitutes for common imports consumed domestically.[28]

Finance officials considered the Zande Scheme to be risky because there was no historical baseline against which to compare its performance. In addition,

[25] Poggo, *The First Sudanese Civil War*, pp. 33–47, and Johnson, *The Root Causes of Sudan's Civil Wars*, pp. 22–39.

[26] Minutes from Ismail Mohd. Bakheit to Ali Baldo, June 19, 1958, NRO Finance 3-A/42/1/3/.

[27] Letter from Khalifa Mahjoub to Directors of EPB, May 29, 1956, NRO Finance 3-A/42/1/4/.

[28] Ibid. For a discussion of the origins of the Zande Scheme and the debate about whether transforming the Azande into a self-sufficient people was an adequate aim of Sudanese economic policy, see the discussion in Chapter 1. The tension between the Equatoria Board's financial mission and the idea of the Zande Scheme as a pilot industrialization project meant to transform southern Sudan is captured by the contradictions in how its administrators thought it should be judged, see Ferguson, *The Zande Scheme*, pp. 24–29.

assessing the feasibility and earnings of the Zande Scheme was difficult because of a lack of reliable data. It was hard to gather data because bookkeepers and other northern staff members resented being posted to a region that they regarded as hostile and alien. In fact, it was often easier for the scheme's managers to recruit staff from India than to get northern Sudanese accountants to work in Nzara in western Equatoria. As the security situation deteriorated, Khalifa Mahjub, the general manager, reported that even his staff car had been "battered by machine gun fire."[29] The only certainty in the eyes of officials in Khartoum was that the Equatoria Projects Board was losing money, but even how much money could not exactly be ascertained. In 1956, finance officials realized that almost eighteen months of accounts had not been properly recorded.[30] Two years later, when the Ministry of Finance and Economics asked the Equatoria Projects Board to explain its ledgers, it could provide only very incomplete information.[31]

Finance officials believed that the only remunerative possibility for the Zande Scheme was for it to become a cashcrop exporter not only of cotton as in the schemes in the Nuba Mountains, Tokar, and Gash Delta but also of tobacco and coffee. The goal was to put part of the income earned from the export of these crops into a reserve fund, which could then be used to promote social welfare and other forms of regional development. The scheme itself was to be run in such a manner that it maximized the potential revenues earned annually.[32]

By the fall of 1958, despite the talk of reorganizing the Zande Scheme, and without any evidence that it had met its goals of regional economic transformation, finance officials declared that the problems of regional poverty and lack of investment that the scheme had been conceived to address had been solved. This statement ignored the fact that the vast inequality between northern Sudan, particularly the central provinces where the Gezira Scheme was located, and the provinces of southern Sudan persisted. Finance officials did not consider local development to be a legitimate aim of economic policy. Therefore, the goal according to the governor of Equatoria, Ali Baldo, was to run the scheme on "an economical basis and avoid losses," even if that meant shutting

29 Minutes of 40th Meeting, Equatoria Projects Board from Khalifa Mahgoub to Sayyid Abdel Rahim Bayoumi, May 7th, 1956, NRO Finance 3-A/42/1/3/ and Minutes from W. Habashi, April 11, 1956, NRO Finance 3-A/42/1/3/.

30 Losses were due in part to the small quantities of cotton grown, a problem that was aggravated by the uprising in southern Sudan of 1954. Expenditures on centralized agricultural schemes often remained high even if the harvest was poor or the price per unit low. Letter from Khalifa Mahgoub to GM, June 18, 1956, NRO Finance 3-A/42/1/4/; Note from M.vT. Salloum, June 16 1956, NRO Finance 3-A/42/1/4/; and Note from Osman Abdel Osman to Governor of Equatoria, July 2, 1956, NRO Finance 3-A/42/1/4/.

31 Letter from Abdel Rahim Ibrahim Shaddad to General Manager, EPB, September 2, 1958, NRO Finance 3-A/42/3/10/.

32 Letter from Ali Baldo to Sayyid Wadie Habashi, February 20, 1958, NRO Finance 3-A/42/3/10/.

down large parts of the Zande Scheme and simply letting it shrivel through neglect.[33]

While to finance officials in Khartoum the financial prospects of the Zande Scheme appeared unknowable, they tended to associate investments in Managil with predictable returns. To Ministry of Finance officials the attraction of Managil was that the likely return on capital could be calculated quickly by looking at historical production data related to the Gezira Scheme dating back to the 1920s.[34] The time depth of the statistical record of the Gezira Scheme of which Managil was simply an extension gave estimates about its potential revenue an extra gloss of reliability. Finance officials' ability to make calculations from information the ministry already possessed took on a renewed importance because of the problems that these officials encountered receiving accurate data from agricultural estates, in particular estates located far away from Khartoum, such as those under the direction of the Equatorial Projects Board.[35] Support for particular projects could be justified even in the face of expected financial loses as long as the duration and magnitude of these losses could be approximated.

The Managil Extension was the centerpiece of the government's strategy to boost exports of cotton, but eventually it did produce large quantities of durra, a grain consumed as a primary foodstuff in Sudan. The first of four planned stages of the extension was scheduled to yield an additional 200,000 feddans of irrigated land.[36] The first phase began in 1956 after finance officials allocated the necessary funds in the budget.[37] The extension also required the construction of new infrastructure, including an elevated irrigation canal, a new dam at Roseires, and the upgrading of large parts of the country's railroad network to enable it to transport larger volumes of cotton.[38]

The Pricing Dispute

The presumption that Sudan could maintain a premium price for its cotton exports, despite intense competition within the international market, led finance officials to argue that the independent republic could continue the economic policies established by the British of capital-intensive development based on

33 Letter from Ali Baldo to Sayyid Hamza Mirghani Hamza, September 23, 1958, NRO Finance 3-A/42/3/10/.

34 Memo. Productive Development in the Period between the Completion of the Managil Extension and the Completion of the Roseires Dam, February 25, 1958, SAD G//S 1166/1/4 and J. Carmichael, "The Marketing of Sudan Cotton," June 11, 1958, SAD G//S 1166/2/4/.

35 Letter from A. I. Shadad to General Manager, Equatorial Projects Board, January 21, 1958, NRO Fin 3-A/28/12/43.

36 One feddan equals approximately one acre, or exactly 1.038.

37 Letter from J. H. A Watkins to J. Carmichael, "Memorandum on economic sit. Prepared by the Embasy in Khartoum," November 11, 1958, SAD G//S 1166/2/4/.

38 Minister of Finance and Economics Ibrahim Ahmed, "The 1956/57 Budget Speech," June 7, 1956, SAD G//S 1166/3/5/. See also Sa 'd Mahir Hamzah, *Iqtisadiyat al-Sudan* (al-Qahirah: Maktabat al-Ahram al-Iqtisadi, 1965) and Daly, *Darfur's Sorrow*, pp. 178–202.

irrigating land to grow cotton. In addition, finance officials believed that they could set a price at which the government sold its cotton without referencing market conditions.

Finance officials made calculations in private about the profitability of expenditures to increase cotton production, even as politicians discussed development as an ideology in public. As early as 1954 arguments were heard inside the Ministry of Finance that the "focus on the quality of a produce that has long brought prosperity to Sudan," namely cotton, might be misguided. But these voices remained marginal within the policy-making hierarchy until Permanent Under-Secretary of Finance Hamza Mirghani Hamza raised them again after the poor cotton sales of the 1957–1958 season.[39] Indeed until 1957, the main question that finance officials focused on was how to expand production of their agricultural exports, primarily raw cotton. The profits that the state expected to earn on its investments were calculated from historical data about the price of cotton combined with several different scenarios about how much additional land could be brought under irrigation. This allowed finance officials to make predictions about the additional income that the state should expect.[40] The possibility that Sudan's total cotton production could be doubled with the completion of the Managil Extensions, thereby doubling the size of the Gezira Scheme, became a guidepost of Sudanese economic policy.

Low prices and poor sales of cotton in the years after 1954 made it necessary for finance officials to contemplate raising capital from abroad to make up for what they believed were temporary and short-term deficits. Yet this instability in the cotton market did not fundamentally alter the government's fixation with cotton. Senior officials held on to the belief that cotton grown on irrigated estates was the best investment that Sudan could make. John Carmichael reflected on this belief when he claimed,

> It is hardly true to say that the Sudan is dependent on cotton. A more correct statement would be that, without cotton, the Sudan could be more or less self-sufficient and self-supporting: with cotton, the Sudan can continue to improve its general standards of living and to lay aside funds for future development.[41]

Carmichael's view was illustrative of a common view held in the department that cotton would propel the country's development. After all, Sudan was one of world's cheapest producers of cotton. Even if cotton prices fell from their current price of LE 40 to as low as LE 7 per kantar at Port Sudan, Sudanese

39 Letter from A. N. Shimmin to John Carmichael, October 2, 1956, SAD G//S 1166/1/2/.

40 The sciences of financial and economic planning and later national income accounting produced essentially conservative and controlled visions of the future, based on literal predictions of the present. Andersson, "The Great Future Debate and the Struggle for the World," pp. 1412–1413.

41 John Carmichael, "Notes for the Minister of Finance and Economics for General Consideration in the Financial and Economic Field," November 24, 1958, SAD G//S 1166/2/5/.

irrigated cotton would remain profitable.[42] It was widely believed that no other crop grown in Sudan could yield the profits that Sudan earned from cotton. The government captured a large share of the difference between the LE 40 per kantar that it sold Sudanese cotton for internationally and the LE 7 per kantar that it cost to export raw cotton. The primary question for government officials marketing Sudanese cotton each year was what price to set for the cotton it sold.[43]

Nevertheless by 1957, John Carmichael, now an advisor to the Ministry of Finance and Economics, found himself advocating increased fiscal austerity and a general reduction in the price the Gezira Schemes Board set for all of Sudan's cotton. Hamza Mirghani Hamza, the permanent under-secretary in the Ministry of Finance and Economics, adamantly rejected Carmichael's proposals.[44] Hamza Mirghani Hamza lost the immediate argument, and the 1958–1959 budget proposed an immediate reduction in expenditures from LS 48 to 38 million. Increased austerity brought about a sharp drop in the support for all development projects other than the Managil Extension Scheme. The development budget for other projects was reduced to LS 5.5 million, and there was even discussion that the third stage of the Managil Extension Scheme should be postponed indefinitely, unless funding from the International Bank of Reconstruction and Development was guaranteed.[45]

Despite his advocacy of financial austerity and setting a lower price for cotton, John Carmichael was perhaps the most emblematic member of the camp that suggested that Sudan's commitment to cotton was sound and that the country as a whole faced little more than a short-term problem in pricing cotton. He thought that the basic structure of the cotton export economy could be preserved, even though Sudan would have to be prepared to face altered terms of trade and perhaps have to find a new partner or partners willing to play the role that Britain had once played as a market of last resort. The answer according to Carmichael was for the country's cotton to be priced correctly.[46]

The 1958 International Bank of Reconstruction and Development mission to Sudan supported the view that Sudan could increase the quantities of cotton it sold if it lowered its price, thereby facilitating economic development. The mission concluded that, following the liquidation of the UK Raw Cotton Commission in 1954, which had bought up to 70 percent of Sudan's cotton crop, the Sudanese authorities had been too slow to adjust their cotton-marketing

[42] An unspoken assumption of his was that the contemplated expansions of irrigated cotton-growing schemes would be able to produce cotton at similar prices. John Carmichael, "Notes for the Minister of Finance and Economics for General Consideration in the Financial and Economic Field," 24 November, 1958 SAD G//S 1166/2/5/.

[43] J. Carmichael, "The Marketing of Sudan Cotton," June 11, 1958, SAD G//S 1166/2/4/.

[44] Memo, John Carmichael, "Notes for the Minister of Finance and Economics for General Consideration in the Financial and Economics Field," SAD G//S 1166/2/5/.

[45] Ibid.

[46] Letter from John Carmichael to Hamza Mirghani, January 4, 1959, SAD G//S 1166/2/4/.

strategies.[47] The adoption of minimum prices and the abandonment of open auctions for cotton had driven away many of Sudan's traditional customers.[48] The assumption was that if Sudan simply adapted the price of its commodities (i.e., cotton) to the changed realities (by lowering its profit margins), it would regain access to its former markets. Carmichael and the members of the IBRD mission both thought that the problem was that Sudanese politicians and officials overestimated their control over their own destiny and that the Sudanese should accept the international market price. Carmichael advised that cotton price fixing by the Sudanese state was futile: the price of cotton was simply the product of "competitive bidding."[49] He argued, "There is no formula for assessing the precise parity from day to day or even month to month. Instead there will be one price at which one spinner will be prepared to carry on using Sudan cotton: another spinner may well have another view."[50] Carmichael was aware of the vulnerability of the Sudanese economy, explaining that "Sudan must sell crop quickly ... because only thus can its foreign reserves be maintained at levels that would permit an uninterrupted program of development."[51] He accepted the necessity that the "existing standards of living might have to be depressed temporarily." Reducing national consumption would increase national savings, which could then be invested in economic development.[52] Because the state could not increase revenue by controlling the price at which it sold its cotton, the answer was to sell more cotton. This could be achieved by irrigating ever more land.[53]

As mentioned, the permanent under secretary to the Ministry of Finance, Hamza Mirghani Hamza, disagreed with Carmichael and the IBRD mission's views about how to market Sudan's cotton. Hamza Mirghani Hamza believed that there had been a series of structural changes in the world's demand for cotton, which would prevent Sudan from increasing or even maintaining its current level of cotton sales while maintaining profitable price levels. He suggested that Sudan not lower the price of its cotton immediately to retain its market share, but instead it should try to obtain the best possible price and funnel the earnings immediately into a diversification fund in the face of what he perceived as a long-term structural transformation in the global cotton market.[54] Mirghani pointed out that the "new markets of China, Japan, Asia

47 Report. IBRD, "The Economy of Sudan," February 25, 1958, SAD 593/8/1–61.

48 Ibid.

49 J. Carmichael, "The Marketing of Sudan Cotton," June 11, 1958, SAD G//S 1166/2/4/.

50 Ibid. 51 Ibid. 52 Ibid.

53 Ministry of Finance, Government of Sudan, "Report on Roseires Dam, Project 1958," November 8, 1958, SAD G//S 1166/1/1/.

54 One part of the disagreement between John Carmichael and Hamza Mirghani Hamza had to do with the extent to which US subsidies of short-staple cotton, particularly selling through the Commodity Credit Corporation, were suppressing the price of cotton only in the short term and to what extent Sudan as a low-cost producer could regain its pricing flexibility in the future once US policy stabilized. Carmichael believed that US subsidies and the large amount of

generally were focused on short staple [cotton]," not the long-staple variety Sudan traditionally produced.[55] He also expressed concern about the structure of the labor market in the country and doubted whether more labor could comfortably be directed toward the further development of Sudanese cotton estates.[56] The debate between Carmichael and Mirghani in many ways grafted onto a larger debate in the decolonizing world about how to jump-start development.[57] Hamza Mirghani Hamza argued a position that might be interpreted as a modified form of "export pessimism."[58] He explained that the export prices of commodities were in long-term decline and that only diversification and increased production for the domestic market would be capable of reversing Sudan's declining terms of trade.

In 1958, when the military regime came to power, those who believed that the reserve price that the Gezira Scheme Board set for Sudanese international cotton sales was too high won the argument within the Ministry of Finance and Economics. Sudanese officials decided that expanded production would offset a reduction in the price per kantar at which cotton was sold. If this was combined with a determined government effort to reduce national consumption and the amount of money spent on political costs such as patronage and labor, finance officials believed that stability could be restored to government revenues and the economy returned to a path of economic growth.[59]

Sudanese politicians did not want to reduce spending. Therefore they sought an approach that would get them out of the bind that Carmichael and Hamza Mirghani Hamza presented: austerity either to ride out a temporary decline in the cotton markets or austerity to pursue economic diversification. Instead, Sudanese politicians focused on raising capital from abroad. Yet, as much as Sudanese politicians would have liked to be able to frame the issue of raising capital from abroad as a technical development question, for the likely

uncertainty that surrounded US pricing policies during the 1950s had artificially lowered the price of cotton, while Hamza Mirghani Hamza believed that the fundamentals of the international cotton market had simply changed. Letter from Hamza Mirghani Hamza to Sir J. Carmichael, February 1, 1958, SAD G//S 1166/1/4/; Memo. J. Carmichael, "Managil Extension," January 27, 1958, SAD G//S 1166/1/4/.

55 Sudan traditionally exported the long-staple variety of cotton often known as Bakarat, which was used in the production of high-quality textiles.

56 One issue was whether there would continue to be sufficient seasonal labor to continue to work the cotton estates. In 1958 Gezira was importing Eritreans, West Africans, Kordofanians and Darfurians as seasonal laborers. Letter. H. M. H. to Sir John [Carmichael], January 2, 1958, SAD G//S 1166/1/4/.

57 For a history of some of the debates surrounding the application of the development paradigm, see Gilbert Rist, *The History of Development: From Western Origins to Global Faith* (New York: Zed Books, 2009), pp. 69–93.

58 Harold James, *International Monetary Cooperation since Bretton Woods* (New York: Oxford University Press, 1996), p. 125.

59 Memo. John Carmichael, "The Marketing of Sudan Cotton," November 6th, 1958, SAD G//S 1166/2/4/.

international donors it was a political issue. As a result, between 1956 and 1958, a fierce political debate ensued about the most appropriate funding strategy for Sudan. One faction believed that Sudan should turn to the United States and Great Britain, while the other faction demanded that Sudan maintain its fraternal alliances with Egypt as a fellow Arab state.

Both strategies ran into immediate problems, because neither the United States nor the USSR was particularly interested in the Sudanese cotton-growing industry. In fact they saw Sudanese production as either competition for its domestic producers or as a bit player on the world market whose demands for support were at best a nuisance. Each country's interest in Sudan was related to military alliances and the looming "Arab Cold War" between the Middle Eastern states that aligned with Egypt, which was aligned with the USSR, and those that aligned with Great Britain and the United States. Unfortunately for the Sudanese, each side in this conflict had its own partisans inside of Sudan's political parties.[60] Prior to Prime Minister Abdallah Khalil surrender of authority to Ibrahim 'Abboud, the leaders of the People's Democratic Party (PDP) were indeed threatened with death if they did not agree to the US gifts of aid and the British gifts of arms. Yet around the same time, the National Union Party (NUP), Southern Liberation Party, and the Anti-Imperialism Front issued a statement on July 1, 1958, condemning the US aid and Sudan's turn to the West. Then al-Azhari violently attacked 'Abdullah Khalil, saying that he was little more than another copy of Nuri al-Said. By October 21, 1958, 'Abdullah Khalil was facing numerous attacks from student unions at University of Khartoum, in Cairo, and the Sudan Workers Trade Union Federation was launching sustained protests against him.[61]

The military appeared to offer a solution. It could end the political infighting that was raising the cost of politics among the northern elite while resisting demands for scarce capital to be siphoned off to social and economic development projects in the periphery. However, not everyone within the ministry agreed, and Hamza Mirghani Hamza left his post once the military regime came to power. He then took a position at the International Monetary Fund, beginning a pattern of rotation that would be followed by other officials between the national government and IFIs.[62]

Conclusion

The elite believed they had an obligation to bring civilization and development to the rest of the nation, of which they were the vanguard. Their feelings of

60 Alden Young, "The Anglo-Egyptian Rivalry, The Cold War and Economic Development in Sudan: 1954–1958," in Massimiliano Trentin and Matteo Gerlini, eds., *The Middle East and the Cold War: Between Security and Development* (Newcastle upon Tyne, UK: Cambridge Scholars Press, 2012), pp. 29–53.

61 Al-Amin '*Al-Fariq Ibrahim 'Abbud*, pp. 47–74.

62 Beheiry, *Glimpses in the Life of a Sudanese Public Servant*, p. 109.

superiority continued even as the language of economics replaced overt discussions of civilizational difference. In the decades after World War II, development with its attendant dichotomy between advanced and backward became a global language that both imperialists and nationalists spoke to one another. Yet, investing the majority of the government's income in the expansion of irrigated cotton meant not only ignoring and likely exacerbating regional inequality within Sudan but also increasing the government's vulnerability to an inherently unreliable source of income. Between 1956 and 1959 finance officials embraced an economizing logic, which imagined the most reasonable futures to be projections from the past. They invested in irrigated agriculture because they were able to project the price of cotton into the future, calculating the potential return on investment. Despite the fact that finance officials knew that their calculations of potential returns could only be tentative because they were dependent on a wide range of factors beyond their control, they preferred the allure of calculability to the obvious unknowns involved in investing in southern Sudan. In addition to the questions about the economic strategy that Sudan should pursue, there were political and cultural unknowns involved in expanding the Equatoria Projects Board. For Sudanese finance officials, diversification and industrialization were conceived of as complementary to but not replacements for the cotton-exporting machine. But by 1959, Sudan's adoption of national income accounting created an international set of metrics against which it was possible to measure the performance of other states.[63]

[63] Cooper, "Modernizing Bureaucrats, Backward Africans and the Development Concept," pp. 64–93, and Speich, "Travelling with the GDP through Early Development Economics' History."

5

The Nation, in Whose Name They Could Act: The Military and National Income Accounting, 1958–1964

Shortly after Sudan's independence in 1956, Sudanese policy makers found themselves confronting a problem common to many developing countries, particularly those in Africa: how to meaningfully distribute the benefits of site-specific investments throughout a vast territory with a dispersed population.[1] After all, at independence policy makers in Khartoum were confronted with responsibility for governing what had previously been the largely autonomous regions of the Anglo-Egyptian Sudan as a united territory. The central triangle from Omdurman to Kosti and Sennar not only dominated the nation's politics but was also significantly richer than the rest of the country, with a per capita income of more than LS 100 compared with an income of significantly less than the national average of LS 30 in many parts of southern and western Sudan.[2] Yet despite the significant income inequality that plagued the newly independent Sudan, economic growth rather than equity became the dominant concern of financial policy makers in Khartoum.

It is tempting to frame the aims of development during the era of decolonization in Africa and Asia as being primarily about improving the living standards of each newly independent country's citizens following years of colonial neglect. However, to think of development in such terms is to ignore the new ability of policy makers to compare their state's performance against the performance of neighboring states and the competitive environment this created.[3] It was in this context that, during the years between 1956 and 1958, Sudanese politicians and policy makers became invested in the expansion of irrigated cotton

[1] W. Arthur Lewis, *Politics in West Africa* (Oxford: Oxford University Press, 1965).

[2] Daly *Darfur's Sorrow*, pp. 185–189.

[3] Spiech, "The Use of Global Abstractions," pp. 7–28; Sophus A. Reinert, *Translating Empire: Emulation and the Origins of Political Economy* (Cambridge, MA: Harvard University Press, 2011), p. 1.

production. They understood this approach to be the fastest and most secure means of increasing the income available to the government in order to build more robust institutions of the state, speeding the moment when Sudan developed state institutions that were comparable to those of its imagined peers.

The use of national income statistics to formulate investment plans based on future targets expanded the horizon for policy makers in which to estimate a potential return on investment; in the process it made potentially uncertain investments in irrigated cotton appear certain once again. Because national income accounting produced simple and quantifiable targets, finance officials and their political masters were tempted to use indicators such as the per capita growth rate as meaningful proxies for the success of government policies and the health of the wider economy. Healthy growth rates, however, blinded officials during the early 1960s to rising regional inequality and the stagnating or declining livelihoods of individual Sudanese citizens as a result of their government's policies, which emphasized investment over consumption.

Once policy makers began to evaluate economic policy on the basis of changes in per capita GDP over time, they became more acutely aware of the disparity between the wealth of the Sudanese state and that of other states. At the same time, this metric made policy makers less aware of the growing disparities in wealth within Sudan. Consequentially, the manner in which data were presented exacerbated the biases that policymakers already held, as it focused their attention on accelerating economic growth at the expense of inequality.

The Rise of Sudan's Ministry of Finance and Economics

Two impulses lay behind finance officials' decision to use changes in national income to judge the economic performance of the government after 1958. The first impetus was the evolution in the global practice of economic data gathering and reporting during the 1950s. This evolution was marked by the widespread adoption of practices like national income accounting and the calculation of per capita GDP.[4] The subsequent prominence in policy making of national income accounting after 1958 fit in not only with international norms but also, when made the centerpiece of the formulation of national development plans, it allowed policy makers to assert that immediate sacrifice would result in future gains over a longer time horizon.[5]

[4] Speich, "The Use of Global Abstractions." P. C. Okigbo *National Development Planning in Nigeria, 1900–92* (Oxford: James Currey, 1989).

[5] Beginning in 1947, the United Nations sought to create a system of national income accounts that could be standardized and deployed by all member states to further the project of international comparison. In 1953, these standards were finally enshrined in a manual, which could be followed by the statistical offices of various states. For a basic timeline of the development of national income accounts please see the website of the United Nations Bureau of Economic and Social Affairs, "Historic Versions of the System of National Accounts," (2012), http://unstats.un.org/unsd/nationalaccount/hsna.asp [accessed June 16, 2012]. The second reason for the spread

For Sudanese politicians and officials in the Ministry of Finance and Economics, the immediate push to transform the way in which financial decisions were calculated and presented was the increased fluctuation in the price of cotton. Before 1958, the primary means of evaluating an investment decision was its impact on the fiscal health of the state and its foreign exchange reserves. Whereas, national planning based on endpoints such as future rises in per capita income both created more abstract goals and extended the timeframe for reaching those goals. From 1954 until 1958, fluctuations in the price of cotton created doubt about Sudanese officials' budgetary projections, reopening the debate about the state's investment decisions. In particular, rising annual budget deficits allowed senior finance officials such as Hamza Mirghani Hamza, the Permanent Under-Secretary of Finance, to ask if it was prudent for the Sudanese government to gamble the state's financial future on the construction of the Managil Extension Scheme and the network of infrastructure necessary to support it. Hamza Mirghani Hamza's rivals within the Ministry such as Mamoun Beheiry and John Carmichael believed that because national income accounts attempted to tabulate the totality of economic activity within a particular economy, finance officials could use this data to model the future impact of investing in cotton cultivation on the economy as a whole, demonstrating how much growth would occur in the future as result of immediate sacrifices.[6] They hoped that by emphasizing the transformation of the Sudanese economy, which according to theory should enable the country to sustain a higher growth rate in the future, they would be able to marginalize the criticisms of Hamza Mirghani Hamza and the export pessimists who argued that investing in the infrastructure for increased cotton production would inevitably weaken the state's financial position.

The desire to marginalize the criticisms of deficit spending and large scale capital investment, owed itself to a commitment of a faction of Sudanese politicians and finance officials, who believed that demonstrating that capital-intensive investment over a short period of time could raise national living standards, despite a few years of sacrifice, would enable them to retain political support for their investment plans. During the 1950s, riots had repeatedly plagued the three cities of Khartoum, Khartoum North, and Omdurman as the various political parties jockeyed for power and protested the increased sacrifices

of national income accounting was that it became a necessity for membership in the United Nations, because the income of member countries had to be calculated so that individual member country dues could be determined. Studenski, *The Income of Nations*, pp. 152 and 155.

[6] Until 1958, finance officials used the simple formula of F = D–A to estimate shifts in the country's ability to retain capital savings. F was the total amount of foreign reserves within the country. D equaled the amount of foreign reserves that were present in government or private banking accounts, and A equaled the amount of money advanced from those accounts.

Memo. "Movements in the Sudan's Foreign Exchange Reserves in the Period 1952–1955 Leading to a General Review and Suggestions as to Future Policy," May 22, 1956, SAD G//S 1166/3/1/.

in individual consumption necessitated by an emphasis on savings and investment in increasing production in the cotton-growing sector.[7]

At independence, the political elite in Khartoum believed that the economic basis of the new state of Sudan could be agriculture, particularly the export of raw cotton. They expected the price of cotton to continue increasing as it had during the first half of the 1950s. However, once the the price of cotton began to level off in 1954 and then to decline in 1957, Sudanese officials were forced to search for new sources of revenue both for the state and the political parties that were rivaling one another for leadership. Beginning in 1954, Sudanese officials committed themselves to funding the expansion of state-managed irrigated cotton schemes. These schemes became a cornerstone of the country's national development efforts. The concentration of political and economic authority in Khartoum after the achievement of self-government in 1954 allowed the bureaucracy of the newly independent Sudan to decide how to spend the government's resources. The government decided to expand irrigation in the southwestern region of the Gezira Plain, planning an undertaking that became known as the Managil Agricultural Extension Scheme. Managil consumed most of the state's development budget from 1955 until its completion in 1962. The construction of the Roseires Dam, a major goal of which was to provide water to the additional land irrigated as part of the Managil Extension, was not completed until 1967. The government decided to prioritize Managil, even with its side effect of exacerbating existing regional inequality and despite fluctuations in the price of cotton and the negative impact of those fluctuations on the government's balance sheet: it made this decision based on faith in finance officials' ability to project the economic growth that this investment would eventually produce.

Within political circles in Khartoum, the decline in the price of cotton that occurred in 1957 was not a reason to turn to alternative types of development, such as the production of new cash crops like sisal, tobacco, tea, or even livestock. Instead, finance officials continued to believe that these crops would produce a subpar return on investment in comparison to exporting cotton. In addition, investments in new crops would have required a dramatic shift in the types of infrastructure investments that were supported by the state. A focus on upgrading Sudan's transportation infrastructure and improving the connection between the various peripheries of the country would have supplanted the current focus on building irrigation works in the most developed areas of the country. This policy change was rejected during the late 1950s and again during the early years of the 1960s, when planning according to national income targets became the norm in Khartoum.

The senior members of the Sudanese bureaucracy remained committed to their earlier policy decisions. This was despite the realization in 1957 by finance

[7] Al-Amin, *'Al-Fariq Ibrahim 'Abbud*, pp. 47–74.

officials that the decreases in the price of cotton would prevent the government from being able to finance from domestic sources alone the Managil Scheme on which its development agenda rested. A scapegoat was needed and was quickly found in the shape of the political parties, which were blamed for increasing spending on consumption that could have been spent on investment. One of the key justifications of the supporters of the military coup that occurred on November 18, 1958, was that the political leaders lacked the discipline necessary to develop the Managil Scheme and to hold off the frivolous demands emerging for investment in the periphery.

The senior officers in the military, who replaced the civilian government for the first time in November 1958, believed that economic growth, particularly within the region of the country spanning Omdurman to Kosti and Sennar, would create increased political and social stability in the core regions of the country and that stability in the periphery would follow, even if not immediately. The size of the cotton sector and its location in the most politically influential area of the country meant that, even with the application of new techniques of economic measurement, its success continued to represent the future of the Sudanese economy in the eyes of government officials in Khartoum.

At first glance, the shift in the way in which officials described, measured, and demonstrated the country's economic performance might appear to be unrelated to whether civilian politicians or military officers ruled in Khartoum. However, both were a response to the same problem. The declining and increasingly unstable price of cotton threatened the political and economic hegemony of the cotton elite, which had inherited political power as the British departed and had their investments in the central regions of Sudan. Their economic privilege was ensured by their ability to continually receive the majority of the state's investments.

Initially, finance officials were able to take for granted that the expansion of the Managil Extension Scheme would be in the interest of the state and Sudanese society at large. However, demand shifts and volatile cotton prices combined to create doubts about the wisdom of the government's investment decisions, therefore necessitating greater clarity about whether the state's policies actually benefited Sudanese society. The introduction of national income accounting and a focus on the growth rate were both attempts by state officials to *justify* their policies to increasingly restless constituencies. Between 1946 and 1964, finance officials went from being government auditors to the articulators of plans against which the government's legitimacy was measured. They did this by transforming a fragmentary and disjointed Anglo-Egyptian Sudan into a national economy. Finance officials began by asserting that they had the authority to coordinate the planning process for the entirety of Sudan without deference to the prerogatives of local or imperial actors. In the process of evaluating individual projects for inclusion in the five-year plans that finance officials designed, they transformed the meaning of development in Sudan. Development projects that emphasized the protection of distinct populations were deemphasized in favor of those that benefited the territory of Sudan as a whole. Finance officials calculated the benefit of various projects to the territory of Sudan by projecting their impact on the central budget. While finance officials developed an evaluative framework for their own use, which determined the viability of projects and their suitability for funding by measuring their impact on the central budget, it was not until the production of national income accounts in 1959 that a unified Sudanese economy was institutionalized.

The military buttressed its legitimacy by claiming that it was putting fiscally responsible technocrats in power in place of feckless civilian politicians. Military leaders made use of new tools such as national income accounting to proclaim that their regime was accountable. In the *Ten Year Plan of Economic and Social Development 1961/62–1970/71*, finance officials articulated clear and measurable goals, with the expectation that if these goals were met, the regime would be rewarded for its sound economic stewardship. Instead, despite raising the growth rate, completing the Managil Extension, and making sustained progress on the Roseires Dam, the military regime was greeted with angry crowds in the streets of Khartoum in October 1964. The October Revolution had begun, and the military had lost its mandate to rule. The senior army officers in Khartoum surrendered in stunned disbelief to the crowds in the capital, in part because they had always assumed that unrest would only occur in the economically marginalized peripheral regions of the country. They had already begun a pacification campaign in the south and were prepared to sustain it. Finance officials and their military overlords believed that economic growth would assure their legitimacy in the wealthiest parts of the country and therefore were largely silent when it did not.

National Income Accounting and the *Ten Year Plan of Economic and Social Development, 1961/62–1970/71*

From the time of its coup in 1958, the military government was committed to the new model of national planning. The major innovation under the military was the introduction of national income estimates. Aside from questions about bureaucratic capacity, the principal complaint of planners had been that they were unable to devise an appropriate means of measuring, evaluating, and calibrating the impact of the government's economic policies. National income accounts addressed that complaint by making the wealth of various nations comparable across time; they allowed political leaders to demonstrate with hard figures how successful their policies were. The publication of economic growth statistics effectively became an annual referendum on the political leadership of the country. Depending on the calculations undertaken, economists and statisticians claimed that the resulting figures could be used to understand economic productivity and the manner in which a society's economic welfare was distributed, as well as to highlight how the different units of the economy and society fit together.[8] Another feature of the national income accounts and the plans constructed based on them was their collective nature: economics professor Paul Studenski emphasized that "the concept of national income is social in nature and differs fundamentally from the private concepts of individual, family, or group incomes."[9] The implication was that national income accounting gave the authors and the policy makers who depended on these accounts a new social object – the nation – in whose name they could act. It was the ability of military leaders to claim that they were acting in the name of the nation that justified the abrogation of the electoral system, which was premised on aggregating individual preferences.

The national income statistics that finance officials produced were aggregates, numbers that described the average and the norm, rather than the individual experience. While national income accounts in theory were composed of three separate calculations that needed to match, in Sudan as in many developing countries only two calculations were made. The first calculation is often referred to as the "output method," and the second technique is called the "expenditure method."[10] The output method was a tabulation of the value of all of the goods and services produced in a given economy, while the expenditure method calculated the total amount of money spent on goods and services. Finance officials used both calculations to estimate the total income of the economy, because output, expenditure, and income should all be equal in a given economy. The major innovation undergirding national income accounting was imagining that the income of a whole society could be accounted for using bookkeeping in a similar fashion to how a single business balances its books.[11] Even as the general formulas for calculating national income became increasingly standardized, the intrusion of politics was clearest in "deciding which receipts of money or of goods and services to include in the concept and computation of national income and which to exclude." The estimator was inevitably forced to rely on arbitrary "escapes from theoretical and practical difficulties," accounting challenges that were compounded by theoretical questions about which activities qualified as economic and which activities should properly be considered non-economic and therefore uncountable.[12] Decisions about what to count and how to count directly affected how finance officials and the public evaluated economic policy, especially the economic plans crafted by the military. For instance, when Sudanese historian Al-Amin 'Abd-Rahman points to the positive aspects of the 'Abboud regime, he emphasizes 'Abboud's

8 Studenski, *The Income of Nations*; Mitchell, *Rule of Experts*.

9 Studenski, *The Income of Nations*, p. 165.

10 Department of Statistics (HQ Council of Ministers), *National Income of Sudan (in Brief). 1955/56. Occasional Statistical Paper No. 2.* (Khartoum, Sudan. 1959).

11 Andre Vanoli, *A History of National Accounting* (Amsterdam: IOS Press, 2005).

12 Studenski, *The Income of Nations*, p. 166.

success in increasing the growth rate, assuming that the lives of ordinary people became easier as a result.[13]

It was in the context of an improving economy that work on a comprehensive development plan for Sudan began to bear fruit.[14] These efforts were coordinated by 'Abd al-Rahim Mirghani, deputy permanent under-secretary within the Ministry of Finance. The economic council headed by the president of the Supreme Council for the Armed Forces, and including the prime minister and key cabinet members, determined policy. Policy proposals were designed by the development committee, a submittee of the Supreme Council, which was composed of the senior civil servants from the different ministries. The earlier efforts at development planning were to enumerate desirable capital projects with their estimated price tags, which were then compared with a series of projections about the amount of revenue that the government would be capable of raising over a defined period of time.[15]

The new 1961 development plan included a macroeconomic framework within which the plan's proposals were situated and against which their impact was estimated.[16] The primary innovation in this iteration of planning was that all of the various proposals developed by government departments and units were "subsequently embodied in a uniform set of summaries and schedules, showing the aims of each proposal, the required investment amount and its phasing, its contribution to the national income, its effects on the balance of payments [and] administrative requirements."[17] A special World Bank Mission and Dr. W. H. Singer, the Special Advisor to the Under Secretary for Economic and Social Affairs of the United Nations, travelled to Sudan and evaluated the macroeconomic framework developed by the Economic Planning Unit inside the Ministry of Finance to ensure that the plan met emerging international norms. The aim of the plan was to ensure that Sudan's economy "not only expand[ed] at an accelerated rate but…at the same time reach[ed] the stage of self-sustaining growth."[18]

[13] Al-Amin, *Al-Fariq Ibrahim 'Abbud wa 'Asruhu al-Dhahabi.*

[14] Economic Planning Secretariat, Ministry of Finance and Economics, *The Ten Year Plan of Economic and Social Development, 1961/62–1970/71* (Khartoum, Sudan: Government Printing Press, 1962), p. 1.

[15] A. R. Mirghani, *Development Planning in the Sudan in the Sixties* (Khartoum: University of Khartoum Press, 1983), p. 10.

[16] The macroeconomic framework included a new iteration of the national income accounts prepared by the Department of Statistics that specifically focused on producing data about capital formation, the output of manufacturing, and capital-output ratios. A study about the structure of the Sudanese economy was also undertaken, papers were written focusing on the building and construction potential of the government machinery and the availability of skilled labor. The principal Sudanese officials working on these studies within the Ministry of Finance were 'Abd al-Rahim Mirghani and Mohammed Khogali. Letter, Abdel Rahim Mirghani to Arie Kruithof, IBRD, October 16, 1961, "Sudan Railway Project – Negotiation 01," Box # 172012B.

[17] *The Ten Year Plan of Economic and Social Development*, p. 1.

[18] Abdel Rahim Mirghani, "Introduction," *The Ten Year Plan of Economic and Social Development*, p. 2.

The publication in March 1959 of *The National Income of Sudan: 1955/56*, Sudan's first series of national income accounts, allowed the military government to equate economic success with political legitimacy. C. H. Harvie and J. G. Kleve were the senior officials within the Department of Statistics in Sudan. They oversaw publication of the National Income Accounts with the help of eleven Sudanese assistants.[19] The Sudanese national income survey followed those carried out in Nigeria and Tanganyika, and many of those surveys' assumptions were held up as lessons for the Sudanese case.[20] Technical advice about how to shape government budgets and accounts for national income accounting came from several United Nations publications, including *Budget Management* and *A Manual for the Economic and Functional Classification of Government Transactions*.[21]

In his introduction to the ten-year plan, Minister of Finance and Economics Ibrahim Ahmed, speaking in the name of the military revolutionary council, stated, "Amongst the most important targets that the blessed Revolutionary Government pursued and is still pursuing is the improvement of the standard of living of the citizens through the development of the resources of the Country." The metric of success was per capita income growth.[22] Previous plans had been collections of public sector capital investments, without a clear estimation of the effects of capital spending on "over-all magnitudes like national income, balance of payments, government revenues, employment, etc."[23] This plan was to be comprehensive. Ahmed defined comprehensive planning as follows:

> Comprehensive economic planning is basically a scientific study of the circumstances and problems that hinder the progress of society, and assessing the natural and human resources available, and drawing out the right projects which aim at changing those circumstances and dealing with these problems in the light of the available resources. It is therefore a process of defining and knowing the problems and resources of society and the best use and effective mobilization of these resources to achieve a stage of progress accepted by society as a target to be achieved in a certain period of time.[24]

According to Ahmed comprehensive planning attempted not simply to establish a schedule of capital spending but also to measure the impact of investment decisions.

[19] C. H. Harvie and J. G. Kleve, *The National Income of Sudan 1955/56* (Department of Statistics, Khartoum: March 1959), p. 1.

[20] Morgan, "Seeking Parts, Looking for Wholes," and A. R. Prest and I. G. Stewart, *The National Income of Nigeria, 1950–1951* (London: H. M. Stationery Office, 1953).

[21] United Nations, Department of Economic and Social Affairs, *A Manual for the Economic and Functional Classification of Government Transactions* (New York: United Nations, 1958).

[22] "Broadcast statement by the Minister of Finance and Economics on the Occasion of the Presentation of the Ten Year Plan of Economic and Social Development 1961/62–1970/71." *The Ten Year Plan of Economic and Social Development*, p. 3.

[23] Memo, R. N. Poduval, "Sudan's Ten Year Plan of Economic and Social Development," United Arab Republic, The Institute of National Planning, Memo. No. 333, May 29, 1963, (Cairo, Egypt), 2.

[24] "Broadcast statement by the Minister of Finance," pp. 4–5.

Internationally, many economic experts argued that what was required for economic development was an increase in the accumulated capital base of a particular country. Therefore economists and other policy makers focused on "the ratio of 'required' investment to desired growth." As noted by the economist Easterly, the formula was as follows: a country that wanted to develop had to go from an investment rate of 4 percent of GDP to 12–15 percent of GDP. Investment had to keep ahead of population growth.[25]

This ratio made it possible to make hypothetical calculations along the following lines. If a country pushed its rate of investment up to 12 percent of GDP, it could increase its GDP by perhaps 3 percent per year. Assuming population growth of 2 percent per year, it could achieve a per capita growth rate of roughly 1 percent per year. Sudanese policy makers chose to set an ambitious target of growing the capital-intensive sections of their economy by 3 percent during the first years of the 1960s, which meant that they would have to find adequate inflows of capital.[26] However, there was a widespread belief in the international community that poor countries could not achieve such high rates of investment from their own savings alone and therefore would need not only to suppress domestic consumption but also to turn to foreign aid.[27] It was the failure of the parliamentary system to create a political climate in which either of these objectives appeared possible that paved the way for and legitimated the military coup.

The ten-year plan projected that per capita income would rise from LS 28–30 to LS 65 by the end of the plan period. This would allow Sudan to surpass the per capita income of Morocco and Tunisia and bring it into the range of such countries as Turkey. The projected figures also demonstrated that the wealth divide within the country would remain quite large, with some regions, particularly western and southern Sudan, considerably below the LS 28–30 per capita income range, even at the end of the plan.[28] Other areas of the country, particularly the area within the triangle formed by Omdurman–Kosti–Sennar (including the three towns of Omdurman, Khartoum, and Khartoum North) as

25 W. Easterly, "The Ghost of Financing Gap: How the Harrod-Domar Growth Model Still Haunts Development Economics," Policy Research Working Paper 1807 (Washington, DC: World Bank Development Research Group, 1997).

26 Mirghani, *Development Planning in the Sudan in the Sixties*, p. 29.

27 Easterly, "The Ghost of Financing Gap."

28 Another feature of the national income accounts was the inclusion of Sudan on a United Nations list of countries ordered by each country's per capita income. Of the fifteen countries listed the United States ranked at the top and Tanganyika at the bottom. Using numbers for 1956, the United States had a per capita income of LS 717, while using 1954 data Tanganyika had a per capita income of LS 17. Sudan was calculated to have the same income per person as Kenya, LS 27, and to have an income higher than that of Pakistan, India, and Nigeria, in addition to Tanganyika. However, the income of the Sudanese was significantly lower than that of the Egyptians, who had a per capita income of LS 40 calculated in 1956, and significantly below the per capita income of the Union of South Africa and the European countries. Department of Statistics, *National Income of Sudan (In Brief)*, p. 9.

well as the Gezira district, had much higher per capita incomes. This was the area of maximum state investment because of schemes such as Gezira and Managil, and its residents already enjoyed incomes above that of Turkey, in the range of LS 65–75 per capita.[29] It was expected that by the end of the plan period, the per capita of this triangle could reach levels as high as LS 110, much higher than the projected national per capita GDP of LS 37. This would be "very high by African standards and probably sufficiently high to sustain self-generating growth."[30] Unequal growth was justified by the assumption that if one continued to invest in the most capital-intensive parts of the economy, growth there would eventually propel growth in other portions of the economy through savings:

> For although at first sight the "imbalance" in the economy between the modern part and the traditional part might be criticized, particularly in respect of the difference in per capita incomes, the Plan in fact turns this imbalance to advantage by using the resulting higher rate of domestic savings in the modern sector to develop both parts of the economy.[31]

It was also estimated that during the life of the plan, the proportion of the population of Sudan involved in the modern sector of the economy would rise from one-quarter to possibly one-third. As the modern sector of the economy grew, finance officials expected that the profits derived from it would be available to fund the development of other parts of the economy, creating a virtuous cycle and leading to a higher national income overall.[32] For the planners, the development strategy would essentially realize a "big push" to propel the most economically advanced sectors and regions of the economy forward.[33] The "big push" did not aim for economic equitability and stability, but rather to maximize growth at the national level.

The objective of the plan was to transform a poor economy with these attributes – a low national income; a total dependence on cotton; idle manpower in the south, east, and west of the country; little skilled manpower; unknown resources; and a rudimentary industrial base – into a growing and increasingly wealthy economy. Planners wanted the population to make the transition from the traditional sector of the economy toward the modern sector of the economy. They also aimed to diversify the economy. However, noticeably missing from Sudanese diversification plans were theories of import substitution based on heavy industrialization. Instead planners intended for industrialization initially to be confined to processes that were complementary

29 *The Ten Year Plan of Economic and Social Development*, p. 40.

30 Federation of British Industries, *Assessment of Sudan's Ten Year Plan* (London: FBI, 1963), p. 4.

31 *The Ten Year Plan of Economic and Social Development*, p. 40.

32 Ibid., pp. 43–44.

33 Poduval, "Sudan's Ten Year Plan," p. 2. For more on the history of the "big push" idea, see H. W. Arndt, *Economic Development: The History of an Idea* (Chicago: University of Chicago Press, 1987), p. 58.

to the agricultural sector, such as the light processing of agricultural goods. A major component of reducing imports was also agricultural diversification, because, while it was mostly self-sufficient in the production of foodstuffs, Sudan imported large amounts of tea, coffee, sugar, and wheat.[34] Finance officials such as Mamoun Beheiry and John Carmichael assumed that for the foreseeable future Sudan would remain an agricultural-exporting economy.[35] Unlike many developing countries, Sudan's policy makers recognized the limitations of their domestic market and never intended to shift the basis of the economy from agriculture to manufacturing. Rather, the government hoped to produce more agricultural products for domestic consumption and at the same time increase agricultural exports in order to fund greater quantities of imports.[36] Planners thought the most promising path toward import substitution was agricultural diversification into such commodities as coffee, rice, and sugar, thereby decreasing the need to import these products.[37]

The Limitations of the Ten-Year Plan

The publication of a national census and the country's first national income survey in 1959 allowed Sudanese finance officials for the first time to evaluate their economic policies according to their impact on the country's national income.[38] In 1962 the *Ten Year Plan of Economic and Social Development* became the first planning document to officially state that increasing the country's national income was the goal of state policy. Therefore, raising the growth rate became the prime indicator of policy success.[39] For the first time, Sudanese policy makers would attempt to tabulate the impact of government spending on economic activity, and not simply the impact of individual enterprises on the government's balance sheet. The success of economic policy, specifically the large-scale investment in cotton cultivation, would now be evaluated by the extent to which this investment increased national income. The goal was to allow government policy makers to demonstrate how their investment decisions, and in particular the concentration of the countries' resources into a few projects, benefited the nation's welfare and not simply a few narrowly defined interests.

Despite the fact that the vast majority of capital expenditure was allocated to a small number of projects located in the central region of Sudan, finance officials presented the plan to the public through radio broadcasts and speeches as an initiative that would benefit the entire country. Officials even acknowledged that the focus would remain on "a wedge-shaped fertile clay plain…situated

[34] Federation of British Industries, *Assessment of Sudan's Ten Year Plan*, p. 2.
[35] "Broadcast statement by the Minister of Finance," p. 6.
[36] Federation of British Industries, *Assessment of Sudan's Ten Year Plan*, pp. 2–3.
[37] *The Ten Year Plan of Economic and Social Development*, p. 29.
[38] Harvie and Kleve, *The National Income of Sudan 1955/56*.
[39] *The Ten Year Plan of Economic and Social Development*.

in the center of the country and ... widening towards the East."[40] The plan did comprise more than 260 individual projects, including coffee schemes in Equatoria and experiments with rice cultivation in Bahr el-Ghazal.[41] Yet aside from generic statements about how the plan "paid attention to the development of backward areas in all parts of the country especially the South," it denied funding to major projects in the western, eastern, and southern regions of Sudan.[42] Although coffee and rice cultivation could play vital roles in import substitution, as late as the 1964–65 budget, money had only been allocated for surveying potential coffee estates in Equatoria and establishing a pilot scheme for rice production in Bahr el-Ghazal.[43] The decision to minimize funding for economic development and social services in southern Sudan would have dramatic consequences, because it increased the alienation of southern communities from the state, even as military conflict was escalating in the south as a response to demands for political autonomy.

The resistance to shifting scarce capital from the expansion of the major preexisting agricultural schemes toward expanding the transportation network further demonstrated the extent to which a limited number of cotton schemes in central Sudan represented the national economy in the imaginations of the Sudanese political elite. Sudanese policymakers continued to debate the merits and challenges of either attempts to integrate additional regions of Sudan into the existing export economy or of rapidly increasing the export potential of the major irrigated schemes. From a purely accounting perspective, increased investment in transportation was considered financially unsound. In a sparsely populated country, an adequate transportation network was judged to be an unaffordable luxury. However, without affordable transportation the expansion of agricultural production into new regions was unprofitable, and

[40] Ibid., p. 10. "Although the arable land in Sudan is estimated at about 100 million acres, only slightly over 7 million acres are cropped. The most developed land agriculturally is the fertile, central clay plains growing practically all cotton. To the west of this, is the 'quoz' area in Kordofan and Darfur provinces where gum arabic and oilseed crops are grown; to the east, are flooded silt plains of Gash and Tokar Deltas, irrigated by seasonal streams, sowing principally cotton and dura (sorghum). The southwest region, chiefly the Equatoria Province, in the tropical rainfall belt, has laterite soil, viable for various tropical crops. In the arid and semi-arid areas in the north, cultivation is confined to the Nile Basin with a uniform cropping pattern consisting of a mixture of food and cash crops." Ibid., p. 27.

[41] Ibid.

[42] Work would not proceed on the Khartoum–Port Sudan Road, the Regeneration of Suakin, the extension of the railway line from Wau to Juba, the exploitation of the Jebel Marra Lands, and the extension of a railway from Nyala to Geneina. Several smaller industrial projects were also not funded.

"Broadcast statement by the Minister of Finance," pp. 8–9.

[43] Similarly, very little work outside of surveying and visits by experts proceeded in Jebel Marra, despite the discovery of water in good quantities. *The Ten Year Plan of Economic and Social Development*, p. 29: "The Ten Year Plan of Economic and Social Development 1961/62–1970/71: Explanatory Memorandum on 1964/65 Development Budgets" (July 1, 1964–June 30, 1965)," pp. 5–31.

therefore the development of new regions of the country could not proceed without loss-making investments.[44] In fact, IBRD officials highlighted the inadequacy of the Sudanese transportation network as "a bottleneck in the development of Sudan."[45] At the same time, the IBRD's transportation analysts were skeptical about the financial feasibility of extending the network to new regions of Sudan.[46] The rationale for ignoring development of the economic peripheries within Sudan came from planners' acceptance of the division of the economy into a modern and a traditional sector. They assumed that the traditional sectors of the economy would eventually wither away to be replaced by the modern sectors of the economy. Indeed, statistics reported between 1956 and 1961 demonstrated that the modern sector grew twice as fast as the traditional sector, which seemed to confirm their expectations.[47]

However, the statisticians tasked with using national income accounts to measure economic performance were relying on a limited set of data. They had good access to data about commodities produced for export, because of the relative ease of acquiring those statistics. The overrepresentation of cotton production in general economic statistics encouraged Sudanese officials to overestimate the extent to which the Omdurman–Kosti–Sennar triangle was the engine of the national economy. However, officials made very little effort to collect data about the subsistence sections of the economy, which they termed the traditional sector, and which they estimated to account for as much as 36 percent of the country's GDP, though formally finance officials did factor this sector into their calculations.[48] They also estimated that more than half of the country's national income was tied up in the traditional sectors of the economy.

The line between the traditional (or domestic) sector of the economy and the modern (export) sector was unclear for several reasons. On even the most capital-intensive agricultural schemes, such as Gezira and the Managil Extension Schemes, farmers devoted a significant amount of their labor and capital to producing grains for subsistence. Conversely, the cultivators of groundnuts and gum arabic in the western regions of Sudan were often not considered to

44 *The Ten Year Plan of Economic and Social Development*, p. 99.

45 Memo, Mr. Burney to Files. "Sudan – General Negotiations," January 29, 1963, WBG "Sudan Railway Project – Negotiations 01," Box # 172012B.

46 Letter, Cecil Hutson to J. A. McCunniffe, October 3, 1960, WBG "Sudan – Expansion of Railways and Water Transport Facilities Project – Administration 03," No. 1741655, Box # 172007B.

47 *The Ten Year Plan of Economic and Social Development*, p. 13.

48 In Sudan, subsistence agricultural production was included in the calculation of per capita income. These prices were figured by deriving the sum at which agricultural products were sold directly from the farm without including marketing and transportation costs. Statistics on subsistence farming were biased toward figures that documented the production of tenants on the major exporting estates, who were allowed to use part of the land to produce foodstuffs that were often also sold in the market. The farm gate value is typically lower than the retail price that consumers pay, because it does not include costs for shipping, handling, storage, marketing, and profit margins of the involved companies. Department of Statistics, *National Income of Sudan (In Brief)*, p. 9.

be part of the modern economy, because they employed "traditional" methods of production, even though both crops were highly profitable and sold to international buyers. Because planners did not consider these to be modern sectors of the economy, they did not invest state resources in improving the small-scale production of such cash crops as grains, gum arabic, or groundnuts. 'Abd al-Rahim Mirghani, citing his own and his colleagues' reading of Dudley Seers' ideas about "uneven development," believed that capital, labor, and land should be steered toward the modern sectors where their productivity could be raised.[49]

The Financial Strain

The vulnerability of the Sudanese economy was evident. The development expenditures programmed within the *The Ten Year Plan of Economic and Social Development* required an additional LS 95 million in loans from abroad, and the LS 56 million already received required interest payments of 5 percent over the next fifteen years. The plan's chief architect, 'Abd al-Rahim Mirghani, expected the burden on the Sudanese economy to be massive. He hoped that the industrialized countries would be lenient in the terms of their loans.[50] One key issue was whether the capital spending that the government was embarking on would produce self-sustaining growth. A second critical question was whether concentrating the bulk of the state's investments in a few development schemes would pay off and yield returns that could be distributed in a sustainable manner. This was particularly important because projections of government revenue during the plan period did not call for taxation to play a major role in raising state revenue.[51]

Despite these concerns, by the 1964/65 fiscal year, four phases of the Managil Extension Schemes had been completed, providing substantially increased export capacity. However, the majority of work on the Roseires Dam was yet to be completed. The foreign currency component of the dam project totaled LS 17,722,841, principally financed by loans secured from the IBRD, the International Development Association, and the Federal Republic of Germany. The cost of constructing the dam continued to rise, as did the cost of completing the Khashm el-Girba Dam.[52] Despite the increased cost of these projects, the 1963 IRBD Mission to Sudan concluded, "The Development plan

49 Mirghani, *Development Planning in the Sudan in the Sixties*, pp. 28–31.

50 "As you know it is now generally recognized and accepted by the industrialized countries that the needs of the underdeveloped countries for capital to finance their development plan should be met by a major part by soft loans otherwise the success of their developmental effects will be endangered." Letter, Abdel Rahim Mirghani to Sayyid Mohammed Hamad el Nil, "Second Sugar Factory at Kashm el Girba," November 15, 1962, WBG "Sudan – Expansion of Railways and Water Transport Facilities Project, Administration 04," Box # 172007B.

51 Poduval, "Sudan's Ten Year Plan," p. 3.

52 "The Ten Year Plan of Economic and Social Development 1961/62–1970/71: Explanatory Memorandum on 1964/65 Development Budgets," pp. 33–35.

was realistic...and that the proposed sale of investment would be within the capacity of the country, provided it could obtain suitable aid from abroad."[53]

The objectives of the ten-year plan were not expected to resolve Sudan's foreign exchange vulnerability in the short term. In fact, experts expected that the programs included within the plan would magnify existing problems. The formulators of the plan understood that Sudan would incur a deficit in its balance of payments, which would require new capital inflows of upward of LS 150 million.[54] One attempt to reduce this deficit was to devote domestic foreign exchange reserves exclusively to the problem of managing short-term fluctuations in the international commodity markets.[55] Heavy capital spending on development projects, the need to service foreign loans, and lower than expected income from exports all meant that there was heavy pressure to reduce other government expenditures on items such as social services and employment.

Reasons for the Failure of the Plan and the Fall of the 'Abboud Regime

By November 1963, the Sudan IBRD Consultative Group, composed of the principal Western creditors to the country, began to express concerns about the country's ability to fund the implementation of its development plan.[56] Sudan had a relatively modest deficit in its balance of payments in 1963 after a poor cotton harvest in 1962.[57] The Sudan IBRD Consultative Group was concerned that the government would be unable to control its spending, and it also identified the concentration of development programs in the central region of the country as a concern. However, the group praised Sudanese officials for their willingness to emphasize commodity-producing projects over social investments.[58]

Predictably the optimistic forecast of cotton harvests on which the plan was based did not materialize, and by January 1964 the Republic of Sudan was forced to return to international lenders, seeking additional loans to fund its

53 Note from Sir D. Ormsby Gore, "Inward Saving Telegram from Washington to FO: IBRD – Sudan," July 27, 1963, TNA FO 371/172364.

54 Poduval, "Sudan's Ten Year Plan," p. 2.

55 *The Ten Year Plan of Economic and Social Development*, p. 46.

56 The Consultative Group was chaired by the IBRD and comprised representatives from the Washington embassies of Belgium, France, Germany, Italy, Japan, Netherlands, Switzerland, and the United Kingdom, as well as from the US State Department and USAID. Letter from Washington, Sir D. Ormsby Gore to FO, "Addressed to FO Telegram No. Eager 232 Saving of November 29: Sudan IBRD Consultative Group," TNA FO 371/172364.

57 "The Sudan's total imports in 1962 were LS 89 million and total exports LS 79 million, of which LS 48.5 million were cotton and cotton seed. This deficit on the visible balance of payments is modest, bearing in mind the development of the Plan and the amounts of foreign aid available." Federation of British Industries, *Assessment of Sudan's Ten Year Plan*, p. 3.

58 Letter from Washington, Sir D. Ormsby Gore to FO, "Addressed to FO Telegram No. Eager 232 Saving of November 29."

development program.[59] In the beginning of February 1964, 'Abd al-Rahim Mirghani traveled to Washington to explain the difficulties that Sudan was having carrying out the *Ten Year Plan*; although he was greeted by sympathetic audiences, he received little new support.[60] To increase its legitimacy internationally and domestically, the Abboud regime in November 1963 had formed the Central Council, an advisory board of civilian experts, to augment the Supreme Council of the Armed Forces as it made executive decisions. By April 1964, however, the Abboud regime was facing increased criticism about its economic stewardship, often from members of its new civilian council.[61] A major complaint raised by the government's critics was that the Khashm el-Girba scheme was significantly over budget, while at the same time Egypt was delaying its payment of the compensation it had promised Sudan for the flooding of Wadi Halfa.[62] The government tried to account for unexpected expenses by raising taxes on tenant farmers, such as those in the Tokar Delta.[63] The Ministries of Defense, Interior, and Information, which were favored by the governing army officers, consistently exceeded their budgets. Criticisms of the government were further fueled by political tensions in southern Sudan, where the decision to cease investing in local economic and social projects exacerbated the ongoing conflict between the periphery and the core regions of the country. Open warfare broke out in the southern region during the early 1960s.[64] However, the immediate concern was not simply the generation of budget surpluses, but finding more foreign exchange for the state to devote to accelerating its development plans.[65] Still, the military regime often won praise from foreign investors for ensuring political stability and for its ability to produce consistent budget surpluses.[66]

A superficial analysis of aggregate economic indicators such as the GDP made the 'Abboud regime's economic stewardship appear modestly successful.

59 Memo. M. A. Burney to Hendrik Van Helden, "Sudan Loan Application for the SR." January 27, 1964. WBG "Sudan – Railway Project – Negotiations 01," Box # 172012B.

60 Letter, Pierre L. Moussa to Mamoun Beheiry, February 27, 1964, WBG "Sudan – Expansion of Railways and Water Transport Facilities Project – Administration 04," Box # 172007B.

61 Bechtold, *Politics in the Sudan*, p. 205.

62 The Sudanese market had become a dumping ground for Egyptian manufactured goods, which were having a difficult time finding alternative markets. Egypt was in need of IMF stabilization funds in 1964 to meet some of its external debts. Memo from Commercial Department, British Embassy in Khartoum, July 4, 1964, TNA FO 371/178613; Letter from A. D. Parsons to P. H. Laurence, April 14, 1964, TNA FO 371/178613; Letter from M. P. V. Hannam to R. W. Munro, July 24, 1964, TNA FO 371/178613.

63 The rate of withdrawal was raised from 5% to 10% for tenants in the Tokar Delta.
Memo, Department of Finance and Economics, "Decision of the Council of Ministers, the 456 Meeting," June 21, 1964, NRO Finance 3-A/28/6/22/.

64 Hasan, "The Sudanese Revolution of October 1964," p. 504.

65 Note, Maurice Bart to Mr. G. Stewart Mason, August 25, 1964, WBG "Sudan – Second Railway Project – Negotiations 02," Box # 172012B.

66 Federation of British Industries, *Assessment of Sudan's Ten Year Plan*, p. 23.

During the first five years of the *Ten Year Plan*, Sudan's GDP increased 20 percent. Excusing the steep economic decline associated with the collapse in the Sudanese economy in 1957–1958, however, the economy scarcely grew any faster during the first years of the plan than it had during the previous years of civilian rule. However, during the second half of the plan period (1965–1971), after the military had been removed from power, Sudan's GDP expanded by 30 percent.[67] By 1965, the military had given way to a transitional civilian government, which came to power following the revolution of October 1964. The new government was formed by the National Front for Professionals and made up of members willing to pursue new social and economic policies. However by April of the following year, the traditional parties such as the Umma and NUP had resumed control of the government, and they had begun to carry out economic policies that were in general alignment with the *Ten Year Plan*.[68] Therefore, the resulting acceleration in the growth rate can be attributed in part to the framework developed by the planners.[69]

Yet this raises the question of why the military regime fell. Bechtold writes that it occurred "surely not because of economic pressures, for the slight drop in foreign exchange reserves affected very few people at the time, and whatever inconvenience resulted was definitely outweighed by the considerable rise in the standard of living since 1958...Economically, [the Supreme Council of the Armed Forces] performed with considerable efficiency; politically, increasing ineffectiveness marked its tenure."[70] One possible explanation for the military regime's downfall can be found by examining the outbreak of violence on October 21, 1964, at the University of Khartoum. It followed a meeting about the government's failed strategy in the South. Recognition among large segments of the Khartoum elite that the military government's strategy of politically and economically marginalizing the periphery was a failed strategy precipitated the end of the 'Abboud regime.[71] The drive for increased economic growth favored the concentration of development in a few defined areas, but such concentration did very little to address questions of regional equity. Therefore, even as economic growth resumed, political unrest continued to fester.

As fighting escalated between the central government and an increasingly complex group of separatist movements in southern Sudan in 1963, the distrust and unfamiliarity that marked relations between the Arabized elite in Khartoum and the largely mission-educated African elites of southern Sudan

[67] Tim Niblock, "Table A.10: Composition of GDP by Economic Sectors, 1955/56–1973/74," in *Class and Power in Sudan*, p. 356.

[68] Ibid., pp. 226–229; Daly, *Darfur's Sorrow*, p. 189.

[69] Daly *Darfur's Sorrow*, pp. 185–189.

[70] Bechtold *Politics in the Sudan*, pp. 213, 202.

[71] Mahgoub, *Democracy on Trial*, pp. 188–192. For a detailed account of the resistance to the 'Abboud regime and the events of October 1964, see Hasan, "The Sudanese Revolution of October 1964," pp. 491–509.

were exacerbated. At the 1965 Khartoum Conference on the Southern Sudan, Aggrey Jaden, the president of the Sudan African National Union, proclaimed,

> The Sudan falls sharply into two distinct areas, both in geographical areas, ethnic groups, and cultural systems. The Northern Sudan is occupied by a hybrid Arab race who are united by their common language, common culture, and common religion; and they look to the Arab world for their cultural and political inspiration. The people of the Southern Sudan, on the other hand, belong to the African ethnic group of East Africa...There is nothing in common between the various sections of the community; no body of shared beliefs, no identity of interests, no local signs of unity and above all, the Sudan has failed to compose a single community.[72]

When Aggrey made this statement in the mid-1960s, it was clear to many northern and southern Sudanese people that the attempt to suppress issues of regional and local identity in the name of national economic development had hopelessly failed. Noted member of the Muslim Brotherhood and lecturer in the Faculty of Law at the University of Khartoum, Dr. Hasan al-Turabi, at a forum on September 9, 1964, argued that the "southern question" could never be solved without addressing issues surrounding Sudan's democracy and centralization. Turabi challenged the legitimacy of the military regime, and after a series of public meetings at the University of Khartoum, the military attempted to reassert its authority. The conflagration that ensued on October 21 eventually led to the overthrow of the government.[73] By April 1965, the United Front, dominated by the Umma and the NUP, had come to power. These two parties continued many of the economic policies of the 'Abboud regime, as well as its civil war in the three southern provinces of Sudan.[74]

In the Sudanese case, national income accounting decreased the visibility of regional inequality and therefore reinforced a tendency of the governments in Khartoum to invest capital in a manner that exacerbated regional inequality rather than alleviating it.[75] The presentation of economic data made it easy for finance officials and military leaders to believe that policies that accelerated the growth rate strengthened the county as a whole. However, the growth rate was not the principal way in which the population judged their well-being. Therefore, despite increasing the growth rate during the 1960s, officials encountered mounting political and social discontent. In 1964, this escalating discontent led to severe riots in Khartoum and the subsequent fall of the military regime.

72 Khartoum Conference on the South, March 1965 documents; speech by Aggrey Jaden (mimeo.), p. 4, cited in George W. Shepherd Jr., "National Integration and the Southern Sudan," *Journal of Modern African Studies* 4:2 (October 1966): 195.

73 Hasan, "The Sudanese Revolution of October 1964," p. 505.

74 Thomas E. Nyquist, "The Sudan: Prelude to Elections," *Middle East Journal* 19:3 (Summer, 1965): 263–272.

75 Simon Mollan, "Business, State and Economy: Cotton and the Anglo-Egyptian Sudan, 1919–1939." *African Economic History* 36 (2008): 95–123.

In theory, reframing the aim of government policy away from particularistic measures, such as the amount of revenue generated by the export of particular commodities, and toward a commitment to counting the total economic activity taking place within the country allowed finance officials to reflect a broader spectrum of the potential drivers of growth in their measurements and eventual decision making. When national income was divided by the population, it provided the real GDP per capita figure that, when compared with previous years, resulted in the growth rate.[76] Aggregate indicators, such as GDP, created a uniform image of economic progress despite the presence of stark inequality within Sudan. These indicators' inability to reflect regional inequality often had the effect of justifying policies that reinforced it. In part, regional inequality was the result of decades of government decisions to invest in certain areas of the country and not other areas.[77] The conventions of national income accounting and the addition of a statistical office to the central government, rather than to the regional authorities, made it easier to visualize the inequality in wealth between Sudan and Britain or Sudan and Turkey than it was to recognize, for example, the inequalities between the Omdurman–Sennar–Kosti triangle and the rest of the country.

[76] Morten Jerven, *Poor Numbers*.

[77] Barbara Weinstein, "Developing Inequality," *American Historical Review* 113:1 (2008): 1–18.

6

A Nation-State Alone Cannot Transform Its Destiny, 1964–1966

The military regime of General Ibrahim Abboud, often referred to as the November Regime, did not fall because it mismanaged the Sudanese economy. In fact, from the time he assumed power in 1958, there was a sustained rise in per capita GDP, allowing the economic policy makers of the 'Abboud period to achieve the stated goals of their plan. Despite these achievements, criticisms of the economic policies of the November Regime came from two directions. The first criticism came from southern elites who, though disgruntled in the 1950s, had largely been willing to participate in politics until the pathway for parliamentary participation was closed in 1958; because southern elites were excluded from the financial bureaucracy, with the military coup they lost their relatively weak voice in financial decision making when parliament was dissolved, and they turned toward armed protest to make their voices heard. The conflict in the southern provinces of Sudan created the atmosphere of crisis that eventually brought down the November Regime.

Criticism also came from a second angle, which in many respects was more influential in shaping policy, because it originated among those inside of the Ministry of Finance. In the years after the 1964 October Revolution, debate resumed on how Sudan fit into the world economy. Previously, the battle over Sudan's place in the world economy had been largely confined to a technical dispute about the correct marketing strategy for Sudanese cotton; however by the mid-1960s, this debate had morphed into a larger discussion about the nature of sovereignty and if the ideal of development within one state was exhausted. As part of a broader trend across the continent, financial technocrats in countries such as Sudan, who found themselves charged with the difficult task of managing a large geographic territory – the largest state in Africa but with a relatively small formal economy – began to shift their attention to transforming the international policy-making environment rather than envisioning development as a national project.

Though today it is often forgotten, African intellectuals and policy makers were among the first to realize that in isolation an individual state would not be able to transform its economic destiny. African intellectuals and policy makers understood independence to be necessary as part of a transnational social movement against racism.[1] Yet, the traps of self-determination were apparent to intellectuals across the continent even before independence was won.[2] Recently, historians have increasingly sought to recover the intellectual projects of African thinkers who imagined alternatives to the nation-state. So far this literature has moved in three directions, all of which are fruitful. The first is the recognition that decolonization as a mid-twentieth-century project did not have the creation of independent nation-states as a fixed destination.[3] This is an insight that can be generalized to apply to the end of empires in general; empires are typically brought down by those seeking to reform them, not by those seeking to overthrow them.[4] The second strand has highlighted the success of African states in mobilizing their position in organizations such as the UN General Assembly to argue for a reorganization of the international economic system, beginning in the mid-1970s through initiatives such as the New International Economic Order and the Lagos Plan of Action for the Economic Development of Africa from 1980–2000.[5] The third direction in which scholarship has developed is the study of groups of countries often labeled as radical.[6] Historians have interpreted these countries as being opposed to the Bretton Woods institutions throughout the period of the Cold War and decolonization, but recent scholarship has called into question whether groupings designed to encapsulate these countries as a distinct bloc, such as "the non-aligned movement" or "Bandung," can readily be identified.[7]

The Sudanese case upends these narratives. The Sudanese elite of the 1950s and 1960s, unlike their peers in countries such as Nkrumah's Ghana, did not argue for a dramatic reordering of the world economy or even a massive program of industrialization; instead they articulated a conservative vision of

[1] Tukufu Zuberi, *African Independence: How Africa Shapes the World* (New York: Rowman & Littlefield, 2015), pp. 13–14. See also Sam Moyn, "Fantasies of Federalism" *Dissent* (Winter 2015), www.dissentmagazine.org/article/fantasies-of-federalism.

[2] Cooper, *Citizenship between Empire and Nation*; Gary Wilder, *Freedom Time: Negritude, Decolonization, and the Future of the World* (Durham, NC: Duke University Press, 2015); and Mitchell, *Carbon Democracy*, pp. 66–86.

[3] W. E. B Du Bois, *The World and Africa: An Inquiry into the Part that Africa has Played in World History* (New York: Viking Press, 1947).

[4] Jeremy Adelman, "An Age of Imperial Revolutions," *American Historical Review* 113:2 (2008): 319–340.

[5] Giovanni Arrighi, "The African Crisis: World Systemic and Regional Aspects"; Gilman, "The New International Economic Order: A Reintroduction," pp. 1–16.

[6] See, for instance, Priya Lal, *African Socialism in Postcolonial Tanzania: Between the Village and the World* (New York: Cambridge University Press, 2015), and Byrne, *Mecca of Revolution*.

[7] Robert Vitalis, "The Midnight Ride of Kwame Nkrumah and Other Fables of Bandung (Ban-doong)," *Humanity* 4:2 (Summer 2013): 261–288.

development. Yet, what defined the independence movement was the concept of inclusion. The political rationale for Sudanese independence was that the *Sudani* could not be integrated equitably into the empires of the British or the Egyptians because of their race. Using a similar logic, the battle against economic discrimination in trade became the underlying principle of Sudanese economic policy. This principle undergirded the Sudanese desire directly after World War II to open the closed administrative zones in order to create a unified market without discrimination. It also provided the imaginary of fair competition that established the Sudanese ideal that Sudanese cotton would be competitive if it was priced correctly, because of its natural low costs.

At independence one Sudanese economic imaginary was that political and economic sovereignty would allow Sudan to successfully compete in the world economy by removing the discriminatory practices that had retarded progress in colonial Sudan during the prior decades.[8] Political economists and economic historians have described the period from 1945 until the beginning of the 1970s as one of the most conducive for economic growth in fact, but perhaps even more definitive of this era was the shared belief of policy-making elites across Africa that the state could be a catalyst for economic and social transformation. Elites who came to power in the wake of independence were prone to believe that political economy held the answers to their society's ills.[9] Yet, the limitations of national development as a project were readily apparent to Sudanese officials even during decolonization's moment of possibility. This insight allows us to rewrite the historiography of development as a story of a policy-making elite committed to national development as a means of creating an equitable place for the Sudanese in the world economy, but simultaneously aware of the sharp constraints that the world economy placed on what was politically or economically imaginable for Sudan.

Despite the fact that the variation in the political economy that African elites often imagined as most beneficial for their societies' future is often ignored in order to create a stylized story about Africa's economic history, this variation is undoubtedly a reality. For instance, Egypt, Kenya, and Nigeria took radically different approaches to questions as basic as the relationship between the state and the private sector.[10] In seeking to bring to light the variation in the postcolonial African political economy, the story of Sudan between 1964 and 1966 highlights the ways in which Sudanese policy makers' consciousness of the

8 Abbas, *The Sudan Question*.

9 Mahmood Mamdani, "Beyond Settler and Native as Political Identities: Overcoming the Political Legacy of Colonialism," *Comparative Studies in Society and History* 43:4 (October 2001): 651; Cooper, "Possibility and Constraint:, pp. 167–196.; Morten Jerven, *Economic Growth and Measurement Reconsidered in Botswana, Kenya, Tanzania, and Zambia, 1965–1995* (New York: Oxford University Press, 2014), pp. 1–28; Cooper, *Africa in the World*.

10 Robert L. Tignor, *Capitalism and Nationalism at the End of Empire: State and Business in Decolonizing Egypt, Nigeria, and Kenya, 1945–1963* (Princeton: Princeton University Press, 1993).

limitations of their own power led them to seek to transform their own state and economy to make it more compliant with what they believed to be the externally determined policy-making orthodoxy controlled by institutions such as the IMF.

The adoption of values such as transparency and stabilization in the middle of the 1960s alters the received narrative of the neoliberal crisis of the African state, which is traditionally dated to the 1981 publication of the Berg Report. Rather we can now see that for cohorts of African bureaucrats such as the Sudanese financial policy-making elite, the internationalization of control over policy making was a well-worn strategy not only to solidify both their own power as experts but also to develop answers to dilemmas that from their very earliest days in power they recognized could not be addressed solely within national units. The Sudanese story demonstrates the ways in which the IMF's view that economic and monetary stabilization were as important if not more important than development arose not in opposition to the development agenda of postcolonial African countries, but rather in collaboration with those countries' financial policy-making elites.

During the 1970s, the capital-intensive development paradigm came under attack across the African continent because of its failure to reduce poverty even where it was successful in increasing economic growth rates.[11] Yet, the first cracks in the Sudanese vision of development occurred not over questions of poverty alleviation, but instead within the elite itself over questions of regional equity and the distribution of government investments.[12] By 1964, the regime had completed the Managil Extension, the Khasm al-Girba Dam, railway lines to Nyala and Wau, the Shambat Road in Khartoum, and the Khartoum-to-Wad Medani road.[13] In a vast country starved of basic infrastructure by the colonial state, the November Regime had concentrated most of its investments in the relatively developed central region of the state; the developmentalist policy makers who made up the November Regime believed that this region held the most economic potential.[14] Yet, to their credit, they did begin extending critical infrastructure into the Sudanese periphery. In an irony, the years before the October Revolution marked the last time for decades that major infrastructural projects, such as the railroads, would be completed in Sudanese regions such as the southern provinces and in Darfur.

Though it was the progress of the war in the southern provinces of Sudan that provided the ostensible reason for the seminar meetings at the University of Khartoum, which eventually gave way to the October Revolution, "those

11 Daniel Speich, "The Kenyan Style of 'African Socialism': Developmental Knowledge Claims and the Explanatory Limits of the Cold War," *Diplomatic History* 33:3 (June 2009): 449–466.

12 W. J. Berridge, *Civil Uprisings in Modern Sudan: The 'Khartoum Springs' of 1964 and 1985* (New York: Bloomsbury, 2015): 15.

13 Bechtold, *Politics in the Sudan.*

14 Alden Young, "Measuring the Sudanese Economy," pp. 44–60.

who participated in the uprising did so as members of the modern, urban economy."[15] The historian Willow J. Berridge noted there was broad participation of "the relatively socially and culturally homogeneous population of Khartoum," but that the revolution's leadership remained limited to the urban professionals: doctors, lawyers, judges, and academics. The October Revolution spread along the communication networks linking provincial secondary schools to the capital. Thus as protests broke out in regions such as Darfur, they repeated the demands of those protestors in the capital. The demands of the uprising were framed by the civil religion of nationalism, rather than of Islam, Marxism, or even of ethnic or regional marginalization.[16] Speaking of political liberty and dressed as a compatriot in the French Revolution, Hassan al-Turabi, who would later become the emblem of Sudan's Islamist movement, commandeered the events of October at a crucial point: he helped steer their focus from the outrages of Sudan's counterinsurgency in the southern provinces toward political liberalism, a politics that benefited Sudan's most enfranchised classes.[17] However, Berridge correctly notes the ultimate irony of the October Revolution: for many of the educated elite, precisely those social groups that actually inherited the decolonizing state, the October Revolution was a second decolonization, this time against the military; in many respects it was a sign of their own unease. Many of those who inherited the colonial state in Sudan suffered an anxiety caused by the distance they felt their education had created between them and the masses they believed their education entitled them to rule. They saw themselves as both dependent on and at the same time superior to the religious sheikhs, the rural notables, and even the proletarian masses on whose mobilization they depended.

In the process, Turabi, though he often styled himself as a revolutionary, and the October events, served to transform the binary that Mahmood Mamdani had outlined between citizens and subjects as the basic colonial legacy in Africa into a triple divide. The 1964 Revolution solidified the formation of what we might imagine as three descending circles of political rights, and Turabi throughout his long career would prove to be a master of all of them. In the first circle centered around Khartoum, citizens enjoyed full political rights, often expressed in civil disputes, while outsiders were kept at bay through genteel discrimination; outside of Omdurman, Khartoum, and Khartoum North and the provincial capitals, the vast majority of northern Sudanese were governed as subjects through the traditional Islamic notables, while in the southern provinces counterinsurgency became a regularized style of governance.[18]

[15] Berridge, *Civil Uprisings in Modern Sudan* pp. 28–29.

[16] Ibid., pp. 13–38. Abdullahi A. Gallab, *First Islamic Republic* (Aldershot: Ashgate, 2008), pp. 57–58.

[17] Berridge, *Civil Uprisings*, pp. 29–30.

[18] Edward Thomas, "Obituary: Hassan al-Turabi (1932–2016)," *Mada Masr* (March 14, 2016). www.madamasr.com/opinion/obituary-hassan-al-turabi-1932–2016 [accessed March

The October Revolution of 1964 led to the fall of the military government and the return of civilians to power. Under the democratic regimes that followed, the war in the southern provinces of Sudan escalated, while finance officials pulled back from their commitment to development, rather than reimagining it in a more inclusive or democratic manner. Mobilizing the rhetoric of accountability, finance officials became increasingly concerned with managing Sudan's place within volatile international markets by controlling the country's debt and balance of payments, at the expense of engineering social transformation.

Counterproductively, Sudanese politicians and policy makers' focus on economic development in order to gain political and economic autonomy entangled Sudan in international debt markets and thereby transformed Sudan from a developmental project at the national level to an object of financial surveillance at the international level. Increased financial surveillance limited the space for political decision making, magnifying political instability as political and financial elites inside of Sudan became increasingly extroverted.

Even as extreme violence was dispatched against the marginalized and wars in the peripheries of Sudan flared, the Sudanese political sphere sought to reconstitute itself by once again confining their political conflicts to the tame playmaking of financial disagreements. Thus we see the proliferation of economics journals such as *the Sudan Journal of Administration and Development* and the *Sudanese Economist*. The proof that the debates that raged in these magazines were not simply the mutterings of a marginalized caste of experts can be found in the increased presence of government ministers in the popular press, often responding directly to lay critics, who made their own calculations of the government's finances based on publicly accessible data. In a phenomenon that dates from the emergence of political arithmetic or the use of financial and demographic reckonings to fight partisan battles for control of the state, the state's critics began to ask for information that did not exist and in the process forced the state to calculate accounts that it had either neglected or never imagined should be kept.[19]

The creation of a vibrant and financially literate public is a cornerstone of the development of a transparent bureaucracy. However, Sudan was pressed to create a tame and public language of financial playmaking under an international spotlight. The strain to fulfill the development ambitions outlined in *The Ten Year Plan for Economic and Social Development of 1960/61* broke the political consensus that had existed in cities such as Khartoum, bringing down the military regime and creating a period of political transition as the various forces that had dominated politics sought to coalesce once again. Numbers

20, 2016]. M. Mamdani, *Citizen and Subject: Contemporary Africa and the Legacy of Late Colonialism* (Princeton: Princeton University Press, 1996).

[19] William Deringer, *Calculated Values: Financial Politics and the Quantitative Age, 1688–1776* (Cambridge, MA: Harvard University Press, in press).

such as the balance of trade, the current account deficit, and the size of the hard currency reserves became topics of political discussion. The numbers that different actors debated were social constructs reflecting huge amounts of both menial and imaginative labor, but they nevertheless reflected the reality that the government found itself in financial straits. These numbers framed what the different actors believed was possible.[20] Meanwhile, Sudan's international creditors led by the International Monetary Fund began to intervene directly into the country's political and economic governance.

After the October Revolution, the veteran politician, Mohamed Ahmed Mahgoub, assumed office as the newly elected (elections were held on April 21) prime minister of Sudan on June 10, 1965. The first challenge his government took up was writing a constitution. The parliamentary regime in power from 1954–1956 that was formed under the Self-Determination Agreement of 1953 was unable to move beyond an interim constitution, even after independence. Part of the problem was the dispute between southern politicians and their northern peers about whether Sudan would grant the southern region federal status or solely adopt a unitary system of government. The second dispute during the 1950s was whether Sudan would adopt a parliamentary or a presidential system of government. It manifested around the specific question of whom to choose as president: Sayyid Abd Al-Rahman al-Mahdi, the leader of Ansar, or his rival Sayyid Ali Mohammed Osman al-Mirghani, the leader of Khatmiyya. Between 1965 and May 25, 1969, when the military once again overthrew the civilian government, questions about how to write the constitution and should Sudan be Islamic or secular, federal or unitary, presidential or parliamentary all resurfaced, only to remain unsettled yet again.[21]

As Sudan prepared to move from the October Revolution toward a transitional government, the events of December 6, 1964, were a reminder that the southern question remained alive. On that day riots broke out between southerners and northerners awaiting the return of Clement Mboro to Khartoum after his visit to Juba as a minister in the newly formed government. Following a peaceful parade to the airport, a dispute broke out among those gathered, because many of the southerners feared that Mboro, whose plane was delayed, had been the victim of foul play. In the clashes that broke out more than 400 southerners and northerners were injured.[22] These clashes were in many ways just a preview of what was to come as the war in the South escalated under successive civilian regimes. Further exacerbating the situation was the decision to schedule national elections on April 21, 1965, without waiting for peace in the southern regions of the country, once again preventing the southern parties that were on the verge of consolidating their legislative power prior to the 'Abboud

[20] Adam Tooze, "Trouble with Numbers: Statistics, Politics, and History in the Construction of Weimar's Trade Balance, 1918–1924," *American Historical Review* 113: 3 (2008): 691.

[21] Mahgoub, *Democracy on Trial*, p. 181. [22] Mahgoub, *Democracy on Trial*, p. 193.

coup in 1958 from institutionalizing their political power ahead of upcoming elections.

The relatively moderate Sudan African National Union (SANU) agreed to attend the Round Table conference organized by the transitional Prime Minister Sirr Al-Khatim Khalifa, which was originally to be held in Juba, but was moved because of the violence there to Khartoum on March 16, 1965. This meeting was meant to provide an opportunity for reconciliation to take place between southerners and northerners, but instead it ended in acrimony. Southern politicians, frequently ignored by their northern colleagues and, after war broke out in 1963, frequently in exile, found themselves forced to address "the Southern Question" in order to win recognition in Khartoum or abroad. "The Southern Question" frequently trapped these politicians into a discourse that was defined outside of the three southern provinces, one that forced individual southern politicians to speak for the South as a whole, even as intense local rivalries limited their appeal.[23] It also pushed them increasingly to speak in the language of race. Mimicking many of the preconceptions of their British, Egyptian, and riverain Arab rivals, southern politicians described themselves as a race apart, African versus Arab.[24] Appealing internationally, they adopted the language of Pan-Africanism, referring to themselves as former slaves versus slave masters.[25] The language of genocide and annihilation became more prominent during the civil war in the second half of the 1960s; this marked a departure from the 1950s, particularly before the rise of the military government in 1958, when many political ideas were advanced, in particular the idea that the Liberal Party led by southerners could provide the political leadership for a united Sudan.[26]

In the midst of the political unrest of the mid-1960s, which questioned the sources of political authority, the consensus surrounding the developmental state collapsed.[27] An illustration of just how macabre the battle over political authority became was the fight between Imam Hadi, Sadiq al-Mahdi, and Muhammad Mahjub for control of the Umma Party. This battle pitted religious authority based on scholarship versus that based on heredity against secular learning and experience in a myriad of combinations. Just as questions

[23] Southern Sudanese politics is not primarily driven by external factors. The memorialization of violence plays a significant role in southern politics. Zoe Cormack, "The Spectacle of Death: Visibility and Concealment at an Unfinished Memorial in South Sudan," *Journal of Eastern African Studies* 11:1 (2017): 115–132.

[24] Justin Willis, "The Southern Problem: Representing Sudan's Southern Provinces to c. 1970," *Journal of African History* 56, no. 2 (2015): 285.

[25] Derek Peterson, "Abolitionism and Political Thought in Britain and East Africa," in Derek Peterson, ed. *Abolitionism and Imperialism in Britain, Africa and the Atlantic* (Athens: Ohio University Press, 2010), pp. 1–37.

[26] Willis, "The Southern Problem," p. 289, and Philip Abbas, "Growth of Black Consciousness in Northern Sudan," *Africa Today* 20:3 (1973): 29–43.

[27] Young, "African Bureaucrats and the Exhaustion of the Development State."

were being asked about who could represent the nation politically, the economic establishment in Sudan was forced to question the feasibility of its development plans. In particular, questions were raised about whether large-scale irrigation could support the Sudanese economy. While government officials and politicians constantly debated the technical details of how large-scale irrigation infrastructure would be made economically feasible through the marketing of cotton, very few officials or politicians questioned the core belief, which had survived from the colonial period through the first decade of independence, that irrigated agriculture was the answer.

During the late 1950s, when Hamza Mirghani Hamza served as the permanent under-secretary in the Ministry of Finance, he became an early believer in "export pessimism." What distinguished Hamza Mirghani Hamza from his peers was his realization that Sudan's problems disposing of its cotton harvest during the late 1950s were not the result of errors in its marketing strategy such as mispricing the harvest or of short-term disturbances such as the introduction of US cotton into the market. Instead picking up on a number of the arguments circulating through organizations such as the International Cotton Association Commission, Hamza Mirghani Hamza came to believe that the terms of trade for commodity-exporting countries were continually in decline compared to those of industrial producers. As a consequence he became an early advocate of the idea that Sudan should diversify its economy away from cotton exporting. Yet, Hamza Mirghani Hamza was attacked for not having a clear vision of how to bring about diversification.

Therefore, those within the Ministry of Finance and the planning arms that it developed later decided that the battle for Sudanese economic development would be fought on the terrain of the price and quantity of cotton. John Carmichael and Mamoun Beheiry believed that Sudan could simply grow more cotton at lower prices that its peers and therefore would, over time, outcompete its competitors. In the late 1950s the assumption that economic competition would take place between national units was dominant, as was the corollary that those units that planned better than their competitors would succeed. With the military coup in November 1958, it became clear that Hamza Mirghani Hamza had lost the battle over economic policy, as the government prepared to embark on a massive plan to construct the Managil Extension Scheme in the Gezira Plain. These investments became the centerpiece of the state's attempt to transform itself into an exporting powerhouse.

Yet his initial defeat became a victory in August 1966, when Mirghani Hamza returned to Sudan, after serving as the first director of the Africa Department of the International Monetary Fund, to become the Minister of Finance in the government of Muhammed Mahjoub.[28] Hamza Mirghani brought home

[28] IMF Archive. "Secretary's Circular No. 66/104: Resignation of Mr. Hamzah Merghani" To: Members of the Executive Board, From: The Acting Secretary, August 16, 1964 [accessed April 27, 2009].

with him a wealth of experience in thinking through the IMF's new initatives of providing stabilization loans for poor commodity-producing countries. His return in the mid-1960s was a marker in an intensification of Sudanese contacts with international networks of finance and economics; however, Sudanese economic thinking had been extroverted from its inception.

While in the late 1950s the impossibility of national development was a minority position, whispered in the halls of the government ministries, by 1960 it was beginning to be discussed even in forums such as the International Monetary Fund. For instance on March 4, 1960, the IMF's executive board was presented with a draft of a proposal titled "Fund Policies and Procedures in Relation to the Compensatory Financing of Commodity Fluctuations."

At first it might be tempting to dismiss this report as merely responding to the demands of developing countries at the United Nations and its various commissions.[29] During the late 1950s, the IMF spent a considerable amount of time out of step with its peer institutions such as the World Bank when considering whether development financing was potentially productive. The perceived pessimism of the IMF reduced its involvement in drawing up Sudan's *Ten Year Program for Economic and Social Development*. Yet, as the plan involved large sums of borrowing in hard currency, which despite speculation otherwise could not all be secured through bilateral financing agreements, the influence of the IMF began to increase. Two of the most notable signs of its increasing influence were its corraling the largest donor countries into a single working group to deal with the issue of Sudan and, even more importantly, opening its doors to Sudanese officials such as Hamza Mirghani Hamza who joined the IMF as political pressures at home made dissent less tolerable.

In "Fund Policies and Procedures in Relation to the Compensatory Financing of Commodity Fluctuations," the IMF acknowledged that it had a role to play in "the provision of compensatory financing to alleviate the difficulties that arise from instability of export earnings in countries largely dependent on the exportation of primary commodities." It defined compensatory financing as any "movements in a country's own official reserves as well as any international borrowing or any other international transfers that are designed to relieve the strain on reserves or to preserve the stability of the exchange rate." This was not a position that the IMF itself was inclined to adopt, but one that was seen as the lesser of two evils of the proposals floated at the seventh session of the United Nations Commission on International Commodity Trade held in 1959. In particular, that commission posited the idea of creating permanent international mechanisms to compensate commodity-producing countries for fluctuations in the price of their exports. For the IMF such a development held out the potential

[29] Vijay Prashad, *The Darker Nations: A People's History of the Third World* (New York: New Press, 2007), and Giuliano Garavini, *After Empires: European Integration, Decolonization, and the Challenge from the Global South 1957–1986* (New York: Oxford University Press, 2012).

of a dangerous encroachment onto authority that it largely reserved for itself. To prevent possible encroachment, the IMF undertook three steps: to define the types of fluctuations that affected commodity-exporting nations, to look at the pros and cons of different types of compensatory finance, and to discuss which measures it interpreted as legal: its 1960 report reflects that research.[30]

By 1960, economists agreed that the fluctuations in the prices of commodities were larger than those of manufactured goods and that these fluctuations systematically disadvantaged commodity-exporting countries. The question was how would the international community respond to this revelation. At the United Nations two recommendations were put forward. The first was to create a series of international agreements aimed at stabilizing the prices of particular commodities. The second approach offset the fluctuations in commodity prices through "compensatory financing." As mentioned, the IMF for historical reasons was largely opposed to the idea of fixing the prices of commodities through international agreement. It believed that compensatory financing offered it a way to move to the center of the policy discussion in developing countries, and what at first appears to be a minor detail at the bottom of the second page of the 1960 report actually turned out to be a major turning point in the IMF's relationship with its member states, particularly with countries such as Sudan. On p. 2, the IMF notes that one of its conditions for contemplating 'compensatory financing' is that the recipient countries open themselves up to "a policy of domestic financial stabilization."[31]

The "policy of domestic financial stabilization" allowed the IMF to insert itself into the internal policy making of countries that were potential recipients of its financing. Just as after World War II, GDP and the annualized growth rate were methods for evaluating the relative performance of various states, so too would the IMF's criterion of domestic financial stability – a policy framework that was distinguished by its hostility to inflation – make possible comparisons between countries. The IMF also continued to be concerned about guaranteeing repayment. The extent to which it was interested in promoting the idea of domestic self-discipline can be seen in the following sentence found later in the report: "Much is said in this paper about the prudence and self-discipline required of the primary producing countries themselves if they are to keep their economies on an even keel despite the fluctuations of world markets."[32] Underlining the IMF's new approach to primary commodity-exporting countries was the concession that price did not play the role of balancing supply and demand among commodity producers that it did among manufacturers. Whereas when manufacturers were confronted by low prices they were liable to restrict supply, primary commodity producers were unlikely to do so, and as a result they

30 IMF, *Fund Policies and Procedures in Relation to the Compensatory Financing of Commodity Fluctuations* (New York: IMF, 1960), p. 1.

31 Ibid., p 2. 32 Ibid., p 4.

would simply absorb the fall in price without effectively moving to restore a balance.[33]

The most vulnerable countries according to the IMF were "a number of small countries like Ghana, Haiti, and Sudan, that are largely dependent on a single product the output of which is subject to wide fluctuations from year to year."[34] However, in a diverse mix of countries such as Finland, Iceland, Indonesia, and Uruguay, the IMF argued that instability was not the result of fluctuations in the international commodity markets, but rather was due to internal conditions and the maintenance of unrealistic exchange rates.

IMF officials had worried for some time that large capital expenditures on development would potentially undermine the stability of vulnerable countries such as Sudan, encouraging unsustainable growth and elevated inflation. As Sudan became reliant on international "compensatory" finance to stabilize its economy, the influence of the IMF's new thinking had two results. The first was to strengthen the suspicion that, acting alone, domestic policy makers could do relatively little to alter their own country's growth trajectory. The second result was that, to qualify for the international financial flows necessary to mitigate against a turbulent world economy, individual countries needed to make their own economies increasingly transparent and compliant with international orthodoxy.

The *Sudanese Economist* and the Politics of Austerity

Following Hamza Mirghani Hamza's return to Khartoum in 1966, qualms within the Ministry of Finance about the feasibility of the government's plans, which had once been marginal, moved from the periphery of government discourse to the center of the conversation about Sudanese economic policy. Debt and transparency also became principal topics of conversation. During the 1960s, Sudanese government administrators became less concerned with the dichotomy between the developed and the underdeveloped world and more concerned with developing a rule-based means of adjudicating divisive questions about scarce resources.

As a consequence of the loss of confidence in the independence generation's development project, the editors of the prominent dailies in Sudan, such as *Al-Ayyam* and *Al Rai' Al Amm*, replaced discussions of "shared sacrifice" and Rostow's "big push" with talk about inflation, budget crises, and debt. Many of these debates were reprinted in the pages of the *Sudanese Economist*, which was in truth part economics journal and part study guide. Circulated by the Sudanese News Agency beginning in 1958 to an elite audience of bilingual readers in Sudan's major towns, the *Sudanese Economist* served as a house

33 Ibid., p. 4; IMF, *Instability in Export Markets of Underdeveloped Countries* (New York; IMF, 1952).

34 IMF, *Fund Policies and Procedures in Relation to the Compensatory Financing*, p 10.

journal for policy makers interested in financial matters. Its editors frequently welcomed new members to the club of financial decision making by publishing the bachelor's, master's, and PhD theses of Sudanese officials, many of whom were returning from study abroad and would invariably go on to become a part of its readership. For instance, the journal published Fatahel Rahman Ibn Idris's honor's thesis on "the Marketing of Groundnuts in Sudan" in its February 1966 issue. It also published Osman Abdalla El Nazeer's master's thesis on the "Effects of Demographic Factors on the Investment Pattern in the Sudan, 1955/56–1970/71" over three issues from June–August 1966. In addition, the journal republished articles from foreign experts on topics that government officials were currently debating and released samples of long lists of statistics and data collected by government agencies prior to their official publication.

For the remainder of this chapter, I focus on the *Sudanese Economist*, particularly on one debate known as "the Economic Controversy," which raged in various Arabic daily newspapers in the spring of 1966, with selected articles being reprinted in the journal. This debate concerned the right of the public to accurate information about the country's balance of payments and the wisdom of the government's taking on debt either from its own central bank or from abroad. The first piece selected by the editor of the journal M. K. Mahdi was by Sayed Bashir Mohamed Said. Originally appearing in *Al-Ayyam* on February 24, 1966, this editorial began with two provocative questions: "What is the reality of the financial situation of the Country?" and "Why did the government fail in collecting its revenue as reflected in the Budget?" The circumstances that prompted the writing of this editorial in one of the highest circulating newspapers in Sudan was a rumor that the Government of Sudan intended to amend the Bank of Sudan Act to allow the government to obtain more loans. The author begins by asserting, "I am writing this and I am confident – according to firm information – that the Government has actually exhausted the limits of borrowing from the Bank of Sudan and that it is about to amend the Bank of Sudan Act to be able to raise its percentage of borrowing."[35]

In effect Sayed Bashir revealed that Sudanese policy makers had fallen victim to the "fiscal dominance" policy dilemma that afflicted France in the 1920s and the European Central Bank in 2012.[36] Barry Eichengreen explains why this dilemma occurs:

> When fiscal policy makers decide, in their wisdom, to run a budget deficit, and there is nothing the central bank can do about it, the central bank will then have no choice but to buy the government's bonds and tolerate a higher rate of inflation than it would

35 Sayed Bashir Mohamed Said, "The Financial Situation," *Sudanese Economist: A Monthly Economic and Commercial Review, A Supplement of the Sudan News Agency*, no. 92 (Khartoum: Modern Press Agency, 1966), p. 21.

36 Thomas Sargent and Neil Wallace, "Some Unpleasant Monetarist Arithmetic," *Federal Reserve Bank of Minneapolis Quarterly Review* 5:3 (Fall 1981): 1–17.

prefer, if it is otherwise impossible to finance the deficit and the alternative is default and financial chaos.[37]

In Sudan in 1966, as in the case of France in the 1920s and Greece recently, allegations that the politicians in power, and the officials who served them, broke laws created an opportunity for other officials to assert their own technocratic authority.

Regardless of the truth in the author's claim that the Government of Sudan was on the verge of raising its own ceiling on borrowing from 15 to 25 percent of annual projected budget revenue, Sayed Bashir was establishing a right to public information about the government's financial policies: he was asserting that he and his readers are part of the public that has the right and responsibility to audit government finances. Sayed Bashir criticized the finance minister's reliance on foreign experts to tell him about economic matters. Sayed Bashir also noted, "The Government has no proper accounts to reflect to the Minister nor to other responsible people the real position of the country."[38]

Writing during Sudan's second experiment with democracy, Sayed Bashir thus asserted the right of the public – the few people educated in English and Arabic in the major cities of Sudan – to know how its money was being spent "on the basis of the real figures and actual accounts not on the basis of false talks and glittering works."[39] Sayed Bashir's dialogue about financial accountability was premised on a discussion of austerity. He challenged the principle that if the government were simply given more capital resources it would be able to translate those resources into faster growth and therefore mitigate the consequences of its assumption of ever-larger amounts of debt. Implicitly, Sayed Bashir asserted the independence of economic expertise from political interests. In the same issue of the *Sudanese Economist* there was also a long article on the "Reorganization of Economic Planning Secretariat and Ministry of Finance and Economics." Similar articles on planning, central banking, and public administration both internationally and within Sudan appeared in the other issues of the journal published in 1966. Yet, even as questions were raised about the efficacy of the government, the journal and many publications like it remained committed to the ethics of professionalization, or the autonomy of economic expertise from politics.

The power of Sayed Bashir's call for the need for government accountability can be seen in the fact that not only were his charges discussed in the Constituent Assembly, but also Minister of Finance Sayed El Sherif Hussein El Hind felt obliged to give an official statement to the Khartoum News Service on

37 Barry Eichengreen, *Hall of Mirrors: The Great Depression, the Great Recession, and the Uses – and Misuses – of History* (New York: Oxford University Press, 2015), p. 47.

38 Said, "The Financial Situation," p. 22.

39 Ibid., p. 23. For a discussion of the Sudanese public sphere, see the work of Sharkey, *Living with Colonialism*, pp. 16–67.

February 27 in response. His response was reprinted in the same issue of the *Sudanese Economist* in which Sayed Bashir's editorial originally appeared.[40] Sayed El Sherif Hussein El Hind began his response with an incredible admission:

> Government accounts were in arrear and remained unclosed for many years and...they therefore did not give a true picture of the government's financial position. He added that all this was clearly declared by the Government many times. He said that the so-called "budget surpluses" which were announced in past budgets were not real surpluses; they were surpluses "on paper" only.[41]

Countering Sayed Bashir's claims honestly, Sayed El Sherif Hussein El Hind thus admitted what was becoming painfully obvious as the 1960s progressed – that many of the statistics that developed states, let alone new states, were using to plan their economies were based on spotty, if not nonexistent, information. The economic adviser to Nigeria in the early 1960s, Wolfgang Stolper, wrote a whole monograph on his efforts to overcome information problems in Nigeria called *Planning without Facts*.[42] Yet, Minister of Finance Sayed El Sherif Hussein El Hind was admitting not only to a lack of knowledge about economic activity inside of the country in general but was also acknowledging that the government knew very little about its own internal accounts.[43]

Despite the fact that the Sudanese state ignored the economic activity of the vast majority of Sudanese people, it still had an enormous impact on their lives. The transformation in government structure from one shaped around three secretariats – civil, legal, and financial – at the end of World War II to one that by the mid-1960s was structured around a powerful Ministry of Finance and a plethora of new organizations, such as a central bank, agricultural banks, planning agencies, and statistical bureaus, altered how the Sudanese accessed their government and the ways in which their government allocated its resources. Through its ability to tax goods and services and to control credit, the Sudanese state, which was by far the largest economic agent in the country, sought to create a unified national market in place of the autarkic, local economies that the late colonial regime had fostered. Morten Jerven has demonstrated that whereas during the colonial period ordinary Africans fled from the counting apparatuses of the colonial state, during the early independence era, African

40 Editor, "Finance Minister's Statement on Financial Situation," *Sudanese Economist* 92 (1966): 24–29.
41 Ibid., 25.
42 Stopler, *Planning without Facts*; Morgan, "'On a Mission' with Mutable Mobiles," pp. 6–7, and "Seeking Parts, Looking for Wholes," pp. 303–325.
43 Steven Pierce, "Looking like a State: Colonialism and the Discourse of Corruption in Northern Nigeria," *Comparative Studies in History and Society* 48:4 (October 2006): 887–914.

citizens sought out the state, expecting that they could marshal its accounts to improve their lives.[44]

The fact that the military dictatorship justified its rule using the language of economics and accounting meant that finance officials, who were the crucial intermediaries with the external funders of the government's agenda, could use the same language to assert their autonomy from the political leadership. Inflation became, as it often had before, the topic where the political and the technocratic blended.[45] Sayed El Sherif Hussein El Hind acknowledged the extent to which he felt threatened by Sayed Bashir's assertion that financial accountability required austerity, and the imposition of a strict limit on the government's ability to borrow, by going on to discuss the relationship between government borrowing and inflation. In a passage that other authors would attack for its lack of adherence to liberal economic theory, Sayed El Sherif Hussein justified why the principal task of the government was to increase the quantity of capital investment in the country, rather than to account for all government spending or worry about inflation. Sayed El Sherif Hussein made the following defense of government policy:

> The Minister said that borrowing in itself will not lead to inflation and that conspicuous consumption is the kind of expenditure which leads to inflation ... It is also true that the countries which follow an economic development policy are subject to this "inflationary tendency" and that development means investment in productive fields in order to achieve more "employment" and "purchasing power" and hence increasing the money supply and increasing the "imports bill" from the developed countries since the underdeveloped countries do not produce the goods they consume. This, the Minister said, is the price of development which underdeveloped countries have to pay and it is a stage through which they must pass before achieving economic peace.[46]

The fact that the minister felt the need to underscore the economic relationship between capital investment and development demonstrates the extent to which the fall of the military regime in 1964 and the armed rebellions in the southern provinces of Sudan had undermined the legitimacy of the growth model. What is striking, however, is that an alternative model of economic development was not proposed by policy makers, even as intense doubts were raised about the possibility of the government amassing sufficient capital to build the infrastructure necessary to develop the entire country.

The heart of the critique of Sayed El Sherif Hussein's official statement to the Khartoum New Service appeared in *Al Rai Al-Amm* on March 1, 1966, and

44 Jerven, *Poor Numbers*; Keren Weitzberg, "The Unaccountable Census: Colonial Enumeration and Its Implications for the Somali People," *Journal of African History* 56:3 (November 2015): 409–428.

45 Charles Maier, *In Search of Stability: Explorations in Historical Political Economy* (Cambridge: Cambridge University Press, 1988), pp. 187–225.

46 Editor, "Finance Minister's Statement on Financial Situation," *Sudanese Economist* 92 (1966): 24–29.

focused on the minister's inability to conform to what his peers understood as orthodox economics. In a quote dripping with contempt, Fareed Atabani, lecturer in the Faculty of Economics at the University of Khartoum, wrote this of the minister:

> H. E. presented to us some economic theories of which I admit my ignorance. It is not surprising since we were taught our economics in the fifties and sixties of the twentieth century, and those of us with limited imagination cannot hope to elevate themselves to those high attitudes of thought... H. E. is talking in a twenty-first century language.[47]

Further ridiculing the minister for his lack of orthodoxy, Atabani wrote, "I know many of the men of the street – maybe all are abnormal – who complain of inflation and its hard impact." He then went on to mention the experience of Latin American countries and their problems with inflation associated with import-substitution policies; in closing, he wrote of the minister, "I would even request him to ponder the fate of Kwame Nkrumah and how he brought his country to disaster though his rank economic policy."[48]

The manner in which the debate concluded was a sign that the purpose of reprinting these discussions was not so much to solve the economic problem of inflation as to create a space where junior government officials could learn how to talk about economics. Therefore the editors of *the Sudanese Economist* gave the final essay in this debate to Ibrahim Elias. In a commentary on Dr. Atabani's critique, Ibrahim took the professor to task for failing to adequately represent the views of the international economics profession, writing,

> Neither the Finance Minister nor for this case, the Finance Ministers anywhere could possibly have available references endorsed by economists to which they could refer to find a straight solution for the problems of inflation. This is not only the case as regards inflation, but in fact there are no tested theories in the field of economic development and development planning, which are unanimously accepted by economists.[49]

Here Ibrahim Elias was emphasizing that it was not appropriate for Fareed Atabani to excommunicate his peer the minister from the profession of economics simply over a policy disagreement. In Ibrahim Elias' opinion the minister was still within the bounds of acceptable economics discourse, regardless of whether his recommendations were the correct prescriptions for the nation. What is also interesting in both Fareed and Ibrahim's responses is that both acknowledge that they are members of an internationally constituted profession, a community that draws its legitimacy from its own internal discourse. Sudanese officials

47 Fareed Atabani, "The Economic Theory of the Twenty First Century," *Sudanese Economist* 92 (1966): 30.

48 Ibid., p. 34. For a discussion of the Ghanaian School of Economics, see Gerardo Serra, "From Scattered Data to Ideological Education: Economics, Statistics and the State in Ghana, 1948–1966," (PhD diss., London School of Economics, 2015).

49 Ibrahim Elias, "On the Economic Problem. A Commentary on Dr. Fareed Atabani's Article," *Sudanese Economist* 92 (1966): 34.

were anxious to see themselves as orthodox members of this community. The importance of enforcing professional standards became clear in Elias's statement: "But most regretfully Dr. Atabani resorted to a style non-analytical and unacademic, in commenting on H. E.'s interview." Elias then elaborated on how an economist should be expected to reason:

> Dr. Atabani wrote in a literary language, not as an economist should have done. He should have been talking in terms of figures and statistics and should have given us a scientific evaluation of the increase or decrease in the national income, which this budget would lead to.[50]

These discussions demonstrate the extent to which elites within Sudanese financial circles were concerned with seeing themselves as holding the same professional standards as their international peers and ensuring that senior government officials did not stray beyond the bounds of acceptable economic discourse. In addition, all of the writers revealed the extent to which the language of economics drew a large part of its authority from its ability to make other countries' experiences comparable. This ability held out the promise that officials in countries such as Sudan could learn from their peers and from other historical examples. In the pages of *the Sudanese Economist*, when members of the finance profession asserted their right to accurate information about the government's spending and demanded that the government shape its policies in accordance with a concept of inflation on which the journal's writers and readers claimed to be the primary judges of government policy inside of Sudan, they were in fact claiming what I term "the right to policy discretion."[51]

Conclusion

While the Sudanese elite knitted together in its own "networks of sociability" and carried literary tropes such as a "New Mesopotamia" over to their economic policy making, the extroversion of Sudanese economic policy was hardly new. Indeed the cosmopolitan nature of Sudanese economic discourses was one of its cardinal features: Sudanese policy makers mixed references to capitalists and socialists thinkers, to the Anglo-American tradition and the Latin American tradition. Ghana and Egypt loomed large as examples of failed economic experiments, even as Sudanese policy makers borrowed heavily from the Prebisch-Singer hypothesis to make sense of the listlessness of Sudan's economy in a postimperial world where the price for cotton only declined.

Policy makers in the Ministry of Finance began to argue about the implications of Sudan's heavy dependence on cotton and that crop's declining terms of trade almost from the moment of independence in 1956. On one side of the argument were officials such as Mamoun Beheiry and John Carmichael who

[50] Ibid., p. 36.
[51] Young, "African Bureaucrats and the Exhaustion of the Developmental State."

believed that, despite declining terms of trade, Sudan could simply outproduce its competitors. On the other side of the argument, meanwhile, were officials such as Hamza Mirghani Hamza, who believed that Sudan should try to diversify away from cotton rather than increasing its investment in capital-intensive monoculture. Hamza Mirghani Hamza lost this battle within the ministry. The third option put forth strongly by the British, and echoed less derisively by the International Monetary Fund, that Sudanese officials should do nothing – neither invest in increasing cotton production nor diversify the economy – was also rejected as trapping Sudan in poverty and a barely transformed colonialism. Instead, the Sudanese chose to embark on a massive building project, expanding the infrastructure of the colonial economy they inherited, but firm in the belief that by making the colonial infrastructure bigger they could deliver on the country's unfulfilled promise. Sudan's vision was to reject industrialization and initially to curtail diversification in favor of export-led agricultural development.

During the 1960s this policy produced reasonable gains, even as it enmeshed the country in large if sustainable amounts of debt. A similar strategy worked for the Ivory Coast, a country with which Sudanese policy makers were creating strong intellectual links through organizations such as the African Development Bank initially headed by Mamoun Beheiry but located in Abidjan. The strategy worked for the Ivory Coast until the early 1980s, but unlike Sudan one of the Ivory Coast's first decisions was rejecting the union with Upper Volta. In a similar manner, the economic policies pursued during the first half of the 1960s were suited to the economic core of Sudan, but they did not produce results in a timely enough fashion to bind together the peripheries of the country. Having foresworn political devolution, not to mention the prospect of partition, Sudanese policy makers had a different challenge than many of their peers in French West Africa, who had immediately rejected the prospect of continuing the federation, or even in Nigeria where the regional governments were empowered to tackle many of the fundamental distributional questions.[52]

Questions of distribution loomed large across the decolonizing world, as the ideologies of development and welfare held out the hope that with planning and state intervention society could be transformed. Under the colonial doctrines of laissez-faire – Adam Smith along the Nile – which obscured colonial officials' utter domination of the economy, they proclaimed that the economy was governed by natural laws and that maintenance, not growth, was the sign of good governance. Political independence buoyed by promises of development held out the possibility of transformation, as people came to see the state as offering the possibility of deliverance even as they fled from the colonial state.

[52] Elizabeth Schmidt, *Cold War and Decolonization in Guinea, 1946–1958* (Athens: Ohio University Press, 2007), and Toyin Falola, *Development Planning and Decolonization in Nigeria* (Gainesville: University Press of Florida, 1995).

Yet who would have access to the scarce resources of the state? As the 1960s wore on, distributional conflicts tore apart a number of the most ambitious political projects across independent Africa; for example, Arthur Lewis blamed the crisis of distribution for the collapse of Kwame Nkrumah's regime in Ghana, distributional conflicts destroyed any hope of a French Federation, and issues of distribution engulfed Nigeria in the Biafran conflict.[53] Within Sudan a similar dynamic awaited as conflict broke out across the South and in regions long neglected by the central state. Rebel movements fought under the banner of development, often demanding more investment from the central government.

In many regions of Sudan, the promises of state-led development never materialized; neglect and counterinsurgency filled the vacuum. For those committed to state-led development of a unified Sudan, counterinsurgency became a tool: violence was seen as necessary to force the recalcitrant into submission, thereby creating a unified political consciousness throughout Sudan. The principle here was that, only by creating a unified political and economic space throughout Sudan, would development occur. At the same time, the opposite interpretation began to gain currency in Sudan and throughout much of the developing world as the 1960s wore on – essentially that the concept of national development was a trap. In the place of national development, Sudanese finance officials who had by now gained increased international experience, began to openly ask if development could only happen through closer integration with the world economy, an integration that had the aim of transforming the world economy.

53 Lewis, *Politics in West Africa*.

Conclusion: Toward a New African Economic History

By the early 2000s, the name Sudan had become a synonym for a "failed state." The causal outside observer would be forgiven for thinking of Sudan as trapped in an endless cycle of postcolonial civil wars, along with its neighbors to the west, Chad and the Central African Republic. For Americans coming of age in the 1990s, news reports of droughts, famines, slavery, and competing bands of youths of either the jihadi or the atavistic variety were likely to conjure up images of the chaos of Mogadishu or the genocide in Rwanda. After 9/11 and the revelation that Khartoum had harbored Osama Bin Laden for a time, the scene was perfectly set to couch Sudan's ongoing conflicts as religious and racial wars, as Muslim Arabs fighting Africans, Christian or not; at the same time the "Save Darfur Movement" made Sudan a cause across college and university campuses.[1] The signing of the Comprehensive Peace Agreement in 2005 between the National Congress Party and the Sudanese People Liberation Army/Movement, the two principal protagonists in Sudan's civil war, shone a spotlight on Sudan's political machinations in the runup to the country's partition in 2011. This partition, the only internationally recognized partition in postcolonial Africa aside from that of Sudan's eastern neighbors Ethiopia and Eritrea, created South Sudan, for now the newest country in the world.

But how did we get to a place where the concept of a failed state and Sudan was conjoined? Two types of explanations are frequently provided: the first attributes the sustained violence in Sudan to the persistence of primordial hatreds between different ethnic and religious groups in Sudan. The narrative tends to coalesce around religious or racial conflicts as the primary motivators of conflict in Sudan.[2] The second set of arguments naturalizes

[1] Mamdani, *Saviors and Survivors*.

[2] Jok, *War and Slavery in Sudan*. An explicit statement of the thesis that the Arab elite has sought to underdevelop Africans in relation to economic development can be found in Yongo-Bure,

structural explanations for the core's violent exploitation of the Sudanese periphery, imagining that Sudan's core-periphery exploitation dates to the nineteenth-century Egyptian conquest of the territory that eventually became Sudan or to the colonial period and the investment decisions of the Anglo-Egyptian Sudanese Condominium.[3] However, to understand policy making during the decade before and after Sudan's independence, the policy makers must be placed back into the intellectual environment of the weary optimism of the decolonization era, an optimism that engulfed the Sudanese.

This study takes seriously questions about policy making and bureaucracy in postcolonial Africa, which places it outside of much of the literature on the African state, which seeks to explain the failure of the African state as a result of the state either being too weak or too strong, rapacious, or predatory in relation to an often poorly defined society.[4] Yet, the institutions of the postcolonial state cannot so easily be dismissed.

This book tries to answer the question of how to judge the early postcolonial Sudanese state by making comparisons both explicit and implicit. The explicit comparison is shaped by the period under study, the era of decolonization. This allows the decision making of British colonial officials to be compared directly with that of the Sudanese officials who replaced them. It is in this comparison that one comes to see both the British and Sudanese as reasonable men, men who when tasked with the object of developing Sudan frequently fell back on similar choices, using similar calculative tools. In particular, I find myself struck by the commonalities that existed across the colonialism–nationalism divide. Political authorities came and went, as did colonialism, nationalism, civilian governments, and military governments, but serious ruptures in the ways in which policy makers defined their mandate occurred at different intervals. The choice of one over the other policy was often determined as much by the tools they used to calculate costs and benefits as by policy makers' ideologies.

The comparisons with policy makers elsewhere in the world are implicit. The Sudanese came under an economizing logic that was similar to that which befell

Economic Development of Southern Sudan; see also El Tom, *Darfur, JEM and the Khalil Ibrahim Story*.

3 Mamdani, *Saviors and Survivors*; O'Fahey, *The Darfur Sultanate*. For an up-to-date discussion of the limitations of both perspectives in application to Darfur see Vaughan, *Negotiating the State at its Margins*; see also Willis, "Violence, Authority, and the State in the Nuba Mountains of Condominium Sudan," pp. 92–93, and Johnson, *The Root Causes of Sudan's Civil Wars*, pp. 2–4.

4 Thus Bayart has asserted that it is a waste of time to study the institutions of the African state, the legal edifices of the state being little more than a shell to hide criminality, and the political networks of clients that in their very internationalism often make state institutions irrelevant. Jean-Francois Bayart, *The State in Africa: the Politics of the Belly* (New York: Longman, 1993), p. 211, and Jean-Francois Bayart, Stephen Ellis, and Beatrice Hibou, *The Criminalization of the State in Africa* (Bloomington: Indiana University Press, 1999), p. 20. See also Patrick Chabal and Jean Pascal Daloz, *Africa Works: Disorder as a Political Instrument* (Bloomington: Indiana University Press, 1999).

policy makers internationally in the middle decades of the twentieth century. The history of Sudan produced outcomes that by the 1980s made the country appear to be a "failed state," but the processes at work in the Sudan of the 1950s and 1960s were the same processes at work globally. After all, Sudanese financial bureaucrats were not particularly corrupt; their behavior can be explained by their adherence to the economizing logic of bureaucracy. Peter Hall writes that policy makers are both "puzzling" and "powering" in their practices.[5] As I analyzed the decisions that policy makers made, I have tried to emphasize how they learned, puzzled, and made mistakes.

Though frequently ignored, the Sudanese interlocutors of the various economic missionaries who alighted on Sudan began to appear everywhere in journals, studies, books, and files as I conducted my research. Their records were often impersonal, but within these records were located evidence of the decision-making processes and the intellectual frameworks that determined how financial policy was made in Sudan. Reading the notes of these officials, it was obvious that their papers had been neglected not just because they were scattered but also because they were not seen by scholars as relevant to the larger story of development as an international science and practice. Instead, these officials were either considered derivative, mere appliers of a science developed elsewhere, or corrupt.[6]

Unfortunately, African economic history today lacks a developed literature capable of creating an accurate portrayal of economic growth in Africa during the decades after World War II.[7] With its focus on localized studies often undertaken with an anthropological focus, the scholarly field of African Studies has exacerbated problems caused by the lack of synthetic works on African economic history or discussions of national or regional policy making. One of the fathers of the anthropological turn in African history, Steven Feierman, acknowledged in 1999 that the success of his methodology was making it increasingly difficult to tell African history at a macrolevel on its own terms.[8]

5 Peter A Hall, "Policy Paradigms, Social Learning, and the State: The Case of Economic Policymaking in Britain," *Comparative Politics* 250:3 (April 1993): 275–296.

6 Max Weber, trans. David S. Owen, and Tracy B. Strong, "Politics as a Vocation," *The Vocation Lectures* (New York: Hackett Publishing, 2004), pp. 32–95.

7 Anthony G. Hopkins. "The New Economic History of Africa," *Journal of African History* 50:2 (2009): 155–177; Gareth Austin, "Reciprocal Comparison and African History: Tackling Conceptual Eurocentrism in the Study of Africa's Economic Past," *African Studies Review* 50:3 (2007): 1–28; Robert H. Bates, John H. Coatsworth, and Jeffrey G. Williamson. "Lost Decades: Postindependence Performance in Latin America and Africa," *Journal of Economic History* 67:4 (2007): 917–943; Morten Jerven, "African Growth Recurring: An Economic History Perspective on African Growth Episodes, 1690–2010," *Economic History of Developing Regions* 25:2 (2010): 127–154.

8 Steven Feierman, "Colonizers, Scholars, and the Creation of Invisible Histories," in Victoria Bonnell, Lynn Hunt, and Richard Biernacki, eds., *Beyond the Cultural Turn: New Directions in the Study of Society and Culture* (Berkeley: University of California Press, 1999), p. 184.

The problem is that the lack of a macro- or even a mesolevel perspective on questions of Sudanese or Nigerian wealth and poverty threatens to lead us to ask the wrong questions. Since the 1960s, scholars ranging across the ideological spectrum from the socialist Walter Rodney to the neoliberal Robert Bates have asked why Africa is so poor. Yet, new economic data and the work of a recent generation of economic historians demonstrate that at an aggregate level Africa is roughly as wealthy as large parts of Asia and Latin America.[9] If African poverty is not exceptional, then the scholarly discussion should shift from asking why African states are so poor to answering new questions such as why many postcolonial states tolerate such drastic levels of domestic inequality. It might be time to redirect Bates's famous question: "Why should reasonable men adopt public policies that have harmful consequences for the societies they govern?"[10] His original question was designed to explain slowing national growth rates during the 1970s, but today we might ask it again to try and explain instead why economic policies were put in place that created localized sites of poverty and how policy officials and the societies they represent have come to tolerate such high levels of inequality.

Following on the work of two waves of scholarship, it is now possible to place postcolonial leaders inside of an intellectual world framed by development as a historical concept.[11] After all, Mahmood Mamdani astutely notes that, for the independence generation – those who went to school during the last days of colonialism, but began their professional careers during the first days of independence – their central assumption was that "the impact of colonialism on their societies was mainly economic" and that the coming of the postcolonial order would make economic sovereignty possible.[12] The challenge for historians who wish to understand the independence era is to distinguish the first-order observations of the politicians and policy makers, who constructed their world with an alluring certainty using developmental and economic rationalities, from the second-order observations that we as historians need to make about how these rationalities affect different actors' decision-making processes, often creating very contingent realities in their wake.[13] Nick Cullather argues

9 GDP calculations for Nigeria are the most important factor in creating a population weighted average for the African continent. Javier Blas and William Wallis, "Nigeria Almost Doubles GDP in Recalculation," *Financial Times* (April 7, 2014). www.ft.com/content/70b594fe-bd94–11e3-a5ba-00144feabdc0. Jerven, *Economic Growth and Measurement Reconsidered* and *Poor Numbers*.

10 Bates, *Markets and States in Tropical Africa*, p. 3.

11 Hodge, "Writing the History of Development (Part 1: The First Wave)," pp. 429–463, and "Writing the History of Development (Part 2: Longer, Deeper, Wider).

12 Mamdani, "Beyond Settler and Native as Political Identities," p. 651.

13 Thanks to Onur Ozgode for this reference and the concept of first- and second-order observations. Nikolas Luhmann, *Art as a Social System* (Palo Alto, CA: Stanford University Press, 2000).

that this distinction allows history to become "the methodology for studying modernization, instead of the other way around."[14]

However, even as the concepts of development theory are decentered into historical categories, economic concepts are still valuable tools for inferring the lived conditions of historical actors. Therefore the historian of economics in Sudan finds it necessary to also tell Sudanese economic history. Intervening directly into the debate about the causes of the "African Crisis" of the 1970s and 1980s, Thomas Piketty ties African states' relatively poor economic performance to the limited ability of these states to tax their societies. Reflecting in 2002 on that, the world systems theorist Giovanni Arrighi provided the following general sketch of the economic and social tragedy unfolding across the continent:

> In 1975, the regional GNP per capita of Sub-Saharan Africa stood at 17.6 per cent of "world" per capita GNP; by 1999 it had dropped to 10.5 per cent. Relative to overall Third World trends, Sub-Saharan health, mortality and adult-literacy levels have deteriorated at comparable rates. Life expectancy at birth now stands at 49 years, and 34 per cent of the region's population are classified as undernourished. African infant-mortality rates were 107 per 1,000 live births in 1999, compared to 69 for South Asia and 32 for Latin America. Nearly 9 per cent of Sub-Saharan 15- to 49-year-olds are living with HIV/AIDS – a figure that soars above those of other regions. Tuberculosis cases stand at 121 per 100,000 people; respective figures for South Asia and Latin America are 98 and 45.[15]

While new economic data raise questions about when Africa's economic recovery began or even if economic output really declined at the rates that scholars initially imagined, Arrighi's quote captures the magnitude of the social and economic disaster that occurred across wide swaths of the African continent during the last quarter of the twentieth century. Yet the failure of African economic growth is not the problem, as Frederick Cooper and Morten Jerven have recently established: "There have been moments of growth in Africa that met or exceeded the fastest contemporaneous world growth ... parts of West Africa in the era of the slave trade, the cocoa boom in West Africa in the colonial era, and the export boom of the 1950s and 1960s, plus – more ambiguously – the recent revival of exports."[16]

Paradoxically as new research raises questions about economic performance in absolute terms, the fiscal history of the African state becomes ever more relevant as a tool for understanding the yawning pockets of poverty. Piketty is largely correct in terms of the story he tells about the relationship between the state's declining ability to collect taxes and thereby direct investment and the subsequent decline in GDP growth, though perhaps not completely for the reasons he suspects. Like many economic historians he underestimates the extent

[14] Nick Cullather, "Development? It's History," *Diplomatic History* 24:4 (2000): 462.

[15] Arrighi, "The African Crisis," p. 5.

[16] Cooper, *Africa in the World*, pp. 32–33.

to which GDP is a proxy for the capacity of the state and overestimates the extent to which it is a proxy for actual economic activity.[17] One answer to the question about how to use time-series income data as historical evidence emerges from Jerven's argument about why the data regarding African economic performance vary so widely not just between countries but also over time for the same countries. He argues that, contrary to the views of data set users who have asserted that any inaccuracies in the numbers produced are random, and therefore can be treated as noise, the income data are biased in defined and historically contingent ways. Jerven's work moves beyond being a merely cautionary tale about the accuracy of historical data into a new form of evidence about the nature and structure of the African state in its own right.[18]

Treating economic indicators as a window into the nature of the state, and not primarily as a view of past economic activity, prepares us to study the variety of independent Africa's paths toward economic development.[19] To study the vast divergences in the structure of political economies across the continent, it is necessary to ground our work in a renewed intellectual history, one that takes seriously the ways in which prior experiences of colonialism, revolution, war, and reconstruction have formed the distinct infrastructures in which individual political and policy elites are grounded.[20] That the political and policy elites of individual African states possess divergent ideas about the aims of development, which are not converging on a Western norm, has been successfully demonstrated by scholars working on "illiberal development" as a distinct vision of political economy in countries such as Angola, Ethiopia, and Rwanda.[21] However, development models that appear

[17] Alden Young, "Are Statistics Useless? The Four Phases of the African State in the 20th Century": Review of Morten Jerven's *Poor Numbers* in *Books and Ideas* (November 12, 2013). www.booksandideas.net/Are-Statistics-Useless-2476.html [accessed April 3, 2016]; Ruth Rempel, "Periodizing African Development History," *African Economic History*: 36 (2008): 125–158.

[18] Jerven, "Measuring African Wealth and Progress," in *Poor Numbers*, pp. 33–55.

[19] Peter A. Hall and David Soskice, "An Introduction to Varieties of Capitalism," in Peter Hall and David Soskice, eds., *Varieties of Capitalism: The Institutional Foundations of Comparative Advantage* (New York: Oxford University Press, 2001), pp. 1–71; and as a framework for intra-African comparisons, see Tignor, *Capitalism and Nationalism at the End of Empire*; see also Hannah Appel, "Toward an Ethnography of the National Economy," *Cultural Anthropology* 32: 2 (2017): 294–322.

[20] Michael Woldemariam and Alden Young, "After the Split: Partition, Successor States, and the Dynamics of War in the Horn of Africa," *Journal of Strategic Studies* (2016); Michael Woldemariam, "Partition Problems: Relative Power, Historical Memory, and the Origins of the Eritrean-Ethiopian War," *Nationalism and Ethnic Politics* 21:2 (2015): 166–190; Pande, *Explaining Pakistan's Foreign Policy*; Fair, *Fighting to the End*.

[21] Will Jones, Ricardo Soares de Oliveira, Harry Verhoeven, "Africa's Illiberal State-Builders," *Refugee Studies Center, Working Papers* no. 89 (January 2013). www.rsc.ox.ac.uk/files/publications/working-paper-series/wp89-africas-illiberal-state-builders-2013.pdf; Ricardo Soares De Oliveira, *Magnificent and Beggarland: Angola since the Civil War* (New York: Oxford University Press, 2015); Verhoven, *Water, Civilization and Power in Sudan;* Elleni

alien to European or US analysts have their roots all the way back at the beginning of decolonization.

Centime Zeleke, "When Social Scientific Concepts Become Neutral Arbiters of Social Conflict: Reading the Ethiopian Federal Elections of 2005 through the Ethiopian Student Movement of the 1960s and 1970s," *Northeast African Studies* 16:1 (2016): 107–139.

Bibliography

Archival Sources

Sudan Archive at Durham, UK (SAD)
R. J. Smith Collection SAD G//S 498/6/
SAD 499/14/1–52/
W. N. Allen Collection SAD 593/8/1–61
J. W. Cummins Collection SAD G//S 636/1/
SAD G//S 635/12/
SAD G//S 635/14/
G. D. Lampen Collection SAD 732/8/
SAD 768/8/
SAD 768/9/
John Carmichael Collection SAD G//S 1166/1/1/
SAD G//S 1166/1/2/
SAD G//S 1166/1/3/
SAD G//S 1166/1/4
SAD G//S 1166/2/4/
SAD G//S 1166/2/5/
SAD G//S 1166/2/6
SAD G//S 1166/2/7/
SAD G//S 1166/3/1/
SAD G//S 1166/3/5/
SAD G//S 1166/4/6/
SAD G//S 1166/4/7/
National Records Office at Khartoum, Sudan (NRO)
Finance 3-A/25/1/2/
Finance 3-A/28/4/ Equatoria Projects Board
Finance 3-A/28/6/22
Finance 3-A/28/8/ Cotton Statistics and International Cotton
Fin 3-A/28/12/43/
Finance 3-A/28/13/47/

Finance 3-A/28/16/63
Finance 3-A/42/1/2/
Finance 3-A/42/1/3/
Finance 3-A/42/1/4/
Fin 3-A/42/2/5/
Finance 3-A/42/3/10/
Finance 3-A/59/1/2/.
The National Archives at Kew Gardens, UK (TNA)
FO 371/80387
FO 371/80404/
FO 371/80531/.
FO 371/96845/.
FO 371/96947/.
FO 371/97019/
FO 371/102739/
FO 371/102752/.
FO 371/102753/.
FO 371/102759/.
FO 371/125959/.
FO 371/125960/
FO 371/150919
FO 371/150965
FO 371/163921
FO 371/172364
FO 371/178613
FO 407/230/
FO 407/232/
FO 407/236/
FO 407/237/
National Archives and Records Administration of the United States at College Park, MD (NARA)
RG 59
World Bank Group Archive, Washington, DC (WBGA)
Records of the International Bank of Reconstruction and Development pertaining to Sudan
Administration
Negotiations
International Monetary Fund Archive, Washington, DC (IMF)
Memos to Members of the Executive Board of the International Monetary Fund pertaining to Sudan and to Hamza Mirghani Hamza

Printed Sources

Abaza, A. F., 1940. *Buhuth al-Iqtisadiya 'an al-Sudan*. Cairo: Dar al-Taba 'at al-Masriya.

Abbas, M., 1952. *The Sudan Question*. London: Faber and Faber.

Abbas, P., 1973. "Growth of Black Consciousness in Northern Sudan," *Africa Today* 20:3, 29–43.

Abu Salim, M., 1992. *Buhuth fi Tarikh al-Sudan: al-Aradi, al-'Ulama', al-Khilafah, Barbar, 'Ali al- Mirghani*. Beirut: Dar al-Jil.

Acemoglu, D., S. Johnson, and J. A. Robinson, 2005. "Institutions as a Fundamental Cause of Long-Run Growth," in Philippe Aghion and Steven N. Durlauf, eds., *Handbook of Economic Growth*, Vol. 1A. Oxford: Elsevier, 386–464.

Adelman, J., 2008. "An Age of Imperial Revolutions," *American Historical Review* 113:2, 319–340.

2013. *Wordly Philosophers: The Odyssey of Albert O. Hirschman*. Princeton: Princeton University Press.

Alacevich, M., 2009. *The Political Economy of the World Bank: The Early Years*. Stanford: Stanford University Press.

Al-Amin, A. R., 2005. *Al-Fariq Ibrahim 'Abbud wa 'Asruhu al-Dhahabi*. Khartoum: 'Abd al-Rahman Ahmed 'Isa.

'Ali, J. S., 2008. *Al-Sira al-Siyasiya 'ala al-Sudan 1840–2008*. Beirut: Sirka Matabi 'a al-Sudan lil 'Amila al-Mahdudat.

Anderson, B., 2006. *Imagined Communities: Reflections on the Origins and Spread of Nationalism*. New York: Verso Press.

Andersson, J., 2012. "The Great Future Debate and the Struggle for the World," *American Historical Review* 117:5, 1411–1430.

Appel, H., 2017. "Toward an Ethnography of the National Economy," *Cultural Anthropology* 32:2, 294–322.

Armitage, D., 2000. *The Ideological Origins of the British Empire*. New York: Cambridge University Press.

Arndt, H. W., 1987. *Economic Development: The History of an Idea*. Chicago: University of Chicago Press.

1984. *The Rise and Fall of Economic Growth: A Study in Contemporary Thought*. Chicago: University of Chicago Press.

Arrighi, G., 2002. "The African Crisis: World Systemic and Regional Aspects," *New Left Review* 15.

Austin, G., 2007. "Reciprocal Comparison and African History: Tackling Conceptual Eurocentrism in the Study of Africa's Economic Past," *African Studies Review* 50:3, 1–28.

Barnett, T., 1977. *The Gezira Scheme: An Illusion of Development*. New York: Routledge.

Bates, R., 1981. *Markets and States in Tropical Africa: The Political Basis of Agricultural Policies*. Berkeley: University of California Press.

Bates, R., J. H. Coatsworth, and J. G. Williamson, 2007. "Lost Decades: Postindependence Performance in Latin America and Africa," *Journal of Economic History* 67:4, 917–943.

Bauer, P. T., 1954, *West African Trade: A Study of Competition, Oligopoly and Monopoly in a Changing Economy*. New York: Cambridge University Press.

Bayart, J. F., 1993. *The State in Africa: the Politics of the Belly*. New York: Longman.

Bayart, J. F., S. Ellis, and B. Hibou, 1999. *The Criminalization of the State in Africa*. Bloomington: Indiana University Press.

Bechtold, P. K., 1976. *Politics in the Sudan: Parliamentary and Military Rule in an Emerging African Nation*, New York: Praeger.

Beckert, S., 2004. "Emancipation and Empire: Reconstructing the Worldwide Web of Cotton Production in the Age of the American Civil War," *American Historical Review* 109:5, 1405–1438.

Beheiry, M., 2003. *Glimpses from the Life of a Sudanese Public Servant* Omdurman, Sudan: M. O. Besheer Center for Sudanese Studies.

Bernal, V., 1997. "Colonial Moral Economy and the Discipline of Development: The Gezira Scheme and 'Modern' Sudan," *Cultural Anthropology* 12:4, 447–479.

1995. "Cotton and Colonial Order in Sudan: A Social History with Emphasis on the Gezira Scheme," in Allen Isaacman and Richard Roberts, eds., *Cotton Colonialism and Social History in Sub-Saharan Africa*. Portsmouth, NH: Heinemann, 96–118.

Bernstein, Henry, 1977. "Notes on Capital and Peasantry," *Review of African Political Economy* 4:10, 60–73.

Berridge, W. J., 2015. *Civil Uprisings in Modern Sudan: The 'Khartoum Springs' of 1964 and 1985*. New York: Bloomsbury.

Berry, S., 1998. "Unsettled Accounts: Stool Debts, Chieftaincy Disputes and the Question of Asante Constitutionalism," *Journal of African History* 39:1, 39–62.

Beshai, A. A., 1976. *Export Performance and Economic Development in Sudan, 1900–1967*. London: Ithaca Press.

Beusekom, M., 2000. "Disjunctures in Theory and Practice: Making Sense of Change in Agricultural Development at the Office Du Niger, 1920–60," *Journal of African History* 41:1, 79–99.

Beusekom, M., and Dorothy L. Hodgson, 2000. "Lessons Learned? Development Experience during the Late Colonial Period," *Journal of African History*, 41:1, 29–33.

Bhattacharyya, D., 2016. "Interwar Housing Speculation and Rent Profiteering in Colonial Calcutta," *Comparative Studies of South Asia, Africa and the Middle East* 36:3, 465–482.

Bjorkelo, A., 2003. *Prelude to the Mahdiyya: Peasants and Traders in the Shendi Region, 1821–1885*. New York: Cambridge University Press.

Bonnecase, V., 2011. *La Pauvreté au Sahel: Du Savoir Colonial à la Mesure Internationale*. Paris: Karthala.

Boone, C., 2014. *Property and Political Order in Africa: Land Rights and the Structure of Politics*. New York: Cambridge University Press.

Byrne, J., 2016. *Mecca of Revolution: Algeria, Decolonization, and the Third World Order*. Oxford: Oxford University Press.

Cain P. J., and A. G. Hopkins, 2002. *British Imperialism: 1688–2000*. London: Pearson Education.

Cairncross, A., 1985. *Years of Recovery: British Economic Policy, 1945–1951*. New York: Methuen and Co.

Chabal, P., and J. P. Daloz, 1999. *Africa Works: Disorder as a Political Instrument*. Bloomington: Indiana University Press.

Clapham, C., ed., 1998. *African Guerillas*. Oxford: James Currey.

Coleman, J., 1971. *Nigeria: Background to Nationalism*. Berkeley: University of California Press.

Collins, R. O., 2008. *A History of Modern Sudan*. New York: Cambridge University Press.

1996. *Hydropolitics and the Jonglei Canal, 1900–1988*. Princeton: Markus Weiner.

1983. *Shadows in the Grass: Britain in the Southern Sudan, 1918–1956*. New Haven: Yale University Press,

1972. "The Sudan Political Service: A Portrait of the 'Imperialists,'" *African Affairs*. 71:284, 293–303.

1996. *The Waters of the Nile: Hydropolitics and the Jonglei Canal, 1900–1988*. Princeton: Markus Wiener.

Conrad, S., 2016, *What Is Global History*? Princeton: Princeton University Press.

Cooper, F., 2014. *Africa in the World: Capitalism, Empire, Nation-State*. Cambridge, MA: Harvard University Press.

2002. *Africa since 1940: The Past of the Present*. New York: Cambridge University Press.

2014. *Citizenship between Empire and Nation: Remaking France and French Africa, 1945–1960*. Princeton: Princeton University Press.

2016. "Commentary on the Essay of Joseph Hodge," *Humanity*, May 3, 2016, http://humanityjournal.org/blog/commentary-on-the-essay-of-joseph-hodge/.

1996. *Decolonization and African Society: The Labor Question in French and British Africa*. Cambridge: Cambridge University Press.

1998. "Modernizing Bureaucrats, Backward Africans, and the Development Concept," in Frederick Cooper and Randall Packard, eds., *International Development and the Social Sciences: Essays on the History and Politics of Knowledge*. Berkeley: University of California Press, 64–84.

2008. "Possibility and Constraint: African Independence in Historical Perspective," *Journal of African History* 49, 167–196.

2001. "What Is the Concept of Globalization Good For? An African Historian's Perspective," *African Affairs* 100:2001, 189–213.

2010, "Writing the History of Development," *Journal of Modern European History* 8:1, 5–23.

Copnall, J. A 2014. *Poisonous Thorn in Our Hearts: Sudan and South Sudan's Bitter and Incomplete Divorce*. New York: Hurst Press.

Cormack, R. 2016, "The Legendary Bookseller of Cairo," *Apollo: The International Art Magazine*, www.apollo-magazine.com/the-legendary-bookseller-of-cairo [accessed January 16, 2017].

Cormack, Z. 2017, "The Spectacle of Death: Visability and Concealment at an Unfinished Memorial in South Sudan," *Journal of Eastern African Studies* 11:1, 115–132.

Crozier, M., S. Huntington, and J. Watanuki, 1975. *The Crisis of Democracy: On the Governability of Democracies to the Trilateral Commission*. New York: New York University Press.

Cullather, N., 2000. "Development? It's History." *Diplomatic History* 24:4, 641–653.

Daly, M. W., 2007. *Darfur's Sorrow: A History of Destruction and Genocide*, Cambridge: Cambridge University Press.

1983. "The Development of the Governor-Generalship of the Sudan, 1899–1934," *Journal of African History* 24:1, 77–96.

1986. *Empire on the Nile: The Anglo-Egyptian Sudan, 1898–1934*. Cambridge: Cambridge University Press.

2002. *Imperial Sudan: The Anglo-Egyptian Condominium, 1934–56*. New York: Cambridge University Press.

Darwin, J., 2009. *The Empire Project: The Rise and Fall of the British World-System, 1830–1970*. Cambridge: Cambridge University Press.

Das V., and D. Poole, 2004. "State and Its Margins: Comparative Ethnographies," in Veena Das and Deborah Poole, eds., *Anthropology at the Margins of the State*. Oxford: James Currey Press, 3–35.

Deane, P., 1955. "The Implications of Early National Income Estimates for the Measurement of Long-Term Economic Growth in the United Kingdom," *Economic Development and Cultural Change* 4:1, Part 1.

Deng, F. M., and M. W. Daly, 1989. *Bonds of Silk: The Human Factor in the British Administration of Sudan*. East Lansing: Michigan State University Press.

Department of Economic Planning, Ministry of Finance and Economics, Republic of Sudan, 1965. *The Ten Year Plan of Economic and Social Development 1961/62–1970/71: Explanatory Memorandum on 1964/65 Development Budgets*. Khartoum: Government Printing Press.

Department of Statistics (H.Q. Council of Ministers), 1959. *National Income of Sudan (in Brief). 1955/56*, Occasional Statistical Paper No. 2 Khartoum: Government Printing Press.

Deringer, W. in press. *Calculated Values: Financial Politics and the Quantitative Age, 1688–1776*. Cambridge, MA: Harvard University Press.

Desrosieres, A., trans. C. Nash, 1998. *The Politics of Large Numbers: A History of Statistical Reasoning*. Cambridge, MA: Harvard University Press.

De Waal, A. 2010. "*Dollarised*," *London Review of Books*, June: 38–41.

2007. "Sudan: The Turbulent State," in A. De Waal, ed., *War in Darfur and the Search for Peace*. Cambridge, MA: Global Equity Initiative, Harvard University.

De Waal, A., & A. H. Abdel Salam, "Islamism, State Power and Jihad in Sudan," in A. De Waal, ed., *Islamism and its Enemies in the Horn of Africa*. London: Hurst, 2004.

Der Wee, H. V., 1984. *Prosperity and Upheaval: The World Economy, 1945–1980*. Berkeley: University of California Press.

Du Bois, W. E. B. 1947. *The World and Africa: An Inquiry into the Part that Africa Has Played in World History*, New York: Viking Press.

Easterly, W. 2002. *The Elusive Quest for Growth: Economists Adventures and Misadventures in the Tropics*. Cambridge, MA: MIT Press.

1997. *The Ghost of Financing Gap: How the Harrod-Domar Growth Model Still Haunts Development Economics, Policy Research Working Paper 1807*. Washington, DC: World Bank Development Research Group.

Economic Planning Secretariat, Ministry of Finance and Economics, 1962. *The Ten Year Plan of Economic and Social Development, 1961/62–1970/71*, Khartoum: Government Printing Press.

Eichengreen, B., 2015, *Hall of Mirrors: The Great Depression, the Great Recession, and the Uses – and Misuses – of History*. New York: Oxford University Press.

Escobar, A., 1995. *Encountering Development: The Making and Unmaking of the Third World*. Princeton: Princeton University Press.

Fair, C., 2014. *Fighting to the End: The Pakistani Army's Way of War*. Oxford: Oxford University Press.

Falola, T., 1995. *Development Planning and Decolonization in Nigeria*. Gainesville: University Press of Florida.

Fawzi, S. 1958. *Muhadirat ʿan Juanib min al-Iqtisad al-Sudan ʿala taliba Qasim al-Darasat al-Iqtisadiya wa al-Ijtimaʿaiya*. Cairo: al-Mutab ʿat al- Kamalit.

Feichtinger, M., and S. Malinowski, 2014. "Transformative Invasions: Western Post 9/11 Counterinsurgency and the Lessons of Colonialism," *Humanity* 3:1, 35–63.

Feierman, S., 1999. "Colonizers, Scholars, and the Creation of Invisible Histories," in Victoria Bonnell, Lynn Hunt, and Richard Biernacki, eds., *Beyond the Cultural Turn: New Directions in the Study of Society and Culture*. Berkeley: University of California Press.

Federation of British Industries, 1963. *Assessment of Sudan's Ten Year Plan* London: FBI.
Ferguson, H., 1954. *The Zande Scheme*. Khartoum: Agricultural Publications Committee.
Ferguson, J., 1994. *The Anti-Politics Machine: "Development," Depoliticization, and Bureaucratic Power in Lesotho*. Minneapolis: University of Minnesota Press.
2015. *Give a Man a Fish: Reflections on the New Politics of Distribution*. Durham, NC: Duke University Press.
2006. *Global Shadows: Africa in the Neoliberal World Order*. Durham, NC: Duke University Press.
2005. "Seeing like an Oil Company: Space, Security, and Global Capital in Neoliberal Africa," *American Anthropologist*, 107:3, 377–382.
Fforde, J., 1992. *The Bank of England and Public Policy, 1941–1958*. Cambridge: Cambridge University Press.
Finance Department, Sudan Government, 1946. *Five Year Plan for Post-War Development*. Khartoum: Finance Department.
1953. *The Sudan Development Programme 1951/56* Khartoum: Finance Department.
Flint, J., and A. De Waal, 2008. *Darfur: A New History of a Long War*. London: Zed.
Frankel, H. S., 1938. *Capital Investment in Africa: Its Course and Effects*. New York: Oxford University Press.
1952. "'Psychic' and 'Accounting' Concepts of Income and Welfare," *Oxford Economic Papers* 14:1, 1–17.
Friedman, B., 2006. *The Moral Consequences of Economic Growth*. New York: Vintage Press.
Frey, M,. and S. Kunkel, 2011. "Writing the History of Development: A Review of the Recent Literature," *Contemporary European History* 20:2, 215–232.
Gaitskill, A., 1959. *Gezira: A Story of Development in the Sudan*. London: Faber and Faber.
Gallab, A., 2008. *First Islamic Republic*. Aldershot, UK: Ashgate.
Garavini, G., 2012. *After Empires: European Integration, Decolonization, and the Challenge from the Global South, 1957–1986*. New York: Oxford University Press.
Gardner, L., 2012. *Taxing Colonial Africa: The Political Economy of British Imperialism*. Oxford: Oxford University Press.
Gifford, P., and W. R. Louis, eds., 1982. *The Transfer of Power in Africa: Decolonization, 1940–1960*. New Haven: Yale University Press.
Gilman, N., 2007. *Mandarins of the Future: Modernization Theory in Cold War America*. Baltimore: Johns Hopkins University Press.
2015. "The New International Economic Order: A Reintroduction," *Humanity* 6:1. 1–15.
Goswami, M., 2004. *Producing India: From Colonial Economy to National Space*. Chicago: University of Chicago Press.
Gusten, R., 1966. *Problems of Economic Growth and Planning; the Sudan Example; Some Aspects and Implications of the Current Ten-Year Plan*. New York: Springer-Verlag.
Hajj Hamad, M. A. Q., 1980. *Al-Sudan: al-Ma' ziq al-Tarikhi wa Afaq al-Mustaqbal*. Beirut: Dar al-Kalimat lil Nashr.
Hall, P., 1993. "Policy Paradigms, Social Learning, and the State: The Case of Economic Policymaking in Britain," *Comparative Politics* 25:3, 275–296.

Hall, P., and David Soskice, 2001. "An Introduction to Varieties of Capitalism," in Peter Hall and David Soskice, eds., *Varieties of Capitalism: The Institutional Foundations of Comparative Advantage* New York: Oxford University Press, 1–71.

Hamzah, S. M., 1965. *Iqtisadiyat al-Sudan*. al-Qahirah: Maktabat al-Ahram al-Iqtisadi.

Harvie, C. H., and Kleve, J. G., 1959. *The National Income of Sudan 1955/56*. Khartoum: Department of Statistics.

Hasabu, A., 1985. *Factional Conflict in the Sudanese Nationalist Movement*. Khartoum: Graduate College, University of Khartoum.

Hasan, Y. F., 1967. "The Sudanese Revolution of October 1964," *Journal of Modern African Studies* 5:4, 491–509.

*al-Hassan, A. M., ed. 1976. *An Introduction to the Sudan Economy*. Khartoum: Khartoum University Press.

Henderson, K. D. D., 1966. *Sudan Republic*. New York: Praeger.

Herbst, J. 2000. *States and Power in Africa: Comparative Lessons in Authority and Control*. Princeton: Princeton University Press.

Hill, R., 1959. *Egypt in the Sudan, 1820–1881*. Oxford: Oxford University Press.

Hinds, A., 2001. *Britain's Sterling Colonial Policy and Decolonization, 1939–1958*. Westport, CT: Greenwood Press.

1991. "Imperial Policy and Colonial Sterling Balances, 1943–1956," *Journal of Imperial and Commonwealth History*, 19:1, 24–44.

Hirschman, D., and E. P. Berman, 2014. "Do Economists Make Policies? On the Political Effects of Economics," *Socio-Economic Review* 12. DOI: 10.1093/ser/mwu017.

Hodge, J. M., 2010. "British Colonial Expertise, Postcolonial Careering and the Early History of International Development," *Journal of Modern European History* 8:1, 24–46.

Triumph of the Expert: Agrarian Doctrines of Development and the Legacies of British Colonialism. Athens: Ohio University Press, 2007.

2015. "Writing the History of Development (Part 1: The First Wave)," *Humanity* 6:3, 429–463.

2016. "Writing the History of Development (Part 2: Longer, Deeper, Wider)," *Humanity* 7:1, 125–174.

Holt, P. M., *The Mahdist State in Sudan, 1881–1898*. Oxford: Clarendon Press, 1958.

Hopkins, A., 2009. "The New Economic History of Africa," *Journal of African History* 50:2, 155–177.

Howell. J., and M. B. Hamid, 1969. "Sudan and the Outside World, 1964–1968," *African Affairs* 68:273, 299–300.

Huntington, S. P., 1996. *The Clash of Civilizations and the Remaking of the World Order*. New York: Simon & Schuster.

1968/2006. *Political Order in Changing Societies*. New Haven: Yale University Press.

Idris, A. H., 2001. *Sudan's Civil Wars: Slavery, Race and Formational Identities*. Lewiston, NY: Edwin Mellon Press.

Immerwahr, D., 2012. "Modernization and Development in U.S. Foreign Policy," *Passport: The Society for Historians of American Foreign Relations Review* 43:2, 22–25.

International Monetary Fund. 1960. *Fund Policies and Procedures in Relation to the Compensatory Financing of Commodity Fluctuations*. New York: IMF.

1952. *Instability in Export Markets of Underdeveloped Countries*. New York: IMF.

Jackson, R., and Carl Rosberg, 1982."Why Africa's Weak States Persist: The Empirical and Juridical in Statehood," *World Politics* 35(1), 1–24.
James, H., 2001. *The End of Globalization: Lessons from the Great Depression*. Cambridge, MA: Harvard University Press.
1996. *International Monetary Cooperation since Bretton Woods*. New York: Oxford University Press.
Jasanoff, S., 2015, "Future Imperfect: Science, Technology, and the Imaginations of Modernity," in Sheila Jasanoff and Sung-Hyun Kim, eds., *Dreamscapes of Modernity: Sociotechnical Imaginaries and the Fabrication of the Power*. Chicago: University of Chicago Press.
2012. "Reason in Practice," in Sheila Jasanoff, ed., *Science and Public Reason*. New York: Routledge: 1–23.
Jensen, S. L. B., 2016. *The Making of International Human Rights: The 1960s, Decolonization and the Reconstruction of Global Values*. New York: Cambridge University Press.
Jerven, M., 2010. "African Growth Recurring: An Economic History Perspective on African Growth Episodes, 1690–2010," *Economic History of Developing Regions* 25:2, 127–154.
2015. *Africa: Why Economists Get it Wrong*? New York: Zed Press.
2014, *Economic Growth and Measurement Reconsidered in Botswana, Kenya, Tanzania, and Zambia, 1965–1995*. New York: Oxford University Press.
2013. *Poor Numbers: How We Are Misled By African Development Statistics and What to Do about It*. Ithaca, NY: Cornell University Press.
2011. "Users and Producers of African Income: Measuring African Progress," *African Affairs* 110:439, 169–190.
Johnson, D., 2003. *The Root Causes of Sudan's Civil Wars*. Bloomington: Indiana University Press.
Jok, J. M., 2001. *War and Slavery in Sudan*. Philadelphia: University of Pennsylvania Press.
Jones, W., Ricardo Soares de Oliveira, and Harry Verhoeven, 2013. "Africa's Illiberal State-Builders." *Refugee Studies Center, Working Papers* no. 89. www.rsc.ox.ac.uk/files/publications/working-paper-series/wp89-africas-illiberal-state-builders-2013.pdf.
Kaplan, R. 1998. *Surrender or Starve: Travels in Ethiopia, Sudan, Somalia, and Eritrea*. New York: Vintage.
Keen, David, 1994. *The Benefits of Famine: A Political Economy of Famine and Relief in Southwestern Sudan, 1983–1989*. Princeton: Princeton University Press.
Kreike, E., 2013. *Environmental Infrastructure in African History: Examining the Myth of Natural Resource Management in Namibia*. New York: Cambridge University Press.
Lal, P., 2015. *African Socialism in Postcolonial Tanzania: Between the Village and the World*. New York: Cambridge University Press.
Latham, M., 2000. *Modernization as Ideology: American Social Science and "Nation-Building" in the Kennedy Era*. Chapel Hill: University of North Carolina Press.
Latour, B., 1988. *Science in Action: How to Follow Scientists and Engineers through Society*. Cambridge, MA: Harvard University Press.
1986. "Visualisation and Cognition: Drawing Things Together," *Knowledge and Society Studies in the Sociology of Culture Past and Present* 6: 1–40.

Leonardi, C. 2013. *Dealing with Government in South Sudan: Histories of Chiefship, Community and State*. Woodbridge, Suffolk: James Currey Press.

2005. *Knowing Authority: Colonial Authority and Local Community in Equatoria Province, Sudan, 1900–1956*. PhD diss., Durham University, UK.

LeRiche, M., and M. Arnold, 2013. *South Sudan from Revolution to Independence*. London: Hurst Co..

Lesch, A. 1998. *The Sudan: Contested National Identities*. Bloomington: Indiana University Press.

Lewis, J., 2001. *Empire State-Building: War and Welfare in Kenya, 1925–52*. Athens: Ohio University Press.

2001. "The Ruling Compassions of the Late Colonial State: Welfare versus Force, Kenya, 1945–1952," *Journal of Colonialism and Colonial History*, 21: 2. http://muse.jhu.edu/journals/journal_of_colonialism_and_colonial_history/v002/2.2lewis.html.

Lewis, W. A., 1965. *Politics in West Africa*. Oxford: Oxford University Press.

Louis, W. R., 1984. *The British Empire in the Middle East, 1945–1951: Arab Nationalism, the United States, and Postwar Imperialism*. Oxford: Clarendon Press.

Low, D. A., and J. M. Lonsdale, 1976. "Introduction: Towards the New Order, 1945–1963," in D. A. Low and Alison Smith, eds., *History of East Africa Vol. III*. Oxford: Clarendon Press, 1–63.

Luhmann, N., 2000. *Art as a Social System*. Palo Alto, CA: Stanford University Press.

Mahgoub, M., 1974. *Democracy on Trial: Reflections on Arab and African Politics*. London: Deutsch.

Mahmoud, F. B., 1984. *The Sudanese Bourgeoisie: Vanguard of Development*? London: Zed Books.

Mahmud, U., and S. Baldo, 1987. *The Dhein Massacre: Slavery in the Sudan*. London: Sudan Relief and Rehabilitation Association.

Maier, C., 1988. *In Search of Stability: Explorations in Historical Political Economy*. Cambridge: Cambridge University Press.

Mamdani, M., 2001. "Beyond Settler and Native as Political Identities: Overcoming the Political Legacy of Colonialism," *Comparative Studies in Society and History* 43:4, 651–664.

1996. *Citizen and Subject: Contemporary Africa and the Legacy of Late Colonialism*. Princeton: Princeton University Press.

2009. *Saviors and Survivors: Darfur, Politics, and the War on Terror*. New York: Pantheon.

Mann, L. 2011. *The Retreat of the State and the Market: Liberalization and Education Expansion under the NCP*. PhD diss., University of Edinburgh, 2011.

Mantena, K., 2007. "The Crisis of Liberal Imperialism," in Duncan Bell, ed., *Victorian Visions of Global Order: Empire and International Relations in Nineteenth-Century Political Thought*. New York: Cambridge University Press, 21–56.

Merry, S. E., 2009. "Measuring the World: Indicators, Human Rights, and Global Governance," *Proceedings of the Annual Meeting (American Society of International Law)* 103: 239–243.

Merton, R. 1973. "The Normative Structure of Science," in Norman W. Storer, ed., *The Sociology of Science: Theoretical and Empirical Investigations* Chicago: University of Chicago Press, 267–278.

Mikhail, A. 2012. *Nature and Empire in Ottoman Egypt: An Environmental History*. New York: Cambridge University Press.
Mills, D. E., 2014. *Dividing the Nile: Egypt's Economic Nationalists in the Sudan 1918–1956*. New York: American University of Cairo Press.
Ministry of Social Affairs, 1958. *First Population Census of the Sudan, 1955/56*. Khartoum: Ministry of Social Affairs.
Mirghani, A. R., 1983. *Development Planning in the Sudan in the Sixties*. Khartoum: University of Khartoum Press.
Mitchell, T., 2011. *Carbon Democracy: Political Power in the Age of Oil*. New York: Verso Press.
1991. *Colonising Egypt*. Berkeley: University of California Press.
2014. "Economentality: How the Future Entered Government," *Critical Inquiry* 40:4, 479–507.
1998. "Fixing the Economy," *Cultural Studies* 12:1: 82–101.
2002. *The Rule of Experts: Egypt, Techno-Politics, Modernity*. Berkeley: University of California Press.
Mkandawire, T. 2015. "Neopatrimonalism and the Political Economy of Economic Performance in Africa: Critical Reflections," *World Politics* 67:3, 563–612.
2002. "Thinking about Developmental States in Africa," *Cambridge Journal of Economics* 25:3, 289–313.
Mollan, S., 2008. "Business, State and Economy: Cotton and the Anglo-Egyptian Sudan, 1919–1939," *African Economic History* 36: 95–123.
Morgan, M. S., 2008. "'On a Mission' with Mutable Mobiles." *Working Paper on the Nature of Evidence: How Well Do 'Facts' Travel?* No. 34/08. London School of Economics, Department of Economic History, 3-52.
2011. "Seeking Parts, Looking for Wholes," in Lorraine Daston and Elizabeth Lunbeck, eds., *Histories of Scientific Observation*. Chicago: University of Chicago Press.
2012. *The World in the Model: How Economists Work and Think*. New York: Cambridge University Press.
Moure, K., 2002. *The Gold Standard Illusion: France, the Bank of France and the International Gold Standard, 1914–1939*. Oxford: Oxford University Press.
Moyn, S. 2015. "Fantasies of Federalism," *Dissent* 62:1, 145–151. www.dissentmagazine.org/article/fantasies-of-federalism.
2013. "On the Nonglobalization of Ideas," in S. Moyn and A. Sartori, eds. *Global Intellectual History*. New York: Columbia University Press, 187–205.
*al-Mukhtar, A. R., 1978. *al-Harif al-Farah: Asrar al-Sudan, 1950–1970*. Khartoum: Dar al-Sahafa.
Newton, S., 1985. "Britain, the Sterling Area and European Integration, 1945–1950," *Journal of Imperial and Commonwealth History*, 13: 3: 163–182.
Niblock, T., 1987. *Class and Power in Sudan: The Dynamics of Sudanese Politics, 1898–1985*. Albany: SUNY Press.
Nimeiri, S., 1978. *Takhtit al-Iqtisadi fi al-Sudan*. Khartoum: al-Khartum lil-Nashr.
Nyaba, P. A., 1996. *The Politics of Liberation in South Sudan*. Chicago: Fountain Press.
Nyquist, T. E., 1965. "The Sudan: Prelude to Elections," *Middle East Journal* 19:3, 263–272.
O'Fahey, R. S., 2008. *The Darfur Sultanate: A History*. New York: Columbia University Press.

Okigbo, P. C., 1989. *National Development Planning in Nigeria, 1900–92*. Oxford: James Currey.

O'Neill, N., and J. O'Brien, eds., 1988. *Economy and Class in Sudan*. Brookfield, VT: Avebury.

Owen, R., 2012. *The Rise and Fall of Arab Presidents for Life*. Cambridge, MA: Harvard University Press.

2002. "The Dog that Neither Barked Nor Bit: The Fear of Oil Shortages," in William Roger Lewis and Roger Owen, eds., *A Revolutionary Year: The Middle East in 1958*. New York: I. B. Tauris, 275–288.

Pande, A., 2011. *Explaining Pakistan's Foreign Policy: Escaping India*. Abingdon: Routledge.

Perham, Margery, 1952. "Editor's Preface," in Mekki Abbas, ed., *The Sudan Question: The Dispute over the Anglo-Egyptian Condominium, 1884–1951*. London: Faber and Faber.

Peterson, D., 2010. "Abolitionism and Political Thought in Britain and East Africa," in Derek Peterson, ed., *Abolitionism and Imperialism in Britain, Africa and the Atlantic*. Athens: Ohio University Press, 1–37.

Pierce, S., 2006. "Looking like a State: Colonialism and the Discourse of Corruption in Northern Nigeria," *Comparative Studies in History and Society* 48:4, 887–914.

Pierre, J., 2012. *The Predicament of Blackness: Postcolonial Ghana and the Politics of Race*. Chicago: University of Chicago Press.

Poduval, R. N., 1963. "Sudan's Ten Year Plan of Economic and Social Development," United Arab Republic Institute of National Planning, *Memo. No. 333*, May 29, Cairo.

Poggo, S., 2009. *The First Sudanese Civil War: Africans, Arabs, and Israelis in the Southern Sudan, 1955–1972*. New York: St. Martin's Press.

Powell, E. T., 2003. *A Different Shade of Colonialism: Egypt, Britain, and the Mastery of Sudan*. Berkeley: University of California Press.

Prashad, V., 2007. *The Darker Nations: A People's History of the Third World*. New York: New Press.

Prakash, G., 1999. *Another Reason: Science and the Imagination of Modern India*. Princeton: Princeton University Press.

Prest, A. R.. and I. G. Stewart. 1953. *The National Income of Nigeria, 1950–1951*. London: H. M. Stationery Office.

Rahal, M., 2012a. "Comment faire l'histoire de l' Algerie independante?," *La Vie des Idees.fr*. www.laviedesidees.fr/Comment-faire-l-histoire-de-l-Algerie-independante.html [January 16, 2017].

2012b. "Fused Together and Torn Apart: Stories and Violence in Contemporary Algeria," *History and Memory* 24:1, 118–151.

Rahim, M. A., 1966. "The Development of British Policy in Southern Sudan," *Middle Eastern Studies* 2.3:227–249.

Rasakh, G., n.d. "Hamza Mirghani Hamza: Wazir al-Malia Al-Sudan," *Sudanyat.com*. http://sudanyat.org/vb/showthread.php?p=569457 [accessed July 26, 2014].

Reinert, S., 2011. *Translating Empire: Emulation and the Origins of Political Economy*. Cambridge, MA: Harvard University Press.

Reining, C., 1966. *The Zande Scheme*. Evanston, IL: Northwestern University Press.

Rempel, R., 2008. "Periodizing African Development History," *African Economic History* 36, 125–158.

Reynolds, M., 2011. *Shattering Empires: The Clash and Collapse of the Ottoman and Russian Empires, 1908–1918*. Cambridge: Cambridge University Press.
Rist, G., 2009. *The History of Development: From Western Origins to Global Faith*. New York: Zed Books.
Roberts, R. 1996. *Two Worlds of Cotton: Colonialism and the Regional Economy in the French Soudan, 1800–1946*. Stanford: Stanford University Press.
Rolandsen, O., 2011. "A False Start between War and Peace in the Southern Sudan: 1956–1962," *Journal of African History* 52:1: 105–123.
Rolandsen, O., and C. Leonardi, 2014. "Discourses of Violence in the Transition from Colonialism to Independence in Southern Sudan, 1955–1960," *Journal of Eastern African Studies* 8:4, 609–625.
Rosenthal, C., 2013. "From Memory to Mastery: Accounting for Control in America, 1750–1880," *Enterprise and Society* 14:4, 732–748.
Rothschild, E., 2014. "Isolation and Economic Development in Eighteenth Century France," *American Historical Review* 119:4, 1055–1082.
Ryzova, L., 2014. *The Age of the Efendiyya: Passages to Modernity in National-Colonial Egypt*. Oxford: Oxford University Press.
Saavedra, M., 1998. "Ethnicity, Resources and the Central State: Politics in the Nuba Mountains, 1950s to 1990s," in Endre Stiansen and Michael Kevane, eds., *Kordafan Invaded: Peripheral Incorporation and Social Transformation in Islamic Africa*. Boston, Brill, 224–225.
Saeed, A. B., 1988. "Merchant Capital, The State and Peasant Farmers in Southern Kordofan," in Norman O'Neill and Jay O'Brien, eds., *Economy and Class in Sudan*. Brookfield, VT.: Avebury, 186–211.
Sanderson, G. N., 1985. "The Ghost of Adam Smith: Ideology, Bureaucracy, and the Frustration of Economic Development in the Sudan, 1934–1940," in M. W. Daly, ed., *Modernization in the Sudan: Essays in Honor of Richard Hill*. New York: Lilian Barber Press, 101–120.
Sargent, T., and N. Wallace, 1981, "Some Unpleasant Monetarist Arithmetic," *Federal Reserve Bank of Minneapolis Quarterly Review* 5:3, 1–17.
Satia, P., 2007. "Developing Iraq: Britain, India and the Redemption of Empire and Technology in the First World War," *Past and Present*, 11:197, 211–255.
*al-Sayyad, M. M. 1957. *Iqtisadat al-Sudan muhadarat ilaqaha 'ala taliba qasm al-dirasat al-iqtisadiyya wa al-ijtima 'aiyya*. Cairo: Ma 'had al-Bahuth wa al-Dirasat al-Arabiyya, Jama't Al-Douwla Al-Arabiyya,
Schaefer, C., 1992. "The Politics of Banking: The Bank of Abyssinia, 1905–1931," *International Journal of African Historical Studies* 25:2, 361–389.
Schmidt, E., 2007. *Cold War and Decolonization in Guinea, 1946–1958*. Athens: Ohio University Press.
Scott, J. C., 1998. *Seeing like a State: How Certain Schemes to Improve the Human Condition Have Failed*. New Haven: Yale University Press.
Serels, S., 2012. "Famines of War: The Red Sea Grain Market and Famine in Eastern Sudan, 1889–1891," *Northeast African Studies* 12:1, 73–94.
2007. "Political Landscaping: Land Registration, the Definition of Ownership and the Evolution of Colonial Objectives in the Anglo-Egyptian Sudan, 1899–1924," *African Economic History* 35: 59–75
2013. *Starvation and the State: Famine, Slavery, and Power in Sudan, 1883–1956*. New York: Palgrave Macmillan

Serra, G., 2015, "From Scattered Data to Ideological Education: Economics, Statistics and the State in Ghana, 1948–1966," PhD diss., London School of Economics.
Shaaeldin, E., 1984. *The Evolution and Transformation of the Sudanese Economy up to 1950*. Khartoum: Monograph Series of Khartoum University Press.
*Al-Shahi, A. 1981. "A Noah's Ark: The Continuity of the Khatmiyya Order in Northern Sudan," *British Society for Middle Eastern Studies, Bulletin* 8:1, 13–29.
Sharkey, H., 2003. *Living with Colonialism: Nationalism and Culture in the Anglo-Egyptian Sudan*. Berkeley: University of California Press.
Shepherd Jr., G. W., 1966. "National Integration and the Southern Sudan," *Journal of Modern African Studies* 4:2, 195.
Sikainga, A., 2002. *"City of Fire and Steel": A Social History of Atbara, Sudan's Railway Town, 1906–1984*. Portsmouth, NH: Heinemann.
1996. *Slaves into Workers: Emancipation and Labor in Colonial Sudan*. Austin: University of Texas Press.
Sivasundaram, S., 2010. "Sciences and the Global: On Methods, Questions, and Theory," *ISIS* 101:1, 146–158.
Slobodian, Q. 2016. "Which 'the Economy'? Complicating the Timothy Mitchell Thesis," Comment at *Historicizing "the Economy" Workshop*, Harvard University. www.academia.edu/28948215/Which_the_Economy_Complicating_the_Timothy_Mitchell_Thesis [January 15, 2017].
Soares De Oliveira, R., 2015. *Magnificent and Beggarland: Angola since the Civil War*. New York: Oxford University Press.
Sousa Santos, B. 2006. "The Heterogeneous State and Legal Pluralism in Mozambique," *Law and Society Review* 40.1: 42–44.
1995. *Toward a New Common Sense-Law, Science and Politics in the Paradigmatic Transition*. New York: Routledge.
Spaulding, J. 2007. *The Heroic Age in Sinna*. Trenton, NJ: Red Sea Press.
Spaulding, J., and L. Kapteijns, 1994. *An Islamic Alliance: Ali Dinar and the Sanusiyya, 1906–1916*. Evanston, IL: Northwestern University Press.
Speich, D., 2009. "The Kenyan Style of 'African Socialism': Development Knowledge Claims and the Explanatory Limits of the Cold War," *Diplomatic History* 33:3, 449–466.
2008. "Travelling with the GDP through Early Development Economics' History," in *Working Papers on the Nature of Evidence: How Well Do Facts Travel*? No 33/2008, London School of Economics, Department of Economic History.
2011. "The Use of Global Abstractions: National Income Accounting in the Period of Imperial Decline," *Journal of Global History* 6:1, 7–28
Star, S. L., 1999. "The Ethnography of Infrastructure," *American Behavioral Scientist* 43:3, 377–391.
Stopler, W. F. 1966. *Planning without Facts: Lessons in Resource Allocation from Nigeria's Development*. Cambridge, MA: Harvard University Press.
Studenski, P., 1958. *The Income of Nations, Theory, Measurement, and Analysis: Past and Present: A Study in Applied Economics and Statistics*, New York: New York University Press.
Thomas, E., 2014. "Obituary: Hassan al-Turabi (1932–2016)," *Mada Masr*. www.madamasr.com/en/2016/03/14/opinion/u/obituary-hassan-al-turabi-1932-2016/ [accessed January 16, 2017].
2015. *South Sudan: A Slow Liberation*. New York: Zed Books.

Tignor, R. L., 1998. *Capitalism and Nationalism at the End of Empire: State and Business in Decolonizing Egypt, Nigeria, and Kenya, 1945–1963*. Princeton: Princeton University Press.

1982. "Equity in Egypt's Recent Past: 1945–1952," in Judah Abu Al-Khaliq, G. Abdel Khalek, and Robert Tignor, eds., *The Political Economy of Income Distribution in Egypt*. New York: Holmes and Meier Publishers, 20–54.

1966. *Modernization and British Colonial Rule in Egypt, 1882–1914*. Princeton: Princeton University Press.

1993. "Political Corruption in Nigeria before Independence," *Journal of Modern African Studies* 31:2, 175–202.

1987. "The Sudanese Private Sector: An Historical Overview," *Journal of Modern African Studies* 25:2: 179–212

2006. *W. Arthur Lewis and the Birth of Development Economics*. Princeton: Princeton University Press.

Tilley, H., 2011. *African as a Living Laboratory: Empire, Development and the Problem of Scientific Knowledge, 1870–1950*. Chicago: University of Chicago Press.

*El Tom, A., 2011. *Darfur, JEM and the Khalil Ibrahim Story*. Trenton, NJ: Red Sea Press.

*El Tom, A. O., and M. A. M. Salih, 2003. "Reviewed Book: The Black Book of Sudan," *Review of African Political Economy* 30:97, 511–514.

Tooze, A., 2016, The Crisis: The Unmaking of the Economy? *Working Paper London Foucault Working Group*. www.adamtooze.com/wp-content/uploads/2016/03/Tooze-Unmaking-the-Economy-2016.pdf [accessed January 20, 2017].

2008. "Trouble with Numbers: Statistics, Politics, and History in the Construction of Weimar's Trade Balance, 1918–1924," *American Historical Review* 113:8, 678–700.

Toye, J., 2009. "Herbert Frankel: From Colonial Economics to Development Economics," *Oxford Development Studies* 37:2, 171–182.

Tvedt, T., 2004. *The River Nile in the Age of the British: Political Ecology and the Quest for Economic Power*. New York: I. B. Tauris.

Unger, R. M., 1996. *What Should Legal Analysis Become?* New York: Verso.

United Nations Bureau of Economic and Social Affairs. 2012. "Historic Versions of the System of National Accounts." http://unstats.un.org/unsd/nationalaccount/hsna.asp. [accessed June 16, 2017].

United Nations, Department of Economic and Social Affairs, 1958. *A Manual for the Economic and Functional Classification of Government Transactions*. New York: United Nations Press.

Vanoli, A., 2005. *A History of National Accounting*. Amsterdam: IOS Press.

Vaughan, C., 2011. *Negotiating the State at its Margins: Colonial Authority in Condominium Darfur, 1916–1956* Ph.D diss., Durham University, UK.

2010. "Reinventing the Wheel? Local Government and Neo-Traditional Authority in Late-Colonial Northern Sudan," *International Journal of African Historical Studies* 43:2, 255–278.

Vaughan, M., 1991. *Curing their Ills: Colonial Power and African Illness*. Stanford: Stanford University Press.

Verhoeven, H., 2015. *Water, Civilization and Power in Sudan: The Political Economy of Military-Islamist State Building*. New York: Cambridge University Press.

Vezzadini, E., 2015. *Lost Nationalism: Revolution, Memory and Anti-Colonial Resistance in Sudan*. Rochester, NY: Boydell and Brewer.

Vitalis, R., 2013. "The Midnight Ride of Kwame Nkrumah and Other Fables of Bandung (Ban-doong)," *Humanity* 4:2, 261–288.

1995. *When Capitalists Collide: Business Conflict and the End of Empire in Egypt*. Berkeley: University of California Press.

2015. *White World Order, Black Power Politics: The Birth of American International Relations*. Ithaca, NY: Cornell University Press.

Wahab, A. R., 1976. "Development Planning in the Sudan: Policy and Organization," in Ali Mohamed El Hassan, ed., *Introduction to the Sudan Economy*. Khartoum: Khartoum University Press, 216–234.

Walz, T., 1978. *The Trade between Egypt and Bilad as-Sudan, 1700–1820*. Cairo: Institute Francais d'Archeologie Orientale du Cairo.

Warburg, G., 2003. *Islam, Sectarianism and Politics in Sudan since the Mahdiyya*. London: Hurst and Co.

Waterbury, J., 1979. *Hydropolitics of the Nile Valley*. Syracuse, NY: Syracuse University Press.

Weber, M., trans. D. S. Owen and T. B. Strong, 2004. *The Vocation Lectures*. New York: Hackett Publishing.

Weinstein, B., 2008. "Developing Inequality," *American Historical Review* 113:1, 1–18.

Weitzberg, K., 2015. "The Unaccountable Census: Colonial Enumeration and Its Implications for the Somali People," *Journal of African History* 56:3, 409–428.

Wilder, G., 2015. *Freedom Time: Negritude, Decolonization, and the Future of the World*. Durham, NC: Duke University Press.

Willis, J., 2015. "The Southern Problem: Representing Sudan's Southern Provinces to c. 1970," *Journal of African History* 56:2.

2003. "Violence, Authority, and the State in the Nuba Mountains of Condominium Sudan," *Historical Journal* 46:1, 89–114.

Willis, J., and El Battahani, A., 2010. "'We Changed the Laws': Electoral Practice and Malpractice in Sudan since 1953," *African Affairs* 109:435, 191–212.

Woldemariam, M., 2015. "Partition Problems: Relative Power, Historical Memory, and the Origins of the Eritrean-Ethiopian War," *Nationalism and Ethnic Politics* 21:2, 166–190.

Woldemariam, M., and Alden Young, 2016. "After the Split: Partition, Successor States, and the Dynamics of War in the Horn of Africa," *Journal of Strategic Studies*. http://dx.doi.org/10.1080/01402390.2016.1182909.

Woodward, P. 1979. *Condominium and Sudanese Nationalism*. London: Rex Collings.

1990. *Sudan, 1898–1989: The Unstable State*. Boulder, CO: Lynne Rienner.

Yongo-Bure, B., 2007. *Economic Development of Southern Sudan*. Lanham, MD: University Press of America.

Young, A., 2013. *Accounting for Decolonization: The Origins of the Sudanese Economy*. PhD diss., Princeton University.

2017. "African Bureaucrats and the Exhaustion of the Developmental State: Lessons from the Pages of the Sudan Economist," *Humanity* 8:1, 49–75.

2012. "The Anglo-Egyptian Rivalry, The Cold War and Economic Development in Sudan: 1954–1958," in Massimiliano Trentin and Matteo Gerlini, eds., *The Middle East and the Cold War: Between Security and Development* Newcastle upon Tyne, UK: Cambridge Scholars Press, 29–53.

2013. "Are Statistics Useless? The Four Phases of the African State in the 20th Century," *Books and Ideas*, November 12, 2013. www.booksandideas.net/Are-Statistics-Useless-2476.html

2014. "Measuring the Sudanese Economy: A Focus on National Growth Rates and Regional Inequality, 1959–1964," *Canadian Journal of Development Studies* 35:1, 44–60.

Young, C., 1997. *The African Colonial State in Comparative Perspective*. New Haven: Yale University Press,

2004. "The End of the Postcolonial State in Africa? Reflections on Changing African Political Dynamics," *African Affairs* 103:410, 23–49.

Young, C., and Thomas Turner, 1985. *The Rise and Decline of the Zairian State*. Madison: University of Wisconsin Press.

Young, T., 1993. "Elections and Electoral Politics in Africa," *Africa* 63:3, 299–312.

Zeleke, E. C., 2016. "When Social Scientific Concepts Become Neutral Arbiters of Social Conflict: Reading the Ethiopian Federal Elections of 2005 through the Ethiopian Student Movement of the 1960s and 1970s," *Northeast African Studies* 16:1, 107–139.

Zuberi, T. 2015. *African Independence: How Africa Shapes the World*? New York: Rowman & Littlefield.

Index

African Studies

1 *City Politics: A Study of Leopoldville, 1962–63*, J.S. La Fontaine
2 *Studies in Rural Capitalism in West Africa*, Polly Hill
3 *Land Policy in Buganda*, Henry W. West
4 *The Nigerian Military: A Sociological Analysis of Authority and Revolt, 1960–67*, Robin Luckham
5 *The Ghanaian Factory Worker: Industrial Man in Africa*, Margaret Peil
6 *Labour in the South African Gold Mines*, Francis Wilson
7 *The Price of Liberty: Personality and Politics in Colonial Nigeria*, Kenneth W. J. Post and George D. Jenkins
8 *Subsistence to Commercial Farming in Present-Day Buganda: An Economic and Anthropological Survey*, Audrey I. Richards, Fort Sturrock, and Jean M. Fortt (eds)
9 *Dependence and Opportunity: Political Change in Ahafo*, John Dunn and A. F. Robertson
10 *African Railwaymen: Solidarity and Opposition in an East African Labour Force*, R. D. Grillo
11 *Islam and Tribal Art in West Africa*, René A. Bravmann
12 *Modern and Traditional Elites in the Politics of Lagos*, P. D. Cole
13 *Asante in the Nineteenth Century: The Structure and Evaluation of a Political Order*, Ivor Wilks
14 *Culture, Tradition and Society in the West African Novel*, Emmanuel Obiechina
15 *Saints and Politicians*, Donal B. Cruise O'Brien
16 *The Lions of Dagbon: Political Change in Northern Ghana*, Martin Staniland
17 *Politics of Decolonization: Kenya Europeans and the Land Issue 1960–1965*, Gary B. Wasserman
18 *Muslim Brotherhoods in the Nineteenth-Century Africa*, B. G. Martin
19 *Warfare in the Sokoto Caliphate: Historical and Sociological Perspectives*, Joseph P. Smaldone
20 *Liberia and Sierra Leone: An Essay in Comparative Politics*, Christopher Clapham
21 *Adam Kok's Griquas: A Study in the Development of Stratification in South Africa*, Robert Ross
22 *Class, Power and Ideology in Ghana: The Railwaymen of Sekondi*, Richard Jeffries
23 *West African States: Failure and Promise*, John Dunn (ed)
24 *Afrikaaners of the Kalahari: White Minority in a Black State*, Margo Russell and Martin Russell
25 *A Modern History of Tanganyika*, John Iliffe
26 *A History of African Christianity 1950–1975*, Adrian Hastings
27 *Slaves, Peasants and Capitalists in Southern Angola, 1840–1926*, W. G. Clarence-Smith
28 *The Hidden Hippopotamus: Reappraised in African History: The Early Colonial Experience in Western Zambia*, Gywn Prins
29 *Families Divided: The Impact of Migrant Labour in Lesotho*, Colin Murray
30 *Slavery, Colonialism and Economic Growth in Dahomey, 1640–1960*, Patrick Manning
31 *Kings, Commoners and Concessionaries: The Evolution of Dissolution of the Nineteenth-Century Swazi State*, Philip Bonner
32 *Oral Poetry and Somali Nationalism: The Case of Sayid Mahammad 'Abdille Hasan*, Said S. Samatar
33 *The Political Economy of Pondoland 1860–1930*, William Beinart
34 *Volkskapitalisme: Class, Capitals and Ideology in the Development of Afrikaner Nationalism, 1934–1948*, Dan O'Meara
35 *The Settler Economies: Studies in the Economic History of Kenya and Rhodesia 1900–1963*, Paul Mosely

36 *Transformations in Slavery: A History of Slavery in Africa,1st edition*, Paul Lovejoy
37 *Amilcar Cabral: Revolutionary Leadership and People's War*, Patrick Chabal
38 *Essays on the Political Economy of Rural Africa*, Robert H. Bates
39 *Ijeshas and Nigerians: The Incorporation of a Yoruba Kingdom, 1890s-1970s*, J. D. Y. Peel
40 *Black People and the South African War, 1899–1902*, Peter Warwick
41 *A History of Niger 1850–1960*, Finn Fuglestad
42 *Industrialisation and Trade Union Organization in South Africa,1924–1955*, Stephen Ellis
43 *The Rising of the Red Shawls: A Revolt in Madagascar 1895–1899*, Stephen Ellis
44 *Slavery in Dutch South Africa*, Nigel Worden
45 *Law, Custom and Social Order: The Colonial Experience in Malawi and Zambia*, Martin Chanock
46 *Salt of the Desert Sun: A History of Salt Production and Trade in the Central Sudan*, Paul E. Lovejoy
47 *Marrying Well: Marriage, Status and Social Change among the Educated Elite in Colonial Lagos*, Kristin Mann
48 *Language and Colonial Power: The Appropriation of Swahili in the Former Belgian Congo, 1880–1938*, Johannes Fabian
49 *The Shell Money of the Slave Trade*, Jan Hogendorn and Marion Johnson
50 *Political Domination in Africa*, Patrick Chabal
51 *The Southern Marches of Imperial Ethiopia: Essays in History and Social Anthropology*, Donald Donham and Wendy James
52 *Islam and Urban Labor in Northern Nigeria: The Making of a Muslim Working Class*, Paul M. Lubeck
53 *Horn and Crescent: Cultural Change and Traditional Islam on the East African Coast, 800–1900*, Randall L. Pouwels
54 *Capital and Labour on the Kimberley Diamond Fields, 1871–1890*, Robert Vicat Turrell
55 *National and Class Conflict in the Horn of Africa*, John Markakis
56 *Democracy and Prebendal Politics in Nigeria: The Rise and Fall of the Second Republic*, Richard A. Joseph
57 *Entrepreneurs and Parasites: The Struggle for Indigenous Capitalism in Zaire*, Janet MacGaffey
58 *The African Poor: A History*, John Iliffe
59 *Palm Oil and Protest: An Economic History of the Ngwa Region, South-Eastern Nigeria, 1800–1980*, Susan M. Martin
60 *France and Islam in West Africa, 1860–1960*, Christopher Harrison
61 *Transformation and Continuity in Revolutionary Ethiopia*, Christopher Clapham
62 *Prelude to the Mahdiyya: Peasants and Traders in the Shendi Region, 1821–1885*, Anders Bjorkelo
63 *Wa and the Wala: Islam and Polity in Northwestern Ghana*, Ivor Wilks
64 *H.C. Bankole-Bright and Politics in Colonial Sierra Leone, 1919–1958*, Akintola Wyse
65 *Contemporary West African States*, Donal Cruise O'Brien, John Dunn, and Richard Rathbone (eds)
66 *The Oromo of Ethiopia: A History, 1570–1860*, Mohammed Hassen
67 *Slavery and African Life: Occidental, Oriental, and African Slave Trades*, Patrick Manning
68 *Abraham Esau's War: A Black South African War in the Cape, 1899–1902*, Bill Nasson
69 *The Politics of Harmony: Land Dispute Strategies in Swaziland*, Laurel L. Rose
70 *Zimbabwe's Guerrilla War: Peasant Voices*, Norma J. Kriger
71 *Ethiopia: Power and Protest: Peasant Revolts in the Twentieth-Century*, Gebru Tareke

72 *White Supremacy and Black Resistance in Pre-Industrial South Africa: The Making of the Colonial Order in the Eastern Cape, 1770–1865*, Clifton C. Crais
73 *The Elusive Granary: Herder, Farmer, and State in Northern Kenya*, Peter D. Little
74 *The Kanyok of Zaire: An Institutional and Ideological History to 1895*, John C. Yoder
75 *Pragmatism in the Age of Jihad: The Precolonial State of Bundu*, Michael A. Gomez
76 *Slow Death for Slavery: The Course of Abolition in Northern Nigeria, 1897–1936*, Paul E. Lovejoy and Jan S. Hogendorn
77 *West African Slavery and Atlantic Commerce: The Senegal River Valley, 1700–1860*, James F. Searing
78 *A South African Kingdom: The Pursuit of Security in the Nineteenth-Century Lesotho*, Elizabeth A. Elredge
79 *State and Society in Pre-colonial Asante*, T. C. McCaskie
80 *Islamic Society and State Power in Senegal: Disciples and Citizens in Fatick*, Leonardo A. Villalon
81 *Ethnic Pride and Racial Prejudice in Victorian Cape Town: Group Identity and Social Practice*, Vivian Bickford-Smith
82 *The Eritrean Struggle for Independence: Domination, Resistance and Nationalism, 1941–1993*, Ruth Iyob
83 *Corruption and State Politics in Sierra Leone*, William Reno
84 *The Culture of Politics in Modern Kenya*, Angelique Haugerud
85 *Africans: The History of a Continent, 1st edition*, John Iliffe
86 *From Slave Trade to 'Legitimate' Commerce: The Commercial Transition in Nineteenth-Century West Africa*, Robin Law (ed)
87 *Leisure and Society in Colonial Brazzaville*, Phyllis Martin
88 *Kingship and State: The Buganda Dynasty*, Christopher Wrigley
89 *Decolonialization and African Life: The Labour Question in French and British Africa*, Frederick Cooper
90 *Misreading the African Landscape: Society and Ecology in an African Forest-Savannah Mosaic*, James Fairhead, and Melissa Leach
91 *Peasant Revolution in Ethiopia: The Tigray People's Liberation Front, 1975–1991*, John Young
92 *Senegambia and the Atlantic Slave Trade*, Boubacar Barry
93 *Commerce and Economic Change in West Africa: The Oil Trade in the Nineteenth Century*, Martin Lynn
94 *Slavery and French Colonial Rule in West Africa: Senegal, Guinea and Mali*, Martin A. Klein
95 *East African Doctors: A History of the Modern Profession*, John Iliffe
96 *Middlemen of the Cameroons Rivers: The Duala and Their Hinterland, c.1600–1960*, Ralph Derrick, Ralph A. Austen, and Jonathan Derrick
97 *Masters and Servants on the Cape Eastern Frontier, 1760–1803*, Susan Newton-King
98 *Status and Respectability in the Cape Colony, 1750–1870: A Tragedy of Manners*, Robert Ross
99 *Slaves, Freedmen and Indentured Laborers in Colonial Mauritius*, Richard B. Allen
100 *Transformations in Slavery: A History of Slavery in Africa, 2nd edition*, Paul E. Lovejoy
101 *The Peasant Cotton Revolution in West Africa: Cote d'Ivoire, 1880–1995*, Thomas E. Basset
102 *Re-imagining Rwanda: Conflict, Survival and Disinformation in the Late Twentieth Century*, Johan Pottier
103 *The Politics of Evil: Magic, State Power and the Political Imagination in South Africa*, Clifton Crais
104 *Transforming Mozambique: The Politics of Privatization, 1975–2000*, M. Anne Pitcher

105 *Guerrilla Veterans in Post-War Zimbabwe: Symbolic and Violent Politics, 1980–1987*, Norma J. Kriger
106 *An Economic History of Imperial Madagascar, 1750–1895: The Rise and Fall of an Island Empire*, Gwyn Campbell
107 *Honour in African History*, John Iliffe
108 *Africans: A History of a Continent*, 2nd edition, John Iliffe
109 *Guns, Race, and Power in Colonial South Africa*, William Kelleher Storey
110 *Islam and Social Change in French West Africa: History of an Emancipatory Community*, Sean Hanretta
111 *Defeating Mau Mau, Creating Kenya: Counterinsurgency, Civil War and Decolonization*, Daniel Branch
112 *Christianity and Genocide in Rwanda*, Timothy Longman
113 *From Africa to Brazil: Culture, Identity, and an African Slave Trade, 1600–1830*, Walter Hawthorne
114 *Africa in the Time of Cholera: A History of Pandemics from 1817 to the Present*, Myron Echenberg
115 *A History of Race in Muslim West Africa, 1600–1960*, Bruce S. Hall
116 *Witchcraft and Colonial Rule in Kenya, 1900–1955*, Katherine Luongo
117 *Transformations in Slavery: A History of Slavery in Africa*, 3rd edition, Paul E. Lovejoy
118 *The Rise of the Trans-Atlantic Slave Trade in Western Africa, 1300–1589*, Toby Green
119 *Party Politics and Economic Reform in Africa's Democracies*, M. Anne Pitcher
120 *Smugglers and Saints of the Sahara: Regional Connectivity in the Twentieth Century*, Judith Scheele
121 *Cross-Cultural Exchange in the Atlantic World: Angola and Brazil during the Era of the Slave Trade*, Roquinaldo Ferreira
122 *Ethnic Patriotism and the East African Revival*, Derek Peterson
123 *Black Morocco: A History of Slavery and Islam*, Chouki El Hamel
124 *An African Slaving Port and the Atlantic World: Benguela and Its Hinterland*, Mariana Candido
125 *Making Citizens in Africa: Ethnicity, Gender, and National Identity in Ethiopia*, Lahra Smith
126 *Slavery and Emancipation in Islamic East Africa: From Honor to Respectability*, Elisabeth McMahon
127 *A History of African Motherhood: The Case of Uganda, 700–1900*, Rhiannon Stephens
128 *The Borders of Race in Colonial South Africa: The Kat River Settlement, 1829–1856*, Robert Ross
129 *From Empires to NGOs in the West African Sahel: The Road to Nongovernmentality*, Gregory Mann
130 *Dictators and Democracy in African Development: The Political Economy of Good Governance in Nigeria*, A. Carl LeVan
131 *Water, Civilization and Power in Sudan: The Political Economy of Military-Islamist State Building*, Harry Verhoeven
132 *The Fruits of Freedom in British Togoland: Literacy, Politics and Nationalism, 1914–2014*, Kate Skinner
133 *Political Thought and the Public Sphere in Tanzania: Freedom, Democracy and Citizenship in the Era of Decolonization*, Emma Hunter
134 *Political Identity and Conflict in Central Angola, 1975–2002*, Justin Pearce
135 *From Slavery to Aid: Politics, Labour, and Ecology in the Nigerian Sahel, 1800–2000*, Benedetta Rossi
136 *National Liberation in Postcolonial Southern Africa: A Historical Ethnography of SWAPO's Exile Camps*, Christian A. Williams

137 *Africans: A History of a Continent*, 3rd edition, John Iliffe
138 *Colonial Buganda and the End of Empire: Political Thought and Historical Imagination in Africa*, Jonathon L. Earle
139 *The Struggle over State Power in Zimbabwe: Law and Politics since 1950*, George Karekwaivanane
140 *Transforming Sudan: Decolonisation, Economic Development and State Formation*, Alden Young

Lightning Source UK Ltd.
Milton Keynes UK
UKHW012109271119
354377UK00012B/332/P

9 781107 172494